LOGOS:
Mathematics
and
Christian Theology

Granville C. Henry, Jr.

LEWISBURG
BUCKNELL UNIVERSITY PRESS

LONDON
ASSOCIATED UNIVERSITY PRESSES

© 1976 by Associated University Presses, Inc.

Associated University Presses, Inc.
Cranbury, New Jersey 08512

Associated University Presses
108 New Bond Street
London W1Y OQX, England

Library of Congress Cataloging in Publication Data

Henry, Granville C.
Logos.

Bibliography: p.
Includes index.
1. Religion and science—1946–   2. Mathematics
I. Title.
BL265.M3H46   261.5   74–25529
ISBN 0–8387–1653–9

Contents

Preface

The part of this work that attempts to show the relationship of mathematics to contemporary theology through the works of Husserl, Whitehead, and Wittgenstein was begun during my doctoral studies. I am greatly indebted to John B. Cobb, Jr., my advisor, for his supervision of my doctoral dissertation. Lewis S. Ford, whether he knows it or not, is responsible for my departure from an orthodox interpretation of eternal objects as understood in contemporary process philosophy. In a conversation that occurred at the annual meeting of the American Academy of Religion in Atlanta, October 1971, he precipitated what has become the last chapter of this book.

As I wrote the book, I condensed some of the material and sent it off as journal articles. These, now published, have come due for acknowledgment and are given footnotes as they occur. I want to thank an unknown reader for Bucknell University Press, whose suggestions I have accepted and whose summary of the issues presented I found better than my summary and have utilized in the Introduction. Also I thank Mrs. Mathilde E. Finch, Editor in Chief, Associated University Presses, Inc., for her patience and skill during the editing process. I, of course, assume full responsibility for all errors of any kind.

A grant from the National Endowment for the Humanities made it possible for me to complete the major part of this book during the academic year 1970–71.

7

Acknowledgments

I thank the following publishers for permission to quote from copyrighted material:

Bucknell Review, for permission to quote from Granville C. Henry, Jr., "Mathematics and Theology," Fall 1972.

Cambridge University Press, for permission to quote from G. S. Kirk and J. E. Raven, *The Presocratic Philosophers,* 1962.

Catholic University of America, for permission to quote from Saint Augustine, *The Free Choice of the Will,* in *The Fathers of the Church,* trans. Robert P. Russell, vol. 59, 1968.

William B. Eerdmans, Publisher, for permission to quote from Gerhard Kittel, ed., and Geoffrey W. Bromiley, trans., *Theological Dictionary of the New Testament,* vol. 4, 1967.

Journal of the American Academy of Religion, for permission to quote from Granville C. Henry, Jr., "Mathematics, Phenomenology and Language Analysis in Contemporary Theology," December 1967.

Journal of the Blaisdell Institute, for permission to quote from Granville C. Henry, Jr., "Mathematical Objectification and Common Sense Causality in Science and Religion," January 1969.

National Council of the Churches of Christ in the U.S.A., for permission to quote from the Revised Standard Version Bible, published by Thomas Nelson and Sons, 1952.

9

Paideia Press, for permission to quote from Granville C. Henry, Jr., "Aspects of the Influence of Mathematics on Contemporary Philosophy," in *Philosophia Mathematica*, December 1966.

Process Studies, for permission to quote from Granville C. Henry, Jr., "Nonstandard Mathematics and a Doctrine of God," Spring 1973.

The Southern Journal of Philosophy, for permission to quote from Granville C. Henry, Jr., "Whitehead's Philosophical Response to the New Mathematics," Winter 1969–70.

Introduction

Does mathematics have any significant relationship to Christian theology? If one views mathematics through the eyes of a professional mathematician doing research and understands theology in a tradition that has sought to isolate itself progressively from science and philosophy, then the answer is, obviously, "Very little." If, however, one accepts mathematics in its full range of pure theory with an extended application in the sciences, or includes within the domain of theology concerns for contemporary philosophical questions, or, for that matter, accepts any traditional Christian theology, then the answer is no longer negative but a positive "Yes." I hope to show in this study that mathematics *has* influenced and *does continue* to influence Christian theology and often quite significantly.

Why study *mathematics* and its relationship to Christian theology rather than *science* and its relationship to Christian theology? After all, mathematics does seem to be a part of science. Might not one be severely limiting the scope of inquiry by focusing on this part, when in fact the *relevance* of the part can be understood only in terms of the general issues of science and religion? The answer, in this case, is dependent upon, first, correcting the misapprehension that mathematics is a part or subdivision of any other discipline. Mathematics is, of course, applicable in varying degrees to almost all disciplines. But it is a subpart of none. Mathematics is no more a subsection of physics than it is of history or philosophy. It is, perhaps, of all disciplines most clearly its own. Mathematics was the discipline that first isolated itself from philosophy and theology and one whose advent preceded science (modern science) by at least nineteen hundred years. During this time, before many of the now standard issues between science and religion were ever raised, mathematics was, in fact, influencing Western theology. Surely, then, the oldest of the "pure disciplines" deserves an analysis of its relationship to the, though waning, still dominant Western religion. To view mathematics as a part of any one science, or to view the study of the relationship between mathematics and theology as exclusively a part of science-religion study, may result in a self-conditioning that can systematically obscure an important part of Christian theology.

Yet, there is a utility in considering mathematics to be *one* among the *many* scientific disciples, especially when its relationship to Christian theology does fit some of the general categories of science-religion study. If mathematics is considered to be a science, then the claim can be made that it was the first science to encounter Christian theology and that, furthermore, its conflict with Christian theology was the first major conflict between science and religion. Such a claim can be fruitful for an analysis of the relationship of both science to religion and mathematics to religion.

I consider mathematics to be *a* science. It is, after all, a body of knowledge, systematically arranged and subject to general laws. It differs from the other sciences, however, in that its content is not primarily empirical. Legitimate mathematical structures need have no reference to the actual world. No other scientific discipline is so oriented. Theories are valid in the nonmathematical sciences to the degree that they describe some actually existing physical, social, or psychological structure. In these disciplines, to propose a theory without an intention that it have a reference to the world is illegitimate. For mathematics, this is not the case.

Many may come to an interest in the problem of the relationship of mathematics to theology through an initial interest in the relationship of science to religion. I know this to be my case personally. In an attempt to assess correctly the relationship of science and religion, I first was led to a study of science (in particular, physics), then to the foundations of science where I saw mathematics to be of great importance, then to mathematics, and finally to the foundations of mathematics. In the transition from science to the foundations of mathematics, one loses, of course, many of the aspects of science that are particularly interesting for the comparison of science with religion. In the transition, however, one also encounters problems of a deeper nature, which are preliminary to the examination of science and its relationship to religion, and which form the background for such an examination. The purpose of this work is to isolate such issues and to examine how they may be used for theology.

The issues that seem to me to be most important are those that affect an understanding of the nature of God—literally *theology*, and of an understanding of Christ—*Christology*. Part I of this book is concerned with a historical analysis of the influence of classical mathematics on classical Christian theology. In particular, I attempt to show how mathematics conditioned an understanding of *word* and *wisdom* that was personified in Christ and determinative of orthodox Christology, how the ontological understanding of *word* and *wisdom* precipitated the traditional problem of faith and reason, and how an understanding of mathematics led to a belief in a particular doctrine of the unicity and immutability of God.

Although mathematics changed markedly in the seventeenth and eighteenth centuries, the basic presuppositions concerning the nature of mathematics remained more or less intact. It was not until the nineteenth century that what in this book is called the Euclidean perspective began to crumble, and in its place more questions than confident answers remained. With the support given by the Euclidean perspective to classical Christian doctrines removed, a multiplicity of new issues has arisen and some of them have been sensitive to *new* developments in mathematics. The historical occasions for the new relevance of mathematics for theology have occurred as a result of the philosophical works of Husserl, Whitehead, and Wittgenstein, the first two of which were professional mathematicians who not only knew the new mathematics but contributed to it. Of the three, Wittgenstein was the only one who knew of Gödel's epochal work and responded to it. The primary issues discussed in this book, though not necessarily listed in the order of appearing, are (1) How a new understanding of the objectification of mathematical realities has affected an understanding of the objectification of God; whether, in fact, God and Christ (as Logos) can be objectified at all and if so what such objectification means. (2) The contribution that contemporary mathematical theory makes to interpreting contemporary theological language, in particular, that of phenomenology and language analysis. (3) The relevance of mathematics to a modern erosion of interest in causation and the possibility of new models of causation that include divine causal action. (4) The theological and Christological relevance of mathematics' loss of its own unity in *one* content and *one* axiomatic system. (5) The relationship of mathematics to a growing secularization of theological belief through the quantification of value. (6) The need for a more refined theological skepticism in order to establish an appropriate relationship between theology on the one hand and mathematics and science on the other. And (7) the need for theology, as well as mathematics, to pursue some metaphysical issues.

These issues are discussed in order that I might make some appropriate suggestions as to new directions that a formulation of Christology and theology might take—especially in regard to the relationship of God and Christ to *possibilities*. I could not resist beginning this task, even before major contemporary problems were discussed and before most of the issues above were presented, in a section at the end of chapter 1 called Christology from a Modern Perspective. This topic is summarized, extended, and placed in relationship to an examination of God's metaphysical relationship to possibilities in the last chapter.

An Example—Exponential Function and Population Increase

Since there is no traditional structure for presenting and

analyzing the relationship of mathematics to theology, I would like to introduce this discussion by means of an example. Any use of pure mathematics for understanding the world, e.g., Ptolemaic astronomy, Newtonian mechanics, Einsteinian relativity, quantum mechanics, contemporary genetic theory, and so on, could be used. The questions asked and relationships established for mathematics and theology are to a large extent example-independent, but not totally so. Christianity is a historical religion, historically founded and sensitive in each age to historical events —some of which are the actions of men taken on their beliefs in particular scientific systems. A choice of mathematical properties of population increase, beginning with Malthus's thesis, will not only permit me to attempt a general analysis of the relationship of mathematics to theology but will also focus our attention on a problem that is of utmost importance for the future of man, and hence of considerable contemporary theological interest in its own right.

In 1798 the Reverend Thomas Robert Malthus wrote *An Essay on the Principle of Population* in response to philosophers and theologians who claimed that the perfectability of man, his happiness, and the general quality of his life, were proportional to the numbers of his population. In the first two chapters, by charming conversation and delicate references to the "passion between the sexes," Malthus gives an apt description of the differences between two *mathematical functions,* the exponential and the linear, which were in his terminology and the general mathematical terminology of the day *geometrical increase* and *arithmetical increase.* For his basic thesis was that

Population, when unchecked, increases in a geometrical ratio. Subsistence increases only in an arithmetical ratio.[1]

The consequences of this thesis, as entailed by the *mathematical*

[1] Thomas R. Malthus, *An Essay on the Principle of Population as it Affects the Future Improvement of Society* (London: Printed for J. Johnson, in St. Paul's Church Yard, 1798), Reprinted as *First Essay on Population* (New York: Augustus M. Kelley, 1965), p. 14.

properties of the functions, clearly contradict the assumption that the happiness of the human race depends favorably on its numbers. In the geometrical increase, whose law the human race ostensibly follows, the rate of increase is proportional to the amount present. The larger the population, the faster it is growing. In the arithmetical increase, to which in Malthus's thesis food resources correspond, the rate of increase is constant. Thus, as population increases, food per person goes down and the quality of life diminishes. A Malthusian position insists that unless the disparity between geometrical increase of population and arithmetic increase of food is checked, mankind faces a prospect of worldwide disaster. These conclusions can be arrived at from the mathematics of the thesis itself, provided that the thesis is, in fact, true.

A large array of evidence indicates that Malthus's second assumption that "subsistence increases only in arithmetical ratio" is false. Certainly it has not been strictly true over extended periods of time. Malthus's predictions concerning an imminent disaster failed to materialize. Food production in the nineteenth century did not remain linear, or at least not linear at the old rate of increase. Changes in the agricultural system, the introduction of fertilizers, and the opening of lands not previously considered as food producing, not only staved off hunger, but made food quite plentiful in the European nations and America during the nineteenth century—in spite of a rapid population increase.

At the height of plenty in 1895, a full century after Malthus's first work, Sir William Crookes in his presidential address to the British Association at Bristol issued another grave warning that the continued increase of food resources could not meet the rising (exponential) increase of worldwide population. Crookes saw no possible way to increase the land area of wheat farming in order to meet sufficiently the needs of the projected population of the 1930s. His analysis and pronouncements gave great shock to a generation steeped in the progress of the nineteenth century. Again, however, the crisis failed to materialize. A new application of science to agriculture and the study of plant genetics and its practical results of plant breeding increased production per acre of lands in cultivation and aided development of new crops that would grow in lands previously unproductive. The resulting increase in food production was so rapid that, in spite of continued large gains in population, a food surplus existed in the developed countries during the thirties, the very period that Crookes picked as crucial, and has lasted into the present decade.[2]

The application of the power of Western science and technology to food production has essentially falsified the assumption of its general linear increase. The availability of food, as represented by the falsification of Malthus's second assumption, has allowed the confirmation within restricted bounds of his first, that "population, when unchecked, increases in a geometrical ratio." The world population has increased in a rough exponential fashion with a *decreasing time for doubling.*[3]

In our day, we again hear the dread Malthusian warning from responsible demographers, biologists, and political scientists—but with a different emphasis. It is not just the lack of food that threatens us—and the prospect of a decreasing sufficiency is imminent—but an intensified rate of depletion of irreplaceable natural resources, those raw materials that feed industrialization and the *means* to produce food and other necessities. Pollution, and an increasing rate of pollution, threaten to overcome the delicate balance of life in the closed system of our isolated planet.

It is not the increase of population that poses such a threat to world stability, but its exponential increase. The outrageous fact that world population is now doubling every thirty-five to forty years—doubling in a fixed finite time is a simple characteristic of elementary exponential functions—makes prospective technological developments seem a sour hope. The poorer nations have

[2] See Sir E. John Russell, *World Population and World Food Supplies* (London: George Allen & Unwin, 1954), pp. 5–6.
[3] Ehrlich points out that world population was about 500 million in AD 1650 and took approximately 200 years to double to a billion in 1850 and about 80 years to double to two billion around 1930. Paul R. Ehrlich, *The Population Bomb* (New York: Ballantine Books, 1968), p. 18. We are shortly to reach a world population of four billion with a presently estimated doubling time of 35 years.

to double their food production every thirty-five years to keep up with their *present* levels of poverty. If it were possible to send unlimited numbers of people to the other planets, we could populate a planet the size of the earth with its present population density in thirty-five years. So also when our solar system became populated, we could populate another like it in thirty-five years. So also our galaxy.

We want to ask two kinds of questions of this model of exponential population increase. The first question has to do with the nature of the pure mathematics itself, in this case the linear and exponential functions, their interpretation, and the interpretation of other mathematical categories that make up their precise meaning. The second question seeks an answer to how the pure mathematics is understood to apply to the world.

Pure Mathematics and Christian Theology

I can almost feel the reader's reaction at this point. What really does an exponential function have to do with God, or any understanding of him by the Christian religion, or, for that matter, with any other major theological interest? If we allow the presumption that the general mathematical tools that are ordinarily used to present mathematical relationships themselves have no mystery or ambiguity, that is, if we grasp an exponential function as a technical example of a technical discipline for which no basic questions are asked, then the exponential function has little relevance for a doctrine of God. I know of no one who is writing on "The Technical Consequences of an Exponential Function for an Understanding of God," or any other comparable topic. But if we allow ourselves to question in any way how we understand, as we do, an exponential function—and remember, such a function, or other well-known mathematical relationship, is generally agreed to be the kind of knowledge that is most precise and objective—then we are on the way toward analyzing the general properties of mathematical existence, first in terms of mathematical concepts and then in terms of general philosophical ones.

In considering the literature about population increase, almost all analyses of the problem presuppose on the part of the author, and often of the reader, a knowledge of some of the mathematical properties of exponential or geometric increase. The mathematical knowledge is an essential ground of the wider discussion. On the surface we might not think that this is true. It might appear that our primary knowledge of population increase is dependent simply upon counting the population. We can look at any graph based on census and *see* the extent of world population increase and from this knowledge extrapolate to most of the problems that such increase entails. Do we need mathematical structures as some subterranean grounding for further understanding?

Essentially, Yes! A graph based on census may indicate population numbers and direction of increase. But it tells us little about the internal structures of population increase that cause the problem. Why, for example, has the population risen so markedly in the last forty years? Is it that families are on the average having far more children now than in previous centuries? This does not appear to be the case on the surface, and data gathered by census indicate that it is not true. Mathematical calculations, based upon an underlying mathematical structure, show that it takes only a few children per family to give us the great rise in population we now have. Three per family will do it! In fact, four children per family (assuming that each person becomes a parent) will insure that over any fixed amount of time the last generation of children will always number more than all of their ancestors put together. Under these assumptions, there will always be more children than (other) people who have lived. These results may be surprising, but they are grounded in the mathematical properties of exponential functions, which are true mathematically independently of population studies.

The power of increase of an exponential function from even a small percentage of increase of the total amount present indicates the possibility for a population explosion comparable to our own to have occurred at any time in world history. That it has not occurred points to a previous *high death rate*. The birth rate may be defined to be the number born per thousand people per year in the population examined. The death rate is the number who die per thousand per year. The difference between the two gives the net increase or decrease per thousand people per year. If the difference is, say 20 per thousand per year, there is a 2% increase, which when held constant guarantees mathematically a doubling period of thirty-five years—which is approximately the present doubling time of world population.

In the long past of mankind the high death rate matched closely the high birth rate and insured relative population stability. The population fluctuated periodically between bounds, with the upper bound over long periods increasing slightly in a roughly exponential fashion. In our century, the decreasing death rate caused primarily by the application of Western science and medicine to the world-wide community has allowed a population explosion that will continue until the disparity between birth and death rates is minimized, either by reducing the birth rate or increasing the death rate—through famine, pestilence or warfare.

The confidence that we have about the general science of demography depends upon the input of statistical fact couched in a general structure of assured mathematical relationships. It is these assured mathematical relationships that allow us to interpret the facts, and, indeed, to seek facts that are relevant. I have used an example dealing with population to point out what we all really know, namely, the importance of mathematics for any science.

In illustrating the domain of pure mathematical structures by a population example, I stand in danger of obscuring the very thing I want to show. One tends to "see through" the mathematics, to use it as an accepted and presupposed background for illustrating the problem at hand. The mathematical structures become an agreed-upon paradigm within which the controversial matters of demography are discussed. Intentional focus is not directed to mathematics but to the content of the subject matter. I have insured that the mathematical relationships recede to background status where they become the unquestioned and presupposed conditions for the study itself.

It is the very stability of pure mathematics as a background of precise scientific discussion that lays claim to theological importance. In what way is an understanding of God related to these mathematical structures that insure the intelligibility of scientific fact? If they are truly "eternal," that is, not subject to change or destruction, do they depend upon God for their validity and existence or are they basically independent? If they are dependent upon God, are they created by Him or part of his "eternal" nature?

These may seem like renewed scholastic questions which, indeed, they are. If, however, the reality and nature of God are again to become the central theological issue, as a common theological consensus seems to indicate, after a lapse of interest in the problem for the first half of this century,[4] then the questions must be asked again in the light of significant changes in the understanding of mathematics. Appropriate answers are necessary if any theology of nature involving the relationships of God to the world are to be had. An adequate understanding of the relationship of science to the Christian religion depends upon an analysis of the relationship of mathematics to God.

In the near future, decisions of vast political import will probably have to be made on the basis of *mathematical models* that relate population, pollution, industrialization, and other factors.[5] A theology of mathematics concerned with God's relationship to the discipline and its content ought to be available, especially to the Christian community, in order to aid it in such decisions. I intend to show that doctrines of Christ have historically been

[4] See Schubert M. Ogden, *The Reality of God, and Other Essays* (New York: Harper & Row, 1963), pp. 1–20.

[5] See Jay W. Forrester, "Counterintuitive Behavior of Social Systems," paper coypright 1971 by J. W. F. based on testimony for the Subcommittee on Urban Growth of the Committee on Banking and Currency, U.S. House of Representatives, on October 7, 1970. Also Forrester, *World Dynamics* (Cambridge, Mass.: Wright-Allen Press, 1971).

related to understandings of mathematics through the concept of *logos*—initially itself a mathematical word.[6] In a traditional and orthodox manner, I think we can formulate and redefine a doctrine of Christ that takes into account the nature of contemporary mathematics and its assumed relationship to God. Decisions in any truly Christian morality are made on the basis of a historical relationship to Christ, understood through participation in the church or by mediation of the Holy Spirit. A doctrine of Christ that forcibly engages the domain of mathematics, and its applications in computer technology, ought to be available to make Christian decisions intelligible regarding technical models.

Answers to questions concerning the nature of pure mathematics have conditioned theological positions of the past. An understanding of the nature of man's rationality, derived essentially from Greek mathematics and Greek philosophical commentaries on it, *affected*, and, perhaps, using stronger language, *created*, the traditional problem of faith and reason in Christian theology. On the basis of a particular understanding of mathematics, God's existence has been given an attempted proof. Answers to the question in a Pythagorean and Platonic form aided the classical Christian formulation of God's immutable nature. In our century, concern with the problem of mathematical existence by three mathematician-philosophers, Husserl, Whitehead, and Wittgenstein, has conditioned aspects of their thought that have had remarkable application in contemporary theology through their legacy of phenomenology-existentialism, process thought, and language analysis. We shall be concerned with these issues in subsequent chapters. I want simply to point out here that this is an important question for theology and one whose answer, as yet unresolved, will be crucially important for an approaching theological synthesis. Any adequate answer should also be important for practical ethical decisions that concern science and technology.

---

[6] See section "Ratio: The Golden Key to Greek Mathematics" below and chap. 1, section "Word and Wisdom."

How Is Pure Mathematics Understood To Apply?

A general method of science is to seek out a set of mathematical functions that characterize a specific subject matter. Sometimes these mathematical functions are of such accuracy in representation and so related in consistency and compatibility that they allow axiomatization with a resulting coherent mathematical structure that then becomes a general theory. Often, however, strict formal axiomatization is neither available nor desirable. Also, real valued functions are not thought to apply exactly to the world, but in some approximate way. The mathematics, though rigid and exactly structured itself, possesses statistical means to allow characterization of physical reality that varies within bounds.

It is the function of science to discover and then justify by experiment and application that these mathematical relationships do apply to the subject matter under examination. One understands *how* they apply by examining successful scientific theories.

An examination of the relationship of pure mathematics, as used within science, to the empirical reality, on which science focuses, is a fascinating though by no means easy study. It is the kind of analysis central to traditional philosophy of science, and one that changes in delightful ways when science changes. One is struck in this study with what Wigner calls "the unreasonable effectiveness of mathematics in the natural sciences."[7] The discipline that needs *no* reference to the physical world is the most powerful means of describing the physical world.

An adequate solution of the general problem of the relationship of pure mathematics to the actual world as represented by the natural sciences would surely affect our theological models and allow a more adequate understanding of the traditional problem of God's relationship to the world, especially if we could solve in some acceptable way the problem presented above concerning

[7] Eugene Wigner, "The Unreasonable Effectiveness of Mathematics in the Natural Sciences," *Communications on Pure and Applied Mathematics* 13 (Jan. 1960). Reprinted in *The Spirit and the Uses of the Mathematical Sciences,* ed. Thomas L. Saaty and F. Joachim Weyl (New York: McGraw-Hill, 1969), pp. 123–40.

God's relationship to mathematical reality itself. A way to consider aspects of the general problem is to examine issues dependent upon it. This is the procedure of some subsequent chapters. We may show, for example, that a "too close" identification of mathematics with the physical world, in which it is assumed that the physical world is expressible precisely only in terms of mathematical theory, can, on the one hand, precipitate a rationalism where the world is assumed mapped by the rational categories of mathematics and, on the other hand, bring forth a skepticism that knows full well that the world, especially the religious element of it, can never be adequately characterized mathematically. The kinds and varieties of the polarities of rationalism-skepticism are dependent upon an assumed understanding of the relationship of mathematics to the physical world. Another issue of interest to religion is the progress of the broad wave of secularization of all matters of conviction, especially that due to the quantification of value. Whether one can quantify value and how one does so is also dependent upon an assumed understanding of the relationship of mathematics to the physical world. Perhaps, however, the issue most interesting to the study of religion is that of cause and effect.

I claimed at an earlier point, as informed by mathematical analysis, that the *cause* of recent population increase was a decrease in the death rate and not a general overall increase in birth rate. The average death rate has fallen faster than the average birth rate worldwide, and thus seems central to an analysis of the problem. Yet it seems odd to single out death rate and call it the cause, when actually it is the difference between birth and death rates that is a significant predictor of population increase. Is it then the mathematical difference between the two that is the cause? In the Aristotelian sense of answering "Why?", perhaps, Yes. But this may seem even odder, for we know that mathematical relationships themselves do not cause anything, that is, have no agency in themselves. The mathematical model is not the "real situation" but a mathematically symbolical expression of it. When one understands how the mathematical model applies to the world, then he can understand how the mathematical symbols and connections represent actual causal connections in the world. And this is the point. It depends on *how* one understands the mathematical system to apply to the world, whether one accepts one mode of understanding causality or another—or none at all.

The clearest understanding of the connections and relations between functions, that is, between the elements of the mathematical model, is a mathematical connection. If the mathematical model is the most precise way of understanding the physical world, then it is only natural to look in the model for some connection that corresponds to what we call cause and effect in the world—that so massively presents itself to us in our ordinary experience. And yet in no formal mathematical model of the natural sciences is there a *mathematical* connection that corresponds to cause and effect exactly in the natural world. We have to, as it were, import our own.

Importation of an understanding of cause and effect to the mathematical model is not strictly independent historically of the model itself. Different models in their applicability to the world tend to promote different understandings of cause and effect. A Newtonian model, which was generally thought in its relationships to the world to be an accurate, comprehensive, and thoroughly universal characterization of the actual movements of mechanical particles, carries with it a rigid and pervasive understanding of cause and effect modeled after the ever-pervasive and exactly determined connections of the calculus in which the model was presented. We can see that the relativistic quantum models of today need not carry such deterministic weight, for we can interpret the relationships mathematically in terms of statistical ones, and accord, if we wish and deem it appropriate, a causal relationship of similar indeterminacy.

We see, however, that the mathematical model does not determine uniquely its particular concept of causality, but the way we view the model's connection to the physical world seems to. If, for example, Heisenberg's indeterminacy principle, as included within quantum mechanical descriptions, is a description of the actual indeterminacy of physical particles, then a traditional Newtonian understanding of causality (as precisely formulated by LaPlace) is obviously in error. But if such a principle is a description of the limitation of our knowledge of the physical world, then we *could* have as tightly bound a causal nexus as LaPlace ever dreamed, only our knowledge of its rigid structure, from the mathematics, is denied.

A similar restructuring can be given to causality in Newtonian science. Look what Hume did to Newtonian causality by interpreting the Newtonian mathematical model as a description of normal regularities. Kant took the Newtonian model and made it descriptive of empirical phenomenal knowledge gained by consciousness. Cause and effect became for him a structurally guided activity of consciousness similar to the synthetic activities that created the mathematical numbers and relationships in terms of *a priori* structures.

The problem of understanding causality is a perennial one, certainly with us in active philosophical discussion since the time of Aristotle. But the factors that have conditioned the discussion have not been constant. Especially is this true in terms of the mathematical background. Mathematics has changed and evolved, and is presently doing so. Also, the understanding and use of mathematics in the physical sciences has changed. These changes have affected understandings of causality and present us with a number of options today.

One of the theologically important possibilities concerning an understanding of causality is its reintroduction into the domain of God's action. A dominant scientific and theological thrust during the present century has been to eliminate an understanding of efficient causation from both science and theology, because these disciplines are highly structured and precisely determined. This, as I shall attempt to show later, has been a result of specific interpretations of mathematics in both theology and science.[8] New perspectives on the relationship of mathematical systems to the world again allow God to be understood as causally active in the

[8] See chap. 4.

physical world, as well as allowing the world, with its increasing population, to be seen as causally related.[9] How God is active in the population explosion, and what our possibilities of action are, in terms of our obligations, remains a matter to be explored.

It will be helpful theologically not only to have an adequate knowledge of God's relationship to pure mathematics, but also to have knowledge of His relationship causally to the world problems that our mathematical models show. If the population problem is as severe as many say, such knowledge will be more than theoretical. It can and, indeed, ought to affect the Christian community in its life and worship.

The End of the Scientific Age

The theological fashion of the day is to speak in absolutes. Sometimes this is a most appropriate way to communicate precisely. In this spirit we can claim that in the last decade we as a culture and a nation have seen the end of an era—the end of the scientific age.

Science has not stopped, nor has its brilliantly successful stepchild, technology. On the contrary, we are today completing more basic research in science and mathematics than in any other period in the history of man. We appear to be on the verge of major new syntheses, breakthroughs to fundamental structures, that will give new sight of a unified, aesthetically beautiful, and basically simple structure of cosmic regularity. In spite of major problems, a fruition of theoretical science seems close at hand. The advent of a new, fundamentally pervasive, scientific paradigm appears imminent. We may have it by the turn of the century.

Our technological accomplishments are dazzling. We have witnessed—literally so by television—the actual trip of men to the moon. Millions of lives have been saved and existence made tolerable by medical science. Modern technology has made us powerful. We have a massive ability to change things.

The "end of the scientific age" is used here in the sense in

9 See chap. 4.

which it was popular to use the phrase "end of the Christian age" during the last decade. This did not mean that Christians had ceased to be, nor that a vitality of Christian thought and theology had waned. It did mean that the general cultural thrust toward interpreting existence by means of the Christian faith had been thwarted, and the Christian claim to represent the general public goals and aspirations had been broken. Christianity has found itself to be one among many religions in Western culture and as such often of less importance than a more pervasive religious secularism. The claim that we were in the "post-Christian era" was simply a claim that Christianity had become relativized and had become *a* cultural force in the large pluralism of religious and secular goals.

It was not just the feeling that Christianity had become irrelevant, or had failed to solve the world's problems, that precipitated an anti-Christian reaction among the general population, and the open recognition by theologians that Christianity had become socially impotent, but the more pointed awareness that Christianity had *created*, and still *creates*, major problems that it can not solve. It was felt that Christianity could not heal its own divisions, which in the past not only separated Christian from Christian but also caused wars and hatred among men in the larger society. It was considered that Christianity left to its own devices and consistent internally with its own historical development could not create a concept and model of human sexuality that does not tend to cripple human sexuality and human love through guilt. Can Christianity today lead, even its own members, in coping with the environmental, pollution, and population crises that it has fostered in association with science through its assumptions and beliefs concerning man's relationship to the physical world?

A major portion of the criticism of the church has come from within the church. If one takes the Gospel seriously, the organization most liable for judgment according to the message and work of Christ is the church itself, that is, those who believe the Gospel. It is not inconsistent for Christians to affirm the "end of the

Christian age" in terms of the meaning above. It is not anti-Christian to see the church under Christian judgment for its failures.

The reasons for claiming the "end of the scientific age" are similar to those for claiming the "end of the Christian age." Science has become relativized as a mode of knowledge and has *created* problems that it cannot solve. It is not unscientific to see the radical limitations of science.

The relativization of its knowledge is a result of the internal development of science and philosophical perspectives of science. There are numerous developments within science that limit what we would have considered previously to be scientific knowledge. We cannot know experimentally according to present relativity theory the actual present condition of anything physically distant from us. We have physical evidence of what a star *was*, not *is*, since there is always a finite amount of time for any transmission of information. We cannot know the exact velocity and position of any particle. Such indeterminacy is a foundational condition of the more adequate theory of quantum mechanics.

More telling for the general feeling of relativization of scientific knowledge is a more thorough cultural awareness of the role that mathematics plays in science. Generally speaking, science has progressed as it has couched its concepts in the categories of mathematics. If one really wants to know, for example, what is the contemporary theory of atomic particles, he has to go to the mathematical structures concerning them. Only secondarily can one bring in the more ordinary intuitions of geometrical physical models.

If one grants that the mathematical explanation of scientific theory is the most accurate, that is, what the theory really states, and if one becomes aware, even minimally so, of the extreme abstraction and limitation of "extraneous" factors involved in the understanding of the mathematics, the limitations of scientific theory become painfully obvious. Can the sterile and purified essentially *mathematical connections*, though beguilingly fascinating in themselves, ever include more than a minimal part of human experience or even of the physical world? I shall say much more about the relationship of mathematics to science and the problem of human knowing at a later stage. Sufficient here, however, is to point out a reason why, among many students today, there is a reaction against science. It is not just that the scientific disciplines are hard or demanding, but that they do not allow one to know and experience the real physical world. Indeed, these disciplines in their mathematical purity often seem to hinder or obscure such experience. Contrast these attitudes with those of many of us who went into the study of the physical sciences because we "knew" they could tell us about the real world and would allow us a more intelligent and fuller experience of it.

These problems of the relativization of the knowledge of science, however, are and have been relatively minor, provided that the general thrust of science and technology does not produce a major crisis in human history and thereby undermine the confidence in the enterprise. There is nothing epistemologically unique or essentially awkward about having a primary mode of interpretation of physical theory, namely, the mathematical one, that when taken exclusively by itself is either paradoxical or problematical, *if the primary mode is complemented by a host of other means of knowing.* Such is the case with science historically. It has always been able to cluster to its mathematical theories a plethora of experiential data, aesthetic media, and practical application. Also, this condition has been manifestly true with Christianity, where its essential assertion correlating the meaning of human existence with the passion, death, and resurrection of Christ, though clearly paradoxical, has brought together a vast array of modes of living, philosophical creations, great art and drama—and thoroughly practical living. Both science and Christianity, however, are under serious question, and are and will be subject to progressive disenchantment among Western men because they co-jointly are producing, with other major forces and developments world-wide, an apparently inevitable crisis in human existence of the gravest magnitude.

The approaching crisis, at its heart a population one, can be simply illustrated in terms of world population projections. According to the computer models of Jay W. Forrester, if we continue roughly our present consumption of natural resources, capital investment, and rate of pollution, the world population will continue to rise exponentially until about the year 2020, when it will reach a maximum of somewhat less than six billion and then fall off.[10] How far it falls off and how fast it falls off depends upon action taken now and during the intervening years. In any case, it appears with startling clarity, at least according to the models, that the drop off will be in the range of billions, due to starvation and increase of pollution.

But can we believe Mr. Forrester's projections, or any other set of them?[11] Most responsible world-population projections have been wrong, but have been wrong consistently in the negative direction. Their estimates have been too low. Forrester's work gives us some means for projection of the approximate date of maximum population, which will be followed by a drop, depending upon the other variables of birth control, industrial investment, and so forth. Depending upon our action, the date will vary. The models are rough and imprecise and probably miss the date by some five, twenty, or fifty years. But the evidence we presently have indicates that the population *will* reach a maximum somewhere in the twenty-first century—and probably within the lifetime of most of us. We will know more about this Population-Maximum date as Forrester's models are modified by other responsible research.

The age of *increase* of population, which we have known for centuries, is coming to an end. The increase in human population, representing the domination of nature by man, has been a most significant factor (perhaps unconsciously) in structuring his political, social, and religious life. The change in era to decreasing,

---

[10] Forrester, "Counterintuitive Behavior of Social Systems," figure 2.

[11] Since originally writing this manuscript, I and Dean R. Fowler have attempted to evaluate the world models and theological issues dependent on them. Granville C. Henry and Dean R. Fowler, "World Models: A Review Essay," *Journal of the American Academy of Religion* 42, no. 1 (March 1974): 114–27.

and then perhaps alternately increasing and decreasing populations, similar in nature to the familiar economic cycles, or almost any repetitive natural phenomena, will require significantly new political, religious, and social organizations.

There appears to be great doubt that science and technology, which have allowed man's natural exponential growth to be in effect, can avert the disaster that will accompany continued growth, that is, without a basic change in the relationship of science to culture. Garrett Hardin, in his article "The Tragedy of the Commons," published in a major science journal, asserts that the population problem has no technical solution.[12] By this he does not mean that science cannot aid in humanitarian means for some relief, or, more important, aid in its understanding, but that science and technology *understood and accepted in their present relationsh'p to society and governmental structure are impotent to avert the disaster.* Only by a fundamental extension of morality, exercised in terms of firm social and governmental control—as Hardin calls it, "mutual coercion mutually agreed upon"—will it be possible to deal with the problem in any minimally acceptable way. Ultimately, this would mean basic and far-reaching changes in the governmental structure of the United States and of every other major nation. It would entail a necessary cooperation among the major powers that has not yet existed. Though Hardin does not enter into detail concerning the nature of preferred governmental structures, and certainly makes no claim for the superiority of any present governmental structure over another, his implication and claim are clear. The presently existing structures of science and technology as they are related to various cultures world-wide have created a major problem, approaching a magnitude of disaster unprecedented in world history, for which science can give *no solution* within the present structures of science and society. Science has created a problem that it cannot solve.

[12] Garrett Hardin, "The Tragedy of the Commons," *Science* 162 (Dec. 1968): 1243–48. Reprinted as chap. 123 in *Population, Evolution, and Birth Control,* 2d ed., ed., Garrett Hardin (San Francisco: W. H. Freeman, 1969).

In its continued use by man, the problem progressively worsens.

What should be the response of Christians to science in this post-Christian and post-scientific age? I think that the various Christian communities should encourage and support with as much force as possible the scientific endeavor as it is carried on as a search for knowledge. Theologians and philosophers of the Christian community ought further to consider and formulate models for action that would range in extent from involving small subsections of the Christian church to larger political models involving the whole society, that first might help alleviate, even in a small degree, the present and approaching crisis, and second might reintegrate the pursuit of scientific knowledge in a different and more effectively human societal context. A New Scientific Age might then come, and also, perhaps, a new Christian one.

It is not clear, however, what specific action Christian communities ought to take in regard to the population crisis. Individually or as a community, one can take well-meaning action that appears intuitively correct, for example, reducing population by enforced birth control, which, within the social system itself, merely accentuates and compounds the problem. A present drastic reduction in the birth rate, for example, according to the preliminary models of Forrester, would stimulate capital investment and the consequent further industrialization to such a degree that the ultimate disaster would be far more spectacular, due to pollution and a renewed population explosion, than the present trend, which will see population decreased by a gradual reduction of natural resources.[13] Forrester's work indicates that we will have to reduce, simultaneously and drastically, population, pollution, depletion of natural resources, and, especially, capital investment. Most surprising, some reduction in food production would be necessary, which is certainly counter to what we would normally think at the present stage.[14] In proposing models for Christian action, we need the best analyses that science can provide. For if our object is to aid and heal nature, of which we are the primary cause of its ruin,

[13] Forrester, figure 5.
[14] *Ibid.*, figure 8.

we need the information of those disciplines whose primary responsibility is the *knowledge* of nature.

I began work on the problem of the relationship of mathematics to Christian theology before I was aware of the crisis of population and technology. I had thought that Malthus was discredited once and for all. As the problems in this regard have become ever more apparent, I have sometimes questioned the relevance of a task that appears not to have immediate regard for the crisis-causing source. Upon second look, however, I see this work as part of the necessary model-proposing activities of the theologian. The models that presently appear to help, involve a cultural asceticism, some considerable denial of present activities and freedoms to acquire and consume nonreplaceable resources and further denial of the freedom to pollute. The political necessities may include a cutback on population increase and reductions in the use of natural resources, in industrial output, and even, perhaps, in food production. These must, can, and ought to be matched in the Christian communities by increased appropriate aesthetic, intellectual, and social opportunities—couched in the relevance of worship.

One of the major sources of intellectual life in Western culture has been mathematics. Of almost equal appeal is its aesthetic dimension. Mathematics combines with the hardest intellectual rigors an aesthetic satisfaction that has engaged Christian thought in the past and has potential for further future correlation for the community of Christ. I am not proposing a simple amalgamation, but, I hope, a genuine synthesis, where mathematics obtains an appropriate place in the necessary re-evolution of Christian theology, as we approach and press through the twenty-first century.

Perspectives on Science and Religion

Science has significantly influenced the Christian religion. Very few in the Western world will deny this.

We appear now, however, to be in a period of transition from an old understanding of the relationship of science and religion to a new one. Most of us who had training in the first half of this century, or who were influenced by the dominant academic and scientific assumptions of that period, thought that science not only presented the truth, but also could arbitrate any differences between itself and religion. Under this influence many committed Christians lost their appreciation for the authority of traditional religion.

The spirit of the present academic age has changed. Those who are now receiving their education are under the impress of a different disillusionment. It is the authority and truth content of science that is now under question. Those who may see science as a discipline that narrowly limits the understanding of their own humanity, however, have not in any significant numbers returned to Christianity in order to find answers to their spiritual and ontological problems. The impact that science had on their fathers in its criticism of traditional Western religion is also felt by them. In general, they look to new fields, to new orientations, and to new religions. Even those who speak from within the community of traditional faith do so from new scientific or philosophical perspectives that allow the old content of religious orthodoxy to be seen and presented in a new light.[15]

A questioning of the authority of science associated with the realization that in its technological power it must be integrated with a viable religion has, however, precipitated a considerable awakening of interest over a broad range of orientations concerning the actual historical relationship of science and religion in Western culture. Many old interpretations are recognized as patently false. Science has not constantly warred with theology nor theology with science, as Andrew Dickson White maintained at the end of the nineteenth century.[16] The problems of science and religion are *not* the result of an encounter between urbane, rational, quick-witted scientists and muddle-headed, believing,

[15] Some new perspectives are process philosophy, phenomenology, language analysis and neo-Hegelianism.
[16] Andrew Dickson White, *A History of the Warfare of Science with Theology in Christendom* (New York: D. Appleton, 1897), 2 vols., (New York: The Free Press, 1965).

intuitive religionists; nor are they a result of a challenge by hard-headed empirically minded scientists and abstract, theoretical, deductive theologians. In fact, there has seldom, if ever, been a clear encounter between scientists as a group and religionists as a group at the level of fundamental research and discovery. The conflicts that have occurred have been primarily between men who shared the same religious faith or the same scientific perspective, or *within* a man who saw and accepted both the truth aspects of science and the claims upon his life by religion.

Isaac Newton, for example, was an avowed Christian who seriously attempted to relate what he knew of science with his religious understanding. The beginning preface of his *Principia,* that work which more than any other established a mechanical universe, states his purpose to create a foundation for natural philosophy; and we are led to believe by his statements that this natural philosophy is of a sort similar in function and grounding to the great natural theologies of his Christian past. The *Principia* closes with a general scholium that is a theological treatise on the nature of God and His relationship to the world. If Newton's deep religious interests were peculiar to him as a scientist, we could dismiss them as a psychological aberration. But his case is not that unusual. From the ecstatic religious mysticism of the Pythagoreans, to the Catholic cleric Copernicus's mathematical reformulation of the solar system, the deep religious concerns of Galileo and Kepler, to the nonorthodox but deep religious motivation of Einstein, religion has formed a significant part of the evolution of science.

The recent focus on the ecological crisis has shown the underlying support that the Judeo-Christian religion has given the development of science, first, by desacralizing nature and second, by insisting that nature can serve man. Understanding that there is a transcendent creator God, Who is assumed to have created a lawful universe that need not, however, correspond to the a-priori mathematical categories of man, has helped further an empirical search to see how, in fact, He did create it.

There is no doubt, though, that the scientific community, which has always been composed of a significant subset of Christians and Jews loyal to their religious traditions, has been appalled and incensed by some extravagant claims of religion, and accordingly has opposed them. Nor is there any doubt that certain segments of Christianity, from scattered Protestant communities to the politically more powerful Roman Catholic Church, have taken positions on scientific matters that have been shown by scientists to be incorrect. There are at times conflicts at local church levels between scientific and religious claims as presented by those who know neither science nor the great theological traditions themselves. We are all familiar with the hostility shown by certain Christian groups to the theory of evolution and how, within these groups, there is considerable effort to attempt to disprove the theory of evolution or, from an epistemological study, to show that it is in fact a theory that reasonable men do not have to accept.

These conflicts, however, seem to be aberrations of a normally widespread compatibility of the Judeo-Christian religion with the evolution, continuation, and basic program of Western science. They are more like sibling fights than conflicts between strange enemies. They have done considerable harm to the spiritual body of the church and have badly marred Christian history. They have affected the ordinary attitudes of Western men and women, both Christian and non-Christian, and have caused deep suspicions and actual wounds that prevent the easy and early reconciliation or appropriate understanding of the relationship of the two. As a result, the relevance of Christianity has been seriously challenged among significant portions of the public at large.

Spiritual pride and untoward political involvement of the Christian church did cause some of the major conflicts with science. The ugly encounter between Galileo and the church could have been prevented if the church had been loyal to its own best enlightened principles and had adhered to its own biblical tradition. Although the causes of the conflicts have been manifold, one among many factors stands out as both surprising and critical. *Previous theological accommodation to science set the stage for conflict with science when science itself changed.* The church often hallowed and made static a scientific doctrine and thus secured its own inability to loose itself from a particular scientific posture when challenged.

The church's theological identification with the philosophical and scientific system of Aristotle in the Middle Ages made it almost impossible to accept the scientific assertions of Copernicus and Galileo. The synthesis of Aristotelian philosophy, Ptolemaic astronomy, the Bible, and the Church Fathers created by the medieval theologians was indeed beautiful to behold. We may have great sympathy with the men who were accustomed to a harmony of reason and faith that was fitted together in one religious-philosophical system. In this perspective, Copernicus's claim that the earth moved appeared to violate the best of *rational* claims. The stability of the earth had been confirmed by centuries of accumulated common sense and scientific calculation. Ptolemaic astronomy declared the earth to be a sphere and rough calculations gave its approximate diameter.[17] In considering Copernicus's hypothesis that the earth rotated, astronomers could calculate the approximate velocity of the surface of the earth if it did in fact complete one revolution in a day. Under these circumstances, from such calculations *and within the perspective of Aristotelian physics*, the wind velocity at the surface of the earth would have made life as presently known impossible.[18] The fact of nominal wind velocities, caused by factors other than the earth's rotation, confirmed the earth's stability. What was rationally justified and commensurate with the overwhelming testimony of sensory experience, the church then clothed with spiritual authority. The stability of the earth became a theological doctrine. If the church had not so seriously identified its theology with an Aristotelian philosophy and physics, the novel perspectives of Copernicus, Kepler, and

[17] *The Almagest,* Book I, 4.
[18] *Ibid.,* Book I, 7.

Galileo would not have appeared so scandalous and could have been reconciled with relative ease to scriptural claims.[19]

The English church, after political separation from the Roman church and after engaging in controversy concerning the appropriateness and correctness of Newtonian physics, found itself in harmony with the natural theology growing out of Newton's work. The Book of God and the Book of the World were seen to be mutually compatible. Arguments from design that presupposed a Newtonian universe were frequently used and often appealed to. God was supposed to have shown his excellence through the fineness of the world and in its precision of operation. There was again a happy accommodation of science and religion, between Newtonian natural philosophy and Christian theology.[20]

When one sees the physical world as essentially mechanical, as a well-tuned machine guided and sustained by its maker; when one sees rational human souls as created by God in time and place and put into a precisely working cosmos that is also governed by precisely working moral laws for the purpose of guidance and salvation, then there is considerable intellectual and religious shock when this same universe appears under Darwinian categories to be evolving and changing under its own rules according to chance rather than according to God's providence. The place of God as seen in the Newtonian scheme is necessarily challenged, and what is in considerable measure a conflict between scientific systems is adapted to theological positions and made a conflict between science and religion.

In emphasizing the fact that accommodation of science to theology set conditions that often precipitated conflicts between theology and science, I do not want to minimize what may be genuinely incompatible elements between an authentic Christianity and the then contemporary versions of science. In each of the

[19] See John Dillenberger, *Protestant Thought and Natural Science, A Historical Interpretation* (Garden City: Doubleday & Co., 1960), chap. 1. (Paperback, Cokesbury.)
[20] *Ibid.,* chaps. 4 and 5.

major conflicts between science and religion here mentioned, there were aspects of science that were then and are now unacceptable from a Christian perspective. Most theologians cannot accept the complete geometrization and mechanization of the physical world, and their elimination of purpose within the world, that attended both Cartesian and Newtonian physics. We do not have to accept such mechanization today under the authority of contemporary physics. It was and is difficult to accept the naturalistic philosophy that was inherent in Darwinism. The elimination of God that occurred in some philosophical positions following Darwin is not only unnecessary (scientifically) but violates Christian sensibilities.

The problem, of course, is determining what is the true nature of authentic Christianity and separating an understanding of it, at least in thought, from the accretions of accommodation with science and philosophy. This is part of the traditional problem of *faith and reason*. We cannot ignore the physical world and theories concerning its understanding, control, and use, because from a Christian perspective God created it and is concerned for us to have an appropriate understanding of it. We are responsible for it.[21] The concepts of science, however, have achieved such generality and comprehensiveness that they have tended to influence and at times dominate theology itself.

A word of caution is in order. We in the Christian community do not want to make the same mistake as in the past by identifying or adapting theology too closely to any one scientific system, for when this changes we will probably again find ourselves in the all-too-familiar situation of conflict *with science*. This may seem no danger in our age of relativism. But there are signs of a possible new and comprehensive scientific paradigm bursting upon Western thought.[22]

It is here, at this particular point in the study of the problem of faith and reason, that a study of the relationship of mathematics to theology is helpful, for mathematics has affected epistemology —the study of how we know—more than any other science. It

[21] *Genesis* 1: 1, 28–29.
[22] See chap. 6, section "Skepticism and the 'New Paradigm.' "

has formed the chief example for rationalistic thought and conditioned skeptical alternatives. I shall present mathematics' relationship to traditional understandings of faith and reason in the next chapter, with an analysis of Augustine's thought. I also hope to show that a contemporary understanding of mathematics allows more room for a traditional (Augustinian) "faith" than even Augustine could accept, and, hence, provides opportunities to create theological models for a contemporary position on the problem of faith and reason that include both the necessary "distance from" and "identity with" contemporary science.[23]

It might seem that in order to show the relationship of contemporary mathematics to contemporary theology and thus aid in the model-building process for more appropriate understanding of the relationship of science to religion, I ought simply to enter into a discussion of contemporary developments in mathematics as they affect contemporary theology. But here a peculiar aspect of the problem comes forth. Theologians and philosophers of religion have shown very little interest in mathematics and its relationship to theology, whereas they have discussed actively other scientific disciplines in an attempt to ascertain their relevance to contemporary theology. Could it be true that mathematics has importance for theology proportional to the current interest in it by theologians? That is, is mathematics only minimally engaged with contemporary theology, as perhaps most theologians suspect and believe? This, of course, could be the case. I am going to try to show that it is not. If mathematics is important for theology, we need some indication why it has not been so recognized by contemporary theologians.

The Hidden Revolution[24]

What kinds of scientific theory, data, and new developments

---

[23] See chap. 1, section "Augustine, Mathematics, and the Problem of Faith and Reason."

[24] See Granville C. Henry, Jr., "Mathematics and Theology," *Bucknell Review* 20, no. 2 (Fall 1972).

are of interest to theologians and philosophers of religion? How do they go about selecting from the vast area of content in science that which is appropriate for or related to theology? In an era of specialization when even good scientists can hardly be expected to keep up with developments within their own general field, on what basis does the theologian choose those areas of science that are relevant for his study? The answer is probably a quite expected one. Those areas of science which are of interest to the theologian are those primarily which have already affected theological doctrines historically. The initial encounter between a new science and a traditional theology conditions the kinds of questions asked later about science and thus forms the selective mechanism for choosing within science those areas which are considered relevant to theology.

As an example, if one asks what content within physics is of interest to theologians and philosophers of religion today, he sees in the literature a preoccupation with relativity and quantum theory.[25] The aspects of relativity and quantum theory that are chosen for consideration are those which allow a reinterpretation of an understanding of God's relationship to the created world and of man's relationship to both God and the created world. These contemporary discussions find a *general acceptance by the theological community* because of the residual effect on present sensitivities of the initial shock of a Newtonian mechanization of the world and the subsequent elimination of the necessity of God's sustaining presence through a refinement of this theory.

Another example, again from the content of physics-chemistry, is the present concern with the theory of entropy. The assumed necessary total increase of entropy (disorder) within any closed system seems ultimately to spell disaster for any divinely guided continuing complexification of the created order, a position that is assumed by most process theology and other theologies that see God working creatively toward some goal from "within" evolution. Teilhard de Chardin has responded to the scientific theory of entropy with a philosophical theology that requires a

[25] This is especially true in process theology.

force of vitalization that ultimately must overcome the apparently necessary asymmetric direction of entropy. The concern with entropy is a *concern* because the consequences of the theory seem to be further evidence against a divine teleology, a problem that has a long history within theology. Theological opinion has been conditioned about what is important in science. One can be sure that developments in any scientific field that relax, modify, or reinterpret the theory of entropy will be met with considerable interest by the theological community.

Notice that the position presented here is in no way a radical one. Put in a different form, it is simply a statement that what is of interest to individual theologians is conditioned by the general theological community, which has its own deep historical roots.

Has mathematics, then, never encountered theology with sufficient force in order, according to the above principle, to condition and to allow a contemporary theological interest in it? The answer, I think, is a firm No. There has already been a major encounter between mathematics and theology, a conflict that has structured traditional theology. It has, however, gone virtually unnoticed as a conflict between science and religion because of the mediation of Greek philosophy. As the first major conflict, it was, I believe, of greater importance than the generally recognized "first conflict," the Copernican one. As theologians become more aware of the nature of this initial conflict of mathematics with early Christian thought, I think they will become more interested in the engagement of mathematics with contemporary theology.

In order to affirm an influence of science on religion, we ought to be able to isolate a particular content that is without doubt scientific and be able to show how it has affected content that is clearly theological. Thus, in order to show an early major encounter between mathematics and theology, I need to establish first that there existed a mathematics that was in fact a-theological and, from my perspective, a-philosophical. This seems to be the easiest of tasks. The mere mention of Euclid's *Elements* brings to consideration a body of mathematical theory unified by a few axioms and having interpretation in (theologically neutral) geometric figure. It is true that Greek mathematicians had isolated mathematics as a distinct theory and practice from other philosophical and theological concerns by the time of Plato. We can agree that by this time they had created the first pure science, but we should also notice that their isolation of mathematics from philosophy and theology was not complete.

If we put ourselves into the perspective of the mathematicians of Euclid's time, we would find that there were many assumptions that they considered to be a part of mathematics proper that we would consider to be philosophical. Assumptions that mathematics is primarily geometrical, that it is one system, that it is discovered and not created, that in its ultimate reality it is transcendent and nonempirical, that in knowing mathematical structures one necessarily knows some ontological structures—these are all assumptions that, due to the further development of mathematics, are philosophical concerns about mathematics. There was definitely an area of overlap between mathematics and philosophy in Greek thought. We can make this judgment because through internal mathematical developments the domain of the discipline has been more clearly defined. Accordingly, from our mathematical perspective we can see a well-developed pure science having its effect on philosophy in ancient Greece.

I am proposing that lying behind Greek philosophy was a genuine science that in itself, through the mediation of philosophy, had an important effect on theology. A justification for this position appears in the next chapter. The fact that a science has an effect on theology *through* a philosophical position is not unusual; in fact, this is the normal route of influence. By philosophical here, I do not mean a position necessarily espoused by a philosopher as consciously philosophical, although such positions have been a considerable factor in the history of science and religion. I do mean those assumptions which, at an early stage, may have been a part of the science but which later are isolated through the continuing development of the science and are then not considered to be a part of the science proper. For example, Newton assumed that his *Principia* did illuminate a mechanical world system, and the philosophical assumptions associated with his (not necessarily mechanical) mathematical and physical system influenced theology heavily. The debate over Darwinism was significant for theology because Darwin's scientific theory of evolution seemed to speak authoritatively on larger philosophical issues, in particular on the questions and problems of philosophical naturalism. We know that the *scientific theory* of evolution need not be necessarily associated with philosophical naturalism, and that it is illegitimate to claim as science what is in effect a philosophical posture. But in each of these cases, and in almost all other major conflicts, the genuine science did engage theology through its philosophical interpretations, and had considerable effect on it. The pattern of influence of mathematics through philosophy to Christian theology is the same as the general pattern of the other major sciences and their influence on theology, but the time taken for transition of influence through philosophy was longer for mathematics. In the case of certain major discoveries, mathematical deduction for example, professional philosophy had at least three full centuries to absorb it before the Christian era. Although Judaism was, of course, in existence during this time, the conflict and encounter with it through Philo occurred at about the same time as the advent of Christianity. This time lag, and other historical exigencies that prevented the early Christian thinkers from dealing with primary mathematical sources and left them with some access to Plato and Aristotle but primarily with secondary neo-Platonism, gnosticism, and religious Stoicism, account in part for the fact that Christians thought they were dealing with a general Greek rationality and religion and not with a science of mathematics.

The Underlying Mathesis

The fact that mathematics engaged philosophy at least three centuries before the Christian era and was to a large extent absorbed by the philosophical disciplines is not a *sufficient* explanation of the general unawareness throughout the history of

Christianity of the relationship of mathematics to theology. The influence of mathematics on theology has differed in principle from that of the other sciences. Normally the physical sciences, and the social sciences as they model their procedures on the physical sciences, are concerned to make statements about the objective structures of the physical world. To the degree that such objective understanding of the world, and man within it, affects theology, we can isolate the particular influences from the sciences on theology. Pure mathematics, however, has essentially affected modes of knowing (what we can know and how we can know it) —*not by the objective content of mathematics but through semiformalized structures associated with mathematics that are only later objectivized and then seen to be a part of the actual content of mathematics.* Thus the philosopher and theologian may not recognize that it is the content of mathematics, which is only later so identified, that affects general perspectives of knowing.

The most obvious example of such a process of influence is found in the history of logic and its mathematical formalization. To the best of our knowledge, the use of *mathematical* deduction was beginning to flourish only at the late date of Plato's Academy and then only in a group of mathematicians peripherally associated with the Academy.[26] Plato makes no use of *axiomatic mathematical* deduction in his works. His student Aristotle, however, championed it and began to formalize it. Logic, according to Aristotle, was part of a general rational faculty that was, of course, applicable to mathematics but in no way limited to mathematics. It was not considered to be in itself mathematical content, for example, geometrical figures, numbers, and the like, but was the tool used to discover and show such content. The continued formalization of logic that was reintroduced by Boole in the nineteenth century and the continued development in the twentieth, has shown that within the ancient logic there is a precise content, a number of systems that in our day are now considered as mathematical. After

[26] See O. Neugebauer, *The Exact Sciences in Antiquity* (Princeton, N.J.: Princeton University Press, 1952), p. 152. (Paperback, Harper Torchbook, 1962.)

a flurry of excitement at the beginning of this century concerning the possibility that this mathematical logic was a precise explication of general logic, and thus could possibly be used to plumb the foundations of reality itself, a more moderate position has been assumed by a host of philosophers and mathematicians concerning it, namely, that its primary interpretation is in mathematical axiomatic systems themselves and associated other scientific systems, and not in a general mode of presenting knowledge and truth. This one fact of the limitation of the scope and applicability of mathematical logic, which itself was brought about by mathematical discoveries, perhaps more than any other affected the mature philosophies of Husserl, Whitehead, and Wittgenstein—those philosophers who more than any others have conditioned contemporary theology—and allowed each to reformulate his basic epistemology and come forth with a new "logic" dependent neither upon a mathematical system nor classical logic.[27] Formal logic, which originally had (in Greek thought) its origins primarily in mathematics, has returned home essentially to this discipline. In the meantime, its influence on general epistemology has been enormous, and has affected Christian modes of knowing considerably in a way that I shall outline later.

I do not seek to ignore the influences of known mathematical content that were stated by philosophers and theologians to have affected their own works. When Plato, Aristotle, Augustine, Aquinas, Descartes, Pascal, and many others, tell us of the influence of mathematics on their own positions, we certainly do not want to dismiss these statements. We may assume that a philosopher who spent the major portion of his early years dealing professionally with mathematics, for example, Husserl or Whitehead, and who later directed the full force of his talents to a general philosophical position, still possessed his knowledge of mathematics and was still motivated to secure solutions to the problems of the foundations and philosophy of mathematics in his larger philosophical endeavors. This is said to emphasize that, in addition to the normal modes of examining the relationship

[27] See chaps. 3 and 5.

of mathematics to philosophy and theology, there is a *perspective about the nature of mathematics itself* that affects this work and forms a presupposition of its success. It is only fair to the reader to outline this orientation for his benefit in understanding the subsequent analysis, and, more important, to invite his critical analysis of it.

The first assumption is that *there is an established body of mathematics*. There is a common feeling amounting almost to a prejudice, spread throughout the nonmathematical academic world and fed by attitudes in the elementary and secondary schools, that mathematics is some eternal structure unified without paradox or ambiguity and given in some absolute fashion never to be changed. Anyone familiar with the contemporary discussions in the foundations of mathematics, or who has examined differences between Formalists and Intuitionists, or, for that matter, examined the history of mathematics, knows that this is not altogether true. Mathematics has changed in the past not only by adding to itself new theories and modes of operation, but by rejecting whole disciplinary areas, for example, astrology and numerology, as well as specific mathematical statements. The contemporary development of set theory within which (almost) all other mathematics can be presented itself contains contradictions unless axiomatized to prevent them. Such axiomatization, however, has seemed to limit the formal adequacy of axiomatic structures to characterize the full properties and powers of set theory itself.[28] It might seem that these difficulties, and many others, would prevent the claim that there is a unified body of content of mathematics, because we cannot say what the content is and have general agreement concerning it among mathematicians. And yet there is general agreement among mathematicians concerning what is and is not mathematics. It is an agreement at the operative level of the discipline where philosophical questions do not enter. And here

[28] The famous theorem of Skolem and Lowenheim maintains that any system that can be formalized in the first-order predicate calculus, if it has a model at all, will have a denumerable one. Set theory so formalized, which does possess nondenumerable members, cannot thus be characterized fully by the system.

the common feeling mentioned above is correct. Difficulties in the foundations of mathematics are all the more striking because of the unification the discipline has *actually* achieved.[29]

In spite of the apparent general agreement on what is mathematical, determined within the community in terms of the cases of mathematics that appear, it is surprisingly difficult to describe this content in general philosophical language. At this level there is disagreement about what the nature and content of mathematics are. It is no longer possible to say that mathematics deals exclusively with number and magnitude, which in part it surely does, because there are examples of solid mathematics —Boolean algebras, for example—that are neither number nor magnitude. Enlarging the domain of mathematics to include pure axiomatic systems and their mathematical interpretations helps considerably in an attempt to describe known mathematical content; but again there is mathematical content, the total content of arithmetic, for example, that can not be presented by any one (rigidly formalized) axiomatic system, no matter how comprehensive it appears to be. Even if we conclude that there are a multiplicity of systems, necessarily infinite in number, that can characterize the theorems of arithmetic, we still seem to depend upon the content of arithmetic itself to justify the completeness of the set of systems. And yet the content of arithmetic, including that which can be built from it, in no way constitutes the totality of mathematical content.

The question whether there are infinite sets in mathematics,

[29] In a recent article, Leon Henkin has proposed that the division of foundational studies into the logicism-formalism-intuitionism scheme, which has been prevalent since the beginning of this century, be given up, since this scheme represents competing *philosophical* viewpoints concerning mathematics that are not relevant to the burgeoning *mathematical* activity in the foundations of mathematics. His suggestion for a division into set-theoretic, algebraic, and constructive aspects captures the mathematical character of recent research. "Each of these strands of the subject supplements the others ; they are interwoven to provide a richly illuminated depiction of a common domain." Leon Henkin, "Mathematical Foundations for Mathematics," *The American Mathematical Monthly* 78, no. 5 (May 1971): 466.

considered objectively existing really or ideally, is essentially a philosophical and not a mathematical question. For whether one views the natural numbers as, say, a (Platonically) existing set or as the creation of the mathematician according to a (finite) rule, the natural numbers in their "infinite" nature, however conceived, are a part of mathematics—and universally agreed to be so. The question whether the continuum hypothesis is true or not is definitely a part of the body of mathematics, even though we know that both its affirmation and negation are compatible with known assumptions regarding universal sets.[30] Here we may expect further *mathematical* developments to clarify the meaning of the results of Gödel and Cohen in order to allow more satisfactory statements concerning the continuum hypothesis itself.

The second assumption is that the *discipline of mathematics is cumulative in regard to content*, that is, in the building up of that body which we assume is agreed on, in a way that no other discipline is. Once proved, a theorem remains true within its systematic theory, although the theory may be enlarged, re-interpreted, more thoroughly formalized, made part of some new theory, and put in various contexts not previously known. Contradiction and anomaly play a vital part in the thrust toward cumulative development. Examples abound throughout the history of mathematics of "saving old content" from rejection because of its paradoxical nature. Irrational magnitudes were kept within the domain of geometry by appropriate definitions of Eudoxus and the deductive context of Euclid's *Elements*. Different geometries, which if thought to portray the properties of space or reflect the structures of consciousness seem to falsify each other, have been ordered as themselves elements of a group through group theory. The contradictions and anomalies of the intuitive calculus of

[30] "If X is the continuum hypothesis, $2^{\aleph_0} = \aleph_1$, then we know from the complementary results of K. Gödel and P. Cohen that both X and non-X are compatible with all known natural assumptions regarding the universe of sets." Abraham Robinson, "Formalism 64," *Logic Methodology and Philosophy of Science, Proceedings of the 1964 International Congress*, ed. Yehoshua Bar-Hillel (Amsterdam: North-Holland, 1965), p. 232.

Newton and Leibniz were eliminated by the logical grounding effected in the Berlin school, and as a result the perplexing, mysterious, and apparently contradictory infinitesimals were eliminated, only to find that in this century we can introduce infinitesimals as an integral part of analysis in terms of new structural foundations involving elements that are themselves infinite sequences or, more generally, in terms of nonstandard models.[31]

Essentially I am claiming that the content of mathematics is cumulative, whereas the philosophical and mathematical interpretations of mathematics are subject to rather wide historical fluctuations. The interpretations of mathematics, and the general principles by which it operates as given by mathematicians and philosophers, are designed *to insure* the cumulative nature of its content. The new interpretations and general principles, however, are normally precipitated by mathematical developments themselves. As a technical discipline, mathematics has enough momentum to go beyond the strictures of any specific philosophy or overview and develop difficulties within that philosophy that then require either an enlarged or a new perspective. For this reason we can claim that developments in mathematics can ultimately affect theology through the general reinterpretation of mathematics as precipitated by its own new content. Historically, the discoveries of paradox and contradiction within the *content of mathematics* have resulted in new orientations (which have affected theology) concerning the nature of mathematics, and not in the rejection of previously proved mathematical content.

Thomas Kuhn maintains that the sciences give the impression of massive cumulative development only within a contemporary paradigmatic approach that synthesizes past scientific achievements.[32] When the history of science is viewed in terms of the paradigms themselves, however, discontinuities appear. The paradigms are different from each other and are not conserved without

[31] See Abraham Robinson, *Non-Standard Analysis* (Amsterdam: North-Holland, 1966).
[32] Thomas S. Kuhn, *The Structure of Scientific Revolutions* (Chicago: The University of Chicago Press, 1962). (Paperback, The University of Chicago Press, Phoenix Books, 1964.)

change in the successive new paradigms. Mathematics shares with
the rest of the sciences a known subjection to paradigmatic
approaches. I cannot underestimate this, for it will be a basis on
which I attempt to show an influence of mathematics on theology.
As the paradigms of mathematics change, so do perspectives on
epistemology, which affect theology. But mathematics differs from
the other sciences in the degree of its own continuity of content.
For example, Newtonian mechanics is true as an abstract
mathematical system, "true" in the sense that it is a consistent
mathematical system, but it has been falsified as an accurate
description of the physical world by the newer paradigms of
relativity theory. Though at one time believed true for both
mathematics and physics, it is no longer considered so for physics.
It will always be true mathematically. Since mathematics makes
no claim to represent actually existing physical or empirical structures of any sort, it is not tied to the historical vicissitudes of
physical discovery and scientific confirmation. Mathematics does,
however, have its own problems in its own foundational grounding.

The third assumption is that *some mathematical relationships
are potentials for matters of fact.* Physically existing sets do have
the properties of Boolean algebras. The use of money corresponds
(most of the time) to the structures of arithmetic. One can rotate
a symmetrical object in a mathematical way that determines a
mathematical group. Most physical movements do conform to the
mathematical structures of physics. And yet each of these
mathematical systems or structures can be understood independently of their factual examples. A mathematical structure considered as a potential for matters of fact means that we can
understand it without reference to an interpretation, but we may
now or someday see it (or may have seen it in the past) as
descriptive of some actual situation.

The whole basis of the use of mathematics within science rests
on the assumption that scientific content can be structured and
exemplified by mathematical structures, that is, that there are
interpretations of mathematical systems in the physical world.
Some of the successfully used mathematical structures in the

physical world were discovered and examined as pure mathematics centuries before their use in science.[33] Others have been discovered (or created) as they were needed for science.

Notice that I have not said either that all mathematical structures are potentials for matters of fact or that any matter of fact can be completely described by mathematical structures. Nor have I said that we have any means for determining mathematically which structures, if not all, are potentials for matters of fact. The problem here is whether there is, or can be, an actually infinite set, that is, whether mathematical systems having an infinite domain of particulars can ever find ingress to the actual world. I do not think that there are an infinite number of actual entities in the present world, but to rule out such a possibility for future cosmic epochs would betray, I think, an unduly harsh philosophical prejudice.[34]

The fourth assumption is a strictly theological one. It is that *God knows mathematics* and not just in part. Not only is the cumulative and corporate knowledge of contemporary mathematicians known by God, but He knows the present perplexing problems harassing the foundations of mathematics and their appropriate solution. Thus, He not only knows the present body of mathematics but knows it in its ultimate true unity and cohesiveness, that is, He knows that body of mathematics, including whatever intrinsic epistemological limitations it has, toward which the understanding of the present mathematical community is working.

It may seem that I have necessarily assigned a platonic reality[35]

---

[33] The most famous example is the development by Apollonius of a detailed analysis of conic sections in the third century B.C. which were finally used by Kepler in the seventeenth century to describe planetary motion. Apollonius, who had implicitly the solution to the problem of planetary motion, is credited with suggesting the theory of epicycles to account for and explain discrepancies in a geocentric universe.

[34] My Whiteheadian language here reflects, I think, also a Whiteheadian position.

[35] The word *platonic* with a small "p" is often used to indicate a position in the philosophy of mathematics that holds mathematical

to mathematical structures by this assumption. I have, in truth, eliminated certain philosophical viewpoints concerning mathematics, for example, the one that mathematics is found exclusively in the minds of men or only within human language. But the more perplexing and still philosophically crucial issue of the true nature of mathematical existence is left open. Whether mathematical relationships do exist somehow in themselves and their properties are discovered by the intellectual activities of men, or whether these relationships are created by some more basic and fundamental activities of consciousness for an essentially human purpose of grasping and understanding, is left open. We do not know on the basis of contemporary mathematics either the answer to this question or *how* God knows mathematics. Such answers are still variable and, though based on the "hard" content of mathematics, have in their philosophically frolicsome nature a sensitive hand in conditioning theology.

There are theological consequences from the above assumptions, however. If God really knows mathematics, and mathematical relationships represent potential structures for matters of fact, then God knows a great deal about the actual possibilities of the present world. We can see the extent of such knowledge not only by an appreciation of the combined knowledge of science but also by an awareness of science's inability to grasp *all* the relevant mathematical relationships attendant on any one event. If God has any input from the present actually existing world, then his foreknowledge of mathematical possibilities for persisting events or complexes is amazingly complete—though, perhaps, not total. Such foreknowledge does not entail, at least from any contemporary mathematical perspective, absolute foreordainment. This would depend upon God's actual causal involvement in the world. These and other matters will be discussed further after specific theological orientations have been introduced.

The above four assumptions allow us to take a certain position

structures to have an existence objective to and independent of consciousness.

in regard to historical procedures. If, in fact, the present body of mathematics is agreed on and cumulative over the past, and is progressing toward some unified and cohesive whole, then we have some authority, based upon our present knowledge, to decide what the content of mathematics was in the past. This works two ways: We can decide that a content that was then thought mathematical is not truly mathematical; or, we can recognize mathematical content where it was then unknown. We can see the more completely mathematical nature of Euclid's *Elements* divorced from what we now know were his more philosophical beliefs that he could not separate from mathematics, and we can see the content of mathematics in past logic where it was not recognized to be at the time. In short, we can see changes in philosophical attitudes based upon mathematical developments that outline more clearly, and separate more adequately, the *true nature* of mathematics—based on our contemporary perspective.

I feel that these are really cautious assumptions; the first three, though philosophical in themselves, are cautious from the viewpoint of most mathematicians, and the last is much more compatible with the Christian tradition than any of its possible contraries. I do not plan to use the assumptions in a "metaphysical" manner, where many consequences are derived—that is not a method I presently approve of. I shall use them to justify a particular historical activity, and as a groundwork for some minimal theological construction based upon this activity. I think it appropriate at this point to give a historical example from the history of mathematics to show the relevance of my analysis to these assumptions as well as to lay a foundation, in terms of a particular model, for an assessment of the influence of mathematics on traditional theology.

Ratio: The Golden Key to Greek Mathematics

Although Greek mathematicians knew of the embryonic development of fractional numbers in both Babylonian and Egyptian mathematics, they did not include these numbers within the body of pure mathematics but relegated them to practical matters, where they languished without benefit of theoretical consideration. There were no symbols for general fractions in Greek mathematics until the time of Diophantus (ca. A.D. 250), and they were not then given the detailed analysis that was accorded geometrical concepts in the older *Elements*. One could, of course, divide a geometrical magnitude into smaller parts, each considered in itself as a magnitude. But the understood relationship of smaller to larger was handled by changing the unit to correspond to the smaller segment rather than by objectifying the smaller as a fractional part of the larger. The unit mathematically was not to be divided, and for some good mathematical reasons. As we shall discover, it was a strange turn of mathematical *competence* rather than naiveté that prevented the Greeks from objectifying fractions.

Let us look at an example. Given two arbitrary line segments, AB and CD, how can we, following Euclidean mathematics, understand their relationship by means of ratio? We may divide AB into smaller equal-line segments (units) so that some number of these segments equals CD. The number of segments in AB compared to the number of such segments in CD is known as the *ratio* of AB to CD—so far a simple comparison by whole numbers. This early understanding of ratio, which became an extremely useful device for the clarification and proving of other mathematical theorems, was held and developed by the Pythagoreans.

One wonders why this Pythagorean understanding of ratio was not used to formalize and objectify fractional numbers. An elementary geometrical construction well known to the Pythagoreans allows a division of AB into any number of equal parts. If we consider AB as a unit length and give names to the individual smaller segments in terms of the known number of such segments in AB—it is done. We have got fractions. Of course, in order really to *have* fractions, one must develop the theoretical relationships between them. *We recognize* that such development was *already had* by the Greeks in terms of their systematic analysis of ratio. It would have been an easy task to adapt this theoretical structure to fractions if the fractional entities themselves had been accepted. The Greeks' refusal to accept fractional numbers, and their inability to develop a theory concerning them, were probably due to a discovered flow in the definition of ratio itself.

The Pythagorean understanding of ratio had a basic assumption that turned out to be its basic flaw. The assumption is that any two line segments AB and CD have a ratio, that is, there is some common unit, perhaps very small, that can measure by enumeration both segments. This assumption seems reasonable. Indeed, it seems self evident. If in the above example, ten parts of AB do not provide a small enough unit so that some multiple of it measures CD, we divide AB into one hundred parts. If that is not sufficient, divide it into a thousand, into a million, into a billion, and so on. Surely we can make the unit small enough so that some number of such units will exactly measure CD, since there is no limit to the smallness of the unit segment that we can employ.

The discovery by the Pythagoreans that this is not so, that there are some incommensurable line segments, was one of the greatest mathematical and intellectual feats of the Western world. It became an irritant that has stimulated some of the best development of mathematics not only in Grecian times but in contemporary ones also. The discovery undoubtedly was precipitated by the difficulty in finding actual ratios among some line segments. In a unit right triangle we can always get an "approximate ratio" by simply measuring (see figure 1 below). Divide the base into, say, twenty segments, and the hypotenuse turns out by actual measurement to be roughly 28, but not quite. Thus the approximate ratio of side to hypotenuse is 20:28. If we divide the base into 40 units, the hypotenuse is approximately 57, and we are getting closer to the "true" ratio.

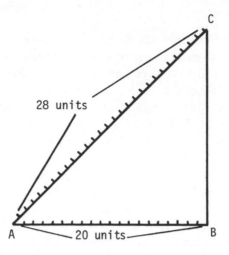

The division of the line segment AB into smaller and smaller units quickly gets beyond the limits of any compass or, for that matter, any possible tool invented to make accurate divisions. In order to pursue the matter ultimately, that is, to either find a ratio or discover that there is none, one has to devise a system of division of AB and AC so that whenever the system is employed some structure remains constant. It would be desirable, for example, that a divided segment of AB have a constant relationship to some divisions of AC that AB as a whole has to AC as a whole.

Consider the following construction. Mark off the length of AB from C along the hypotenuse CA, determining the segment CA_1 (see figure below). Draw A_1C_1 perpendicular to CA. Triangle AA_1C_1 is similar to ABC. Next mark off AA_1 from C_1 along C_1A, determining C_1A_2. Draw A_2C_2 perpendicular to C_1A. The triangle AA_2C_2 is similar to ABC. The process can be continued indefinitely, producing a sequence of triangles, AA_1C_1, AA_2C_2, AA_3C_3, etcetera, each of which is similar to ABC.

If we assume that AB is commensurable (has a ratio) with AC, this means that there is some (largest) unit AP, so that multiples of it measure both AB and AC. We can show by using elementary theorems of geometry that if AB and AC are commensurable

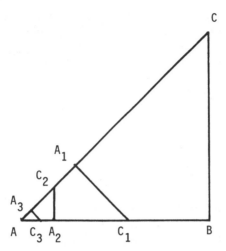

with respect to AP, then the sides of any of the triangles produced above are commensurable.[36] Surely then, since AA_1, AA_2, etcetera, can be made smaller and smaller—smaller than any assumed AP that measures both AB and AC—something is very wrong. The Pythagoreans, who probably worked with some figure like the one above, assessed the situation correctly when they claimed that such contradiction meant that the original assumption was wrong and that AB and AC could not be commensurable, that is, could not have a ratio in any previously defined sense.[37] Yet, as shown

[36] It is sufficient to show that if AB and AC are commensurable, so are AA_1 and AC_2. The commensurability of sides of all other triangles follows, since they are constructed in the same way as triangle AA_1C_1.

If AB is commensurable with AC (with respect to some length AP) then AA_1 is commensurable with respect to AP since AA_1 is AC minus AB. $A_1C_1=C_1B$ (Triangles A_1CC_1 and BCC_1 are congruent). $AA_1=C_1B$ (since $AA_1=A_1C_1$) and thus C_1B is commensurable with respect to AP. This proves AC_1 is commensurable with respect to AP since AC_1 is equal to AB minus C_1B. See Carl B. Boyer, *A History of Mathematics* (New York: John Wiley & Sons, Inc., 1968), p. 81.

[37] The oldest known extant proof of the theorem is referred to by Aristotle, who says simply, "the diagonal of the square is incommensurate with the side, because odd numbers are equal to evens if it is

earlier, the Pythagoreans could get a closer and closer approximation to what they thought must be a true ratio.

The logical scandal of the discovery of incommensurables threatened the very foundations of Pythagorean mathematics, for it challenged their mathematical-religious belief that all things could be represented by connections between whole numbers. They had found exact examples in mathematics itself that could not be so represented. To give up a concept of ratio would have been for the Pythagoreans tantamount to giving up the rational foundations of mathematics itself, for ratio and proportion had been the means that they showed forth proofs in an elegantly simple manner. In short, ratio had become for them an overarching metaphysical connective.

The mathematical solution to the problem of incommensurables was finally given by Eudoxus, a contemporary of Plato.[38] He utilized a new concept of ratio, one that not only allowed an appropriate "connection" between incommensurable magnitudes, but also included the old understanding of ratio and thereby retained all the old mathematics utilizing this understanding. The unity of the discipline of mathematics was thus retained.

As we look at the definitions of ratio in Euclid's *Elements* where the redefined Eudoxan view is presented, we find a curious thing. Euclid's definition of ratio: "A ratio is a sort of relation in respect of size between two magnitudes"[39] is, from our perspec-

---

supposed to be commensurate" (*Anal. Prior*, 41a26). The actual proof of the theorem appeared in the texts of Euclid as X, 117, but is now generally believed to be an interpolation.

[38] His definition appears as Definition 5, Book V, of the *Elements*. "Magnitudes are said to be in the same ratio the first to the second and the third to the fourth when any equal multiples whatever be taken of the first and the third, and any equimultiples whatever be taken of the second and the fourth, the former multiples alike exceed, are alike equal to, or alike fall short of, the latter equimultiples respectively taken in corresponding order" Thomas L. Heath, *The Thirteen Books of Euclid's Elements*, 2nd ed., 3 vols. (New York: Dover, 1956), 2: 114. Put in algebraic symbolism: If A, B, C, D are magnitudes, the ratio of A and B is equal to that of C to D when for arbitrary (whole) numbers p and q, $pC \lesseqgtr qD$ according as $pA \lesseqgtr qB$.

[39] Book V. Definition 3, Heath, 2: 114.

tive, strictly metaphysical. It tells us nothing mathematically and is never used again in the *Elements*. It serves no mathematical purpose and is never referred to. The Eudoxan understanding of ratio, which follows Euclid's definition and is introduced with the words "Magnitudes are *said to be in the same ratio* . . ."[40] is extremely useful mathematically. The body of material following from his definition is, perhaps, the most sophisticated and elegant in all of the *Elements*.

What has happened is that the original Pythagorean metaphysical understanding of ratio has been modified but strengthened and carried into the very body of Euclidean mathematics itself. *Ratio* is a translation of the Greek word *logos*. The *Elements* as it uses the redefined concept of ratio to present beautiful and comprehensive mathematical structures is really, from the viewpoint of the mathematicians, characterizing the properties of a metaphysical logos. The involved history of the word *logos,* its extreme importance for Greek philosophy and religion, and its multiple meanings make it illegitimate for us to claim that its general philosophical meanings arose exclusively out of generalized mathematics. I think what is clear beyond dispute, however, is that its use in mathematics, its deliniation and characterization as ratio, more thoroughly rationalized and mathematized its philosophical and religious usage, and affected Christian theology in a way that I shall outline in chapter 1.

If, from a Euclidean perspective, we believe that ratio, literally *logos,* is an overarching (mathematical) structure, semiformalized but primarily intuitively grasped by some process of participation, then there is some shock involved in our perception of logos as no more than simple arithmetical properties of ordinary arithmetical objects. This possibility has always been present for an understanding of ratio. Ratio and proportion can be understood as really *no more than* the properties of fractions. A is to B as C is to D simply put is $A/B=C/D$.

I call upon the reader's experience in learning mathematics in elementary or early secondary school. If he were under some

[40] Book V, Definition 5, Heath, 2: 114.

older system of instruction, he probably spent weeks on the properties of ratio and proportion. Later (or perhaps earlier) in a separate section, he learned to manipulate fractions. Was there a basic difference in attitude between the study of ratio and proportion and the study of fractions? Was not the theory of ratio and proportion more theoretically connective and were not fractions themselves more nearly manipulatable objects? Commenting on the Greek use of ratio, Boyer maintains:

> Such a view, focusing attention on the connection between pairs of numbers, tends to sharpen the theoretical or rational aspects of the number concept and to deemphasize the role of number as a tool in computation or approximation in mensuration.[41]

The subsuming of ratio and proportion under the properties of fractions is not, of course, as simple as I have made it out to be. The theory is simple if one is dealing with rational numbers. When one includes irrational numbers, however, an elaborate theory is needed, a theory that was actually worked out in the nineteenth century by Dedekind, Weierstrass, *et al.* Had the Greeks not known of incommensurables, they probably would have developed fractions that reflected the properties of ratio. Instead, because they knew too much, they redefined *ratio* to handle incommensurables, effectively blocking any development to entify fractions, and reemphasized the authority of logos structure.

I am using our assumptions, at least two of them, in the manner indicated.[42] Since we can accept that the present body of mathematics is well agreed upon and did achieve its present unity through a cumulative development, we can see that the Greek emphasis on ratio and proportion, without having a commensurate understanding of the objects of fractions, weighted their predisposition toward viewing the nature of mathematical reality as an abstract, metaphysical *logos*. We may sever Euclid's

[41] *A History of Mathematics,* p. 58.
[42] See section "The Underlying Mathesis" above.

definition of ratio (*logos*) from a more purely refined mathematical presentation of his content because we know it to be essentially a philosophical or metaphysical view. We know this. He probably did not.

The Euclidean Perspective

There are many mathematical aspects of the *Elements* other than the use of ratio that contributed toward a specific philosophical viewpoint. The *Elements* was compiled shortly after the death of Aristotle and has in it the best of the cumulative development of Greek mathematics. It affords us the best source for an examination of the mathematics, and the presuppositions associated with it, that influenced Plato and Aristotle, and from there conditioned the development of classical Christianity. I shall call these fundamental presuppositions of the *Elements* the Euclidean perspective.

Chief among the characteristics of the Euclidean perspective is an emphasis on geometrical symbolism. The *Elements* is concerned as much with number theory as it is with geometry, but both are described by geometric variables. This is a very interesting fact, perhaps expressing the Greek mathematician-philosopher's contempt for the common *logistica*, which "does not consider number in the true sense,"[43] perhaps motivated by a much deeper necessity.

The reason for the use of geometric symbols instead of arithmetic ones may be obvious enough. It is that one may see and understand relationships more easily when in pictorial form than in other symbolism. Proposition 2 of Book II, *If a straight line be cut at random, the rectangle contained by the whole and both of the segments is equal to the square on the whole,* which is equivalent to the statement that for any given line segment AB and any arbitrary point C on AB, the area of ADFC and CFEB

[43] Scholium to Plato's *Charmides*, Ivor Thomas, ed., *Selections Illustrating the History of Greek Mathematics*, 2 vols. (Cambridge, Mass.: Harvard University Press, 1951), 1: 17.

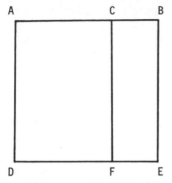

is equal to that of ADEB, where ADEB is the square of AB, and CF is drawn parallel to either AD or BE, is obvious by inspection. One notes that the whole is made up of the two parts, and that is sufficient to see that the proposition is true. Euclid proves the theorem and his proof can be made rigorous in terms of modern standards very easily.

If we translate the proposition into number theory, noticing that the length of line segment corresponds to a number and that a rectangle represents the product of two numbers whose "sides are the numbers which have multiplied one another,"[44] the algebraic representation is:

$$(a + b)(a + b) = a(a + b) + b(a + b)$$

for any positive real numbers a and b. It is intuitively clear that the geometrical presentation is true, whereas the algebraic identity is by no means obvious on inspection.

A deeper reason for emphasis on geometrical magnitude may be that the mathematicians were not able to formulate the foundation of incommensurables algebraically but could and did do so geometrically. Whether they could have formulated such a theory algebraically if they had discovered and used fractions and created symbols for irrational numbers is an open question. It is a fact that they did not. As they worked with geometrical symbolism they became wedded to it. Their intuition was unable to surmount geometrical thinking by numerical or algebraic means. Thus, the axiomatic method of Euclid comes to us in geometrical form. In this form it has conditioned the thinking and intuition of mathematician and philosopher alike for over two thousand years.

Geometrical symbolism carries along with it the presentations associated with spatial relationships. Indeed, geometry has been defined traditionally as the science of space. A mathematics that is characterized *exclusively* in geometrical symbolism as in the

[44] *The Elements,* Book VII, Definition 16. Heath, 2: 278.

Elements allows one to assume a relationship between mathematical form and the human subject comparable to that observed between space and the human subject. Just as one is perceived to be necessarily spatial, that is, subject to spatial relationships, so is he presumed to be subject to mathematical relationships in a similar way. Implicit in this understanding of the nature of mathematics is the belief that mathematics is a description of necessary relationships to which each existent entity must conform. Mathematics becomes a description of an overarching reality that includes the mathematician as a part of this reality.

This fundamental mathematical presupposition is common to the philosophies of both Plato and Aristotle. In Platonic philosophy the geometrical figures that represent numerical and spatial relationships were given an ideal and transcendent status. The mathematical figures were presumed to be descriptive of the ideal forms, which were thought more real than and prior to any phenomenal manifestation of them. Aristotle dissolved the realm of Platonic transcendent forms and considered them as existing in the things themselves. Since the form, according to Aristotle, is that which characterizes anything in its final state and is that thing in its actuality, it is, as in the philosophy of Plato, the locus of primary reality.

The second fundamental characteristic of the Euclidean perspective is the emphasis upon and use of the axiomatic method. The axiomatic method of the *Elements* has four different types of logical constructs: definitions, postulates, common notions, and propositions. The definitions describe or point to the basic things that the propositions are about, points, lines, figures, etcetera. They refer *extra*-system to entities that are the object of examination. Postulates are regarded as permissible constructions but have a logical status with the common notions. Both common notions and postulates may be called axioms. The axioms are basic assumptions, or that which is perfectly obvious, about the things that the definitions describe. Propositions are statements about the things the definitions describe that are proved by means of the axioms.

The definitions in the *Elements* occupy a position in relationship to axioms and propositions that has been thought to be natural and appropriate for two thousand years, but which was seen to be in error by formalistic developments in the nineteenth century. The definitions come *first* in the *Elements* before the postulates, the common notions, and the propositions. They attempt to describe and characterize the nature of things *outside the system* about which the axioms and propositions speak. They present the nature of the subject matter of the *Elements*: points, lines, triangles, squares, etcetera. They denote the objects to be examined.

In the latter part of the nineteenth century, after a more rigid formalization of the axiomatic method had occurred, definitions were found to be, in Russell's terminology, "theoretically superfluous." In contemporary axiomatic formal systems, they follow the undefined terms (or may occur anywhere in the mathematical system) and consist of appropriate combinations *of* the undefined terms. Hence, they refer only to *intra-system* in contradistinction to the *extra*-system reference of definitions in the *Elements*. There is no necessary reference of definitions to anything outside the system.

The emphasis upon geometric symbolism and the descriptive use of definitions enhanced for the Greek mathematicians the objective status of transcendent mathematical objects. The very form of the axiomatic method suggested that mathematical relationships are "out there" and objective to the observer. This confirmed the feeling of the general "thereness" that *geometrical* figures appear to have as they are ingressed in phenomenal objects.

The use of both geometrical symbolism and the axiomatic method provided a natural *unity* for mathematics. The multiplicity of different mathematical relationships in the *Elements* are each formulated in geometrical symbolism. The unity of the multiplicity of relationships is found in the unity of an abstracted space. Just as all spatial relationships are *in* the one universal space, so are all mathematical relationships, that is, geometrical ones, in an abstracted mathematical space. The whole of Euclidean mathematics is deduced from the firm foundation of a few unquestioned axioms and intuitively clear definitions. Mathematics is seen to be unified in *one* axiomatic system. There was only one axiomatic system in the days of Euclid, and the unity of mathematics was presumed to be a simple matter. This may be contrasted with the multiplicity of different axiomatic systems that have come into being since the nineteenth century, and the problem thereby posed for the unity of mathematics.

In short, the Euclidean perspective presents a view of mathematics as one transcendent system, geometrically structured, discovered and not created. In this perspective, *logos* is both technical ratio and cosmic structure. In knowing mathematics one necessarily knows some ontological structures. Such a perspective sets before the theologian and philosopher the standard of an ordered, unified body of thought that is true (in some ways) of all reality. The theology of Augustine and Aquinas, for example, partakes heavily of this standard. Though acutely sensitive to the volitional aspects of human existence coming from the Hebrew-Christian tradition, each theologian sought a truth that is independent of volitional choices of particular men, individual cultures, or historical groups, and that is relevant to all men and all things. If the religious content of the Christian faith has been structured, as I intend to show, in terms of changes in mathematics and presuppositions, then we would expect that changes in mathematics and Euclidean presuppositions would precipitate changes in the structure of contemporary religious thought. The burden of my later chapters is to show these mathematical and theological changes.

A Note on Causality

Throughout this work I speak frequently of mathematics as "influencing," "conditioning," "affecting," and "structuring" theology. I am affirming that there is *some* causal connection between mathematics and theology. Essentially, the above words refer to a connection of *antecedent condition*. I maintain that had not mathematics been a certain way, then theology would not have been as it was or is. But how different theology would have been if mathematics had not "influenced" it is very difficult to present in any analytical, scholarly manner. Obviously any particular theological position has a vast multiplicity of antecedent conditions, some few of which are mathematical. The question is whether these mathematical conditions are *really significant.* Surely the *exact* theological position would not have been as it was had not the mathematical factors been present, but would it have been *that* much different without mathematical influence? I am sure that the reader is aware that I feel that the mathematical conditions are *significant,* otherwise there would be no sense in attempting to write this book. But I am aware that the actual significance is elusive and difficult to present. What does one do when he "knows" that mathematics has affected theology in an important manner? He does, I think, something like what I have done in succeeding chapters, but with an awareness that any convincing will depend on the reader's experience of the ubiquity of mathematics and the importance of theology.

LOGOS:
Mathematics
and
Christian Theology

PART I

Classical Mathematics and Traditional Theology

1
Word and Wisdom

Word and Wisdom

> In the beginning was the *logos,* and the *logos* was with God,
> and the *logos* was God. He was in the beginning with God; all
> things were made through him, and without him was not any-
> thing made that was made. In him was life, and the life was
> the light of men. The light shines in the darkness, and the
> darkness has not overcome it.
> . . . And the *logos* became flesh and dwelt among us, full of
> grace and truth.[1]

So John begins his Gospel and clearly identifies Christ with
logos. By his use of the term he provides a channel through which
Greek philosophical concepts, Greek science, and Greek religion
can get at the heart of the Christian religion. For John's Gospel is
Holy Scripture for Christianity and was recognized to be Scripture
by the early fathers and theologians. John is making a theological
statement concerning Christ and his relationship to God, really
one of the few such statements in the New Testament. As such it
achieved immense authority for subsequent theologians and
especially for those who were concerned with the problem of the

[1] John 1. From the Revised Standard Version Bible, and used by
permission.

relationship of Christianity to Greek religion and philosophy, which includes every major theologian from the time of John to the breakdown of the medieval synthesis in the fifteenth and sixteenth centuries.

Did John intend to introduce Greek philosophical, scientific, or religious interpretations for the person of Christ? A broad consensus of contemporary New Testament scholars maintains that the *logos* Christology of John must be understood in its peculiarly Hebrew context. To deviate from this context and emphasize Greek meanings is to make a major error in interpretation. Certainly John intended that Jesus as word, *logos*, be understood as the address or word of creative power of God, that is, the word of God understood in its Old Testament usage. This is one of the meanings that *logos* did not have traditionally in Greek literature. Where *logos* is used for concrete utterance, and it is used frequently in this manner, the emphasis is on the connected element in speech, the examination of which can often discover and resolve whatever issue is in question within the context of the words themselves.[2] Clearly though, the term *logos*, with its pregnant philosophical and theological Greek history, could not be effectively isolated from its heritage, especially in Hellenic lands and culture, without considerable effort and intentional focus. A very real problem for all of the early Christian theologians was to capture and maintain for the word *logos*, and other Greek philosophical and mathematical words, that which was uniquely Hebrew and peculiarly Christian. In this activity, however, the very concern for the encroachment of Greek philosophy and religion necessarily modified, though in no way completely dominated, the essentially Jewish and Christian concepts.

Bultmann maintains that the *logos* doctrine of John is not derived from Greek philosophical tradition or from Stoicism, nor was it transmitted to the Evangelist by Philo, but came primarily and directly from the tradition of cosmological mythology that

---

[2] *Theological Dictionary of the New Testament*, vol. 4, ed. G. Kittel, trans. Geoffrey W. Bromiley (Grand Rapids, Mich.: Wm. B. Eerdmans, 1967), s.v. *lego*.

had its roots within the general Palestinian ethos.[3] The eighth chapter of the book of Proverbs presents most clearly these cosmological mythological developments that led to *logos* Christology. *Chochmah,* the wisdom literature of the Hebrews, is a special term applied to a "faculty of acute observation, schrewdness of discovery or device, cleverness of invention."[4] It is found normally in the form of proverbs that are limited almost exclusively to the observations of relations of human life and not concerned with nature. Thus, the hypostatization of Hebrew wisdom into a personal being, in *Proverbs,* who is the first-born child of the creator —"The Lord created me at the beginning of his work"; who works with God in the creation—"When he established the heavens, I was there"; who aids him in the historical process —"By me kings reign and rulers decree what is just"; and who woos men (like a female goddess)—"I love those who love me"; is a theological change of considerable magnitude.[5] Von Rad calls the transition "astonishing" and complains that "we have no means of bridging the great gap between Proverbs 10–29 on the one hand and Proverbs 1–8 on the other."[6]

Some scholars see Greek influence as the only explanation of so radical a change in Hebrew wisdom. Eichrodt declares:

> Jews must have found their point of contact with Hellenism in the sense of wonder which they shared in their contemplation of the cosmos, and have managed to incorporate this into their concept of wisdom.[7]

Ringgren admits that there may be some dependence on Greek ideas, but dismisses the endeavor to determine Greek influence

[3] Rudolf Bultmann, *Theology of the New Testament,* trans. Kendrick Grobel, 2 vols. (New York: Charles Scribners Sons, 1955), 2: 64.

[4] S. R. Driver, *An Introduction to the Literature of the Old Testament* (New York: Meridian Library, 1956), p. 392.

[5] Proverbs 8. From the Revised Standard Version Bible, and used by permission.

[6] Gerhad Von Rad, *Old Testament Theology,* 2 vols., trans. D. M. G. Stalker (New York: Harper & Row, 1962), 1: 41.

[7] Walter Eichrodt, *Theology of the Old Testament,* 2 vols., trans. J. A. Baker (Philadelphia: Westminster Press, 1967), 2: 85.

since, as he maintains, there is absolutely no evidence for this position.[8] Since there is evidence to indicate an autonomous development within the general Palestinian culture and some further evidence to claim that the Hebrew hypostatization of wisdom was essentially a Jewish development, much contemporary scholarship has focused within the boundaries of Palestine and has tended to dilute an ostensible influence from the larger Hellenistic culture.

Albright is the chief anti-Hellenist in this regard. He claims that the relatively homogenous Canaanite-Phoenician culture, from which the Hebrews came, developed its own didactic wisdom literature at a very early age, probably in the early third millennium, and is thus as old as Egyptian didactic books.[9] He attempts to show that verse 22 of Proverbs 8, "The lord created me at the beginning of his work" is a transparent reflection of a Canaanite statement "El created me at the beginning of his dominion," which itself harks back to an ancient Baal epic where El brought forth wisdom before he conquered the primordial dragon.[10] Albright concludes that the entire content of Proverbs is probably pre-exilic, and this would be especially true of the material in Proverbs 8.[11]

Although the ubiquity of wisdom literature in the ancient Near East, including Egypt and Greece, is generally recognized, since each culture understood wisdom to be truly universal and did not hesitate to borrow from one another, some scholars, narrowing Albright's claim that Hebrew wisdom literature arose in the general Sumero-Phoenician culture, see a unique Jewish character to the hypostatization that occurred in Israel. Deboer seeks to show that the person of wisdom developed out of the traditional use of the

[8] Helmer Ringgren, *Word and Wisdom, Studies in the Hypostatization of Divine Qualities and Functions in the Ancient Near East* (Lund, 1947), p. 148.

[9] W. F. Albright, "Some Canaanite-Phoenician Sources of Hebrew Wisdom," in *Wisdom in Israel and in the Ancient Near East*, ed. Martin Noth and D. Winton Thomas (Leiden: E. J. Brill, 1960), p. 4.

[10] *Ibid.*, p. 7.

[11] *Ibid.*, p. 13.

Hebrew word for counsel or counsellor.[12] The functions of coun-
sellors Ahitophel and Nathan to David, for example, were similar
to functions attributed to Wisdom as the divine counsellor of God.
Whybury believes that Wisdom is a personification of an attribute
of Yahweh and not of the general God, El.[13] All recognize, however, even if we grant that the initial hypostatization of wisdom
in Proverbs 8 was a genuinely Jewish development, Wisdom did
acquire for herself traits that are different from her Hebrew self
from non-Israelite sources.

Let us assume that the positions of Ringgren, Whybury, and
Deboer are correct, that the hypostatization of wisdom in Proverbs
8 is a hypostatization of an attribute of Yahweh, or that even if
an attribute of El (Albright), then the personified attribute was
understood in terms of the general context of the Hebrew religion
and was implicitly guided by the continuing historical nature of
Yahwistic religion. Although we grant that the wisdom literature
was understood by the Hebrews to include general characteristics
of the human situation, that is, what is wise for *all* men, the
nature of Hebrew wisdom did have certain characteristics that
distinguished it from *sophia* and *logos*.

Hebrew wisdom, which grew out of an understanding of human
activities (What is wise *for men* to do as most shrewd and practical?) and which was tied to Yahwistic religion (What is best for
men to do in their relationship to God?), differs basically from
logos, which indicates a more abstract structural context pertain-
ing to the general cosmos and, when related to "wisdom"
concerning man through speech, pertains to the context of ordered
discourse.

Before the advent of Pythagorean mathematical philosophy,
the word *logos* had implicit in its use certain structural potential
meanings that were compatible with its later mathematical accretions. *Logos* comes from the verb *lego*, which means in the oldest

[12] P. A. H. De Boer, "The Counsellor," *Wisdom in Israel and in the
Ancient Near East*, pp. 44–45.
[13] Roger N. Whybury, *Wisdom in Proverbs, the Concept of Wisdom
in Proverbs 1 through 9* (London: S. C. M., 1965), p. 87.

literature *to gather*. *Lego* in Homer often means *to count*, which is a gathering one after another of similar things. Also, but less frequently used in Homeric literature, the word means *to enumerate*, a process where one recalls from memory things of a same kind. After the writings of Homer, a further step was taken in the evolution of the meaning of *lego*. A complete enumeration of things or events became a narration, *logos*. Contemporary with this use we find *lego* meaning *to say*, and *logos*, the noun form, meaning *speech, saying,* or *word*.[14]

Logos was used by the Pythagoreans to mean mathematical ratio.[15] It was, of course, a technical use where a precise meaning could be attributed in terms of a narrow context. Wittgenstein has warned us, with numerous careful examples, that the meaning of a word must be understood in terms of relatively small language games. The varieties of meanings of words must be separated in terms of the varieties of language games in which they participate. Mathematical technical words are normally so exactly determined by their mathematical context that we have no difficulty in seeing that they have essentially different meanings in their wider usage. It may be quite arbitrary what actual word is used mathematically, since the meaning of the word is determined by the system itself. A mathematical *group* could be called by any other name and still be a "group." The meaning attributed to *group* mathematically is so exquisitely precise that we can effectively sever this meaning from the meaning of *group* (a group of people, etc.) in ordinary language.

But *group* is not an important philosophical word. Furthermore, the evolution of its meaning from a group (collection) of permutations to its more precise mathematical use at the hands of Galois in 1830 occurred so quickly that no linguistically philosophical import can be attached to the mathematical developments. The word *group* did not go through the kind of evolution that *infinity* and *function* did. They have a long history of first being used for

[14] *Theological Dictionary of the New Testament,* 4: 72.
[15] See Introduction, section "Ratio: The Golden Key to Greek Mathematics."

semi-formalized, basically intuitive, and general concepts that were later more thoroughly objectivized and formalized mathematically. The history of the formalization of these words has considerably affected their general philosophical usage. To *infinity* today we normally assign some one meaning or set of meanings out of a host of precisely determined mathematical ones. The older intuitive meanings, though still used in some contexts—neo-Thomism, for example—are really so vague and the range of possible mathematical meanings so exact, that the mathematical usage has virtually taken over the meaning of the word. The word *function* is a different matter. Its use is rampant throughout the different sciences, and in most cases reflects an *older* mathematical one where it is thought to reflect some actual structural connection. Its more recently accepted definition as a certain kind of set of ordered pairs (of numbers) is so completely formalized that, in this mathematical meaning, it has become technical in the way that *group* has. Its mathematical meaning is severed from its general usage, although the general usage, at least in science, reflects an older mathematical one. Thus, we could trace an actual influence on the current meaning of the word *function* from a previously understood mathematical one.

It appears that the degree to which a mathematical word can be isolated from the same word's general meaning is roughly proportional to the degree to which the mathematical concept or object is formalized and objectivized mathematically. This is certainly true for the words *function* and *infinity*. Both were assumed to refer to some general epistemological or cosmological structure and their mathematical characterization as it proceeded first served the purpose of showing forth or plotting out these structures, and only later, when the formalization reached an advanced stage, did it become possible to isolate radically their mathematical meanings from their general scientific or philosophical ones. In the meantime, however, the mathematical development had essentially modified their philosophical meanings.

One of the reasons why the relationship of mathematics to the developing meanings of *logos* has been ignored or dismissed is the assumption that *logos* in Greek mathematics was a technical word like *triangle* or, as mentioned above, *group*, which can and ought to be separated from ordinary usage. *Logos*, as I outlined in some detail in the Introduction, was not formalized in the way that we formalize today or that was begun in later Greek mathematics. As ratio, *logos* was the overarching structural means by which the properties of the more technical aspects of mathematics—triangles, squares, and the like, were proved and presented. The mathematical crisis of the discovery of incommensurable magnitudes could have dethroned the essential mathematical position of *logos* and forced the elevation of some other mathematical means of proof, but the successful extension of the meaning of *logos*, ratio, by Eudoxus allowed *logos* to be an even more comprehensive structure that could be used in even more elaborate and general ways of presenting mathematical content. There was no incompatibility in assuming that the mathematical understanding and use of *logos* were an actual discovery of the *logos* reality to which the word referred.

The Pythagoreans thoroughly ontologized mathematics. Numbers were understood by them to be the basic reality of the universe both as means to describe the world and as its basic physical content. Aristotle's summary of Pythagoreanism is probably as close to an accurate general summary of Pythagorean thought as we have from antiquity.[16] His basic claims: that the Pythagoreans identified the elements of all things with numbers, that their position of ontologized mathematics was a result of their original discoveries of mathematizing music (discovering that harmony was expressible as *ratios* of numbers), and that they believed the whole heaven to be musical number (the music of the spheres), are borne out by other evidence and sources.

Since the Pythagoreans ontologized number, and saw the harmony and connection of the universe to be expressible as (ratios of) number, one might think that they would have ontologized ratio (*logos*) itself as a super reality that connects and orders all things. There is, however, little evidence to support this.

[16] Aristotle, *Meta.* A5, 985b23.

They did view the universe as a connected whole, possessing an orderliness that was characterized by, and was seen to be, number. This orderliness was, however, *cosmos*. The contemplation (*theoria*) of *cosmos* had a salvific function resulting in purification (*katharsis*).

Logos was first given a metaphysical status by Heraclitus. This was done in order to achieve some invariance, some stability in the midst of radical change and destructive illusion. Heraclitus, like all presocratics and ancient man as a whole, was struck by the dominance of change in the world. He became part of a universal quest, one evidenced by both mythology and philosophy, to find some order in change. His method, however, differed from that of his predecessors. One found stability, not by minimizing the reality of change or by declaring it to be illusion, but by emphasizing it and intensifying it to the point where any personal psychological stability was almost impossible. His names of "the obscure" and "the riddler" are quite appropriate, for he fiercely equated opposites and made no attempt to present his thought coherently. This was done in order to show the universality and radicality of flux and change. For only if one could grasp and be torn and almost destroyed by change, could he then, according to Heraclitus, understand the measure, the order, the *logos* inherent in all change. *Logos,* the structure, connection, and way of change is common in all things. It unites all things. It is their ultimate explanation. It is also, according to Heraclitus, the truth of religion. Knowing and being grasped by *logos* is salvation and the only way to lead a true ethical life. Yet *logos,* as Heraclitus understood it, is both the structural plan of things and the substance of them. *Logos* was thought to be a part of the physical world, just as the Pythagoreans thought number to be physical.

Heraclitus chose what was then a mathematical word to use as the name of the interrelating principle of all things. It was through his use of the word that it later acquired many of its metaphysical, cosmological, and nonmathematical connotations. On the authority of fragments that today we have no real reason to doubt, Heraclitus apparently knew, and knew quite well, the teachings of Pythagoras. With typical acrimony, while admitting that Pythagoras practiced inquiry more than any other man, Heraclitus commented, "Learning of many things does not teach intelligence, if so it would have taught Hesiod and Pythagoras, and again Xenophanes and Hecataeus."[17] Heraclitus's particular objection to the thought of Pythagoras was that it was essentially dilettantism, a polymathy based upon a mistaken method. Logic-chopping does not give wisdom. Heraclitus apparently believed that Pythagoras did not perceive the true logos that was available within one's inmost being and gave coherence to the whole, but tried to relate disparate and extraneous material from many sources by an objective method.[18]

Was Heraclitus's concept of *logos*, that order amid chaos and structural change that relates opposites, derived from a Pythagorean understanding of *logos*, which was an essential mathematical connection between numbers? There are marked similarities between the two beliefs. Both emphasized the measure of things as description of phenomena. To both Heraclitus and the Pythagoreans, the arrangement of things was more important than their material nature, although both understood arrangement itself to have some material form. Heraclitus was a generation younger than Pythagoras. He knew of Pythagoras's philosophy; it was in effect a rival system of his own. In sum, due to the priority of Pythagoras's concept of cosmos, his actual technical use of ratio to structure numbers and their relationships, and the similarities between an implicit ontologized Pythagorean ratio and a Heraclitian *logos*, Heraclitus was probably indebted to Pythagoras for an initial understanding of and emphasis on arrangement and (logical) structure. But his mature position, a *logos* made metaphysical, a concept of a unified rational structure that correlated the change in all known things, was his own and went far beyond that of Pythagoras. In any case, whether he was dependent upon

[17] Diogenes Laertius IX, I (DK22AI), trans. G. S. Kirk and J. E. Raven, *The Presocratic Philosophers* (Cambridge: Cambridge University Press, 1962), p. 182.

[18] See J. A. Philip, *Pythagoras and Early Pythagoreanism* (Toronto: University of Toronto Press, 1966), p. 178.

Pythagoras historically or not, his concept of *logos* was compatible with the concept of numerical structure that had been welded and systematized by ratio in Pythagorean thought. As the later philosophers and commentators looked back to the two who were contemporaries, the compatibility of mathematics and metaphysical *logos,* especially in the light of the subsequent cumulative and brilliant development of mathematics, did further mathematize and rationalize the cosmic structure of Logos itself. A combination of *logos* and logic was especially true of the thought of the Stoics, whose philosophy had at points a direct contact with Hellenized Judaism and Christianity.

A disclaimer on my part is perhaps wise at this juncture of the discussion. The reader is perhaps mildly annoyed at, if not positively hostile to, my attempt to show that *logos* had some mathematical meaning, when his knowledge of almost any period of Christian thought, or of Greek philosophy, shows irrefutably that *logos* had many meanings, often without any apparent mathematical connection. I grant that *logos* is one of the more complex words in Greek literature. For its use in philosophy and religion, it is difficult to choose a particular meaning to fit each case. The genius and perplexity of the word is that it may have a number of different meanings—simultaneously. In its ambiguity, it may express precisely a combination of meanings the author intended and perhaps some he did not. As is evidenced by the literature employing the word, one can sum up and conjoin philosophical and metaphysical understandings, as well as a host of technical meanings, in the one word.

Thus any attempt to isolate a particular meaning for the word, and specifically a mathematical or cosmological one, and claim that this is what a theological or philosophical writer had *exclusively* in mind, is bound to err on the side of narrowness of concept. But conversely, to discover a technical mathematical meaning, and then to dismiss it from consideration in the larger philosophical and theological context because it is technical, is to err in another direction, especially if the technical meaning gave impetus to the growing abstract and rational processes of consciousness that were developing so rapidly in the historical period under examination.

The *Theological Dictionary of the New Testament* gives several senses in which *logos* was used in the Greek and Hellenistic world. I list these in abbreviated form as given.

> a. "Counting up," "recounting," the sum of individual words to form the comprehensive construct "speech" or "language," "sentence" or "saying." Because *logos,* as distinct from *mythos,* which is developing or invented narrative or tradition in the poetic or religious sphere, always refers to something material, it is either that which is at issue, or that which is recounted of someone, i.e., good or bad repute, saga, history.
>
> b. "Account," "reckoning," "result of reckoning" (a) in a more metaphysical sense as the principle or law which can be calculated or discovered in calculation or often the reason which is the product of thought and calculation, the argument or explanation; (b) as an economic or commercial term; "reckoning," "cash account," "account," etc.
>
> c. As a technical term in mathematics: "proportion," "relation," "element." . . . Here the orderly and rational character implicit in the term is quite clear. With the interrelation of mathematics and philosophy, *logos,* as the rational relation of things to one another, then acquires the more general sense of "order" or "measure."
>
> d. From the second half of the 5th century it is used subjectively for man's ratio, his ability to think, "reason," the human "mind" or "spirit," "thought."[19]

Notice that in each of the above meanings, even when considered as mental activity, *logos* has the original meanings of "counting," "reckoning," "explaining," which are more ancient than the development of abstract, systematized, and deductive mathematics. If the discipline of pure mathematics had not arisen on Greek soil, *logos* would still have had many of the meanings above, which in their combined total would have made the word different in meaning from the Old and New Testament divine word. With the development of mathematics, a system that presented a structured all, independent of mythological or religious commitment, a system that could be seen to plot out the very

---

[19] *Theological Dictionary of the New Testament,* 4: 77.

being and structure of the cosmos by "counting," "reckoning," and thus "explaining," *logos* acquired a metaphysical dimension that it has maintained ever since. Even if we grant what seems to me highly improbable, that *logos* could have acquired this metaphysical cosmic dimension without contact with abstract mathematics, we still must admit that, once having achieved a metaphysical meaning, the word was enriched immensely by mathematics' confirming the existence (as was thought by all major Greek philosophers) of exactly delineated, structural, metaphysical relationships and actually showing forth their detailed structure.

It would be helpful to be able to compare the development of philosophical sensitivities in other cultures in their relationship to the advent of abstract mathematics, in order to allow a more objective perspective on this development in Greece. But we have no other example comparable in any way to the kind of mathematics developed in Greece between the sixth century B.C. and the third. The Babylonians discovered the "Pythagorean Theorem" perhaps as much as a thousand years earlier than the Greeks, but gave no proof or had no means to give proof of the theorem. Only in Greece did mathematics begin to be structured as a unified whole by means of deduction. Only in Greece were mathematics and structures relevant thereto taken into the very thought forms of the intellectual culture itself and represented in the manifold meanings of *logos*.

Wisdom, Word, and the Problem of Faith and Reason

The development of Israel's later tradition of "theological wisdom," in which wisdom was made a hypostasis of God and was examined extensively in its (actually *her*) relationship to God, served for the Hebrews an important theological function. If, indeed, Yahweh is the one God who created the world and in whom dwells true wisdom, how does one most appropriately relate the traditions of Israel to new knowledge coming from other cultures? The easiest way to accommodate new knowledge without challenging Hebraic priorities was to consider God to have possessed wisdom and to have disseminated this same wisdom to the other cultures, but only in part. The problem for and threat to the historical religion of Israel, however, was obvious.

If we grant with Ben Sirach that wisdom can be identified in part with the Torah, then it is an easy step to assume that Torah-wisdom is but a subset of a larger universal wisdom.[20] If wisdom thus becomes autonomous and separated from the historical life of Israel, through participation in this wisdom one might to be capable of getting at the same wisdom that is found in the Torah. The religious problem for the Hebrews, then, was the ostensible existence of an autonomous wisdom in which one could participate and achieve salvation, knowledge, and revelation independently of the historical-religious tradition of the Jews.

Certain canonical Old Testament Scriptures resist the claim of an autonomous wisdom. This is exactly what the author of Job 28 sought to do.

> But where shall wisdom be found, and where is the place of understanding? Man does not know the way to it and it is not to be found in the land of the living. The deep says that it is not in me, and the sea says that it is not with me. It can not be gotten for gold, and silver cannot be weighed for its price. . . . Behold the fear of the Lord is wisdom, and to depart from evil is understanding.[21]

The fierce invective of Koheleth serves essentially the same purpose. Wisdom is acknowledged as legitimate, but only as coming from God. In short, the response of the community of Israel to other apparently legitimate cultural claims to truth was to include them under the domain of wisdom, but to insist that wisdom is given primarily by God and peculiarly to Israel. Only incidentally was it shed abroad to the other nations.

As the concept of wisdom assumed important theological

[20] Ecclesiasticus 24:23.
[21] From the Revised Standard Version Bible, and used by permission.

functions in Israel, it came in contact with the religious uses of *spirit* and *word*. In the fifth chapter of Daniel, wisdom is described as a characteristic of possession by the spirit. Wisdom is identified as the breath (spirit) of God in the *Wisdom of Solomon*, which is "more moving than any motion," since "she passes and goes through all things by reason of her pureness." [22] She also "makes all things new, and in all ages enters into holy souls and makes them friends of god and prophets." [23] In the *Wisdom of Sirach*, wisdom was "created before all things," [24] and "came out of the mouth of the most high and covered the earth as a cloud." [25] The ease with which the creative word coming out of the mouth of God is confused with spirit (breath) that does also, is quite apparent in this case. Wisdom covers the function of both.

In the New Testament, Paul's doctrine of Christ reflects the wisdom literature in his Christological formula (Col. 1: 15–17) and in his claim that Christ is himself the incarnate Wisdom of God. An almagation of the functions of wisdom with those of word, as I have mentioned earlier, underlies the *logos* doctrine of John. The claim that Christ is the *logos* of the Father by John allowed a freedom of identification of Christ with wisdom and word by the church fathers and early theologians. They shamelessly used a passage from the *Wisdom of Solomon*:

> Thine almighty word leaped from heaven out of thy royal throne as a fierce man of war to the land of destruction, and brought thine unfeigned commandment as a sharp sword,[26]

which refers to the passover destruction of the Egyptians' eldest sons, for Christ's incarnation. Quite typical of general belief are the statements of Athanasius that "the Son of God . . . is the very Word and Wisdom of the Father" [27] and of Augustine that "the

---

[22] Wisdom of Solomon, 7: 24, 25.
[23] *Ibid.*, 7: 27.
[24] Ecclesiasticus 1: 4.
[25] *Ibid.*, 24: 3.
[26] Wisdom of Solomon, 18: 15.
[27] Athanasius, *De Decretis*, chap. 4. From *A Select Library of Nicene and Post Nicene Fathers of the Christian Church*, ed. Schaff and Wace (Grand Rapids: Wm. B. Eerdmans, 1957), 4: 159.

Wisdom of God, that is, the Word co-eternal with the Father, hath builded Him . . . a human body in the virgin womb."[28]

As the incarnate Logos became more thoroughly identified with Hebrew Wisdom in the early church, the initial problem of the relationship of the historic Hebrew faith to a ubiquitous and autonomous *Wisdom* became more intense and is not inappropriately called the problem of (Christian) faith and *reason*. Although there are significant differences on the nature of *faith* between the Hebrew and early Christian communities—for one thing Christian faith became more intensely individual as contrasted with essential Hebrew communal salvation—the primary differences between the problems of *faith and wisdom* and *faith and reason* center on the differences between Hebrew wisdom and Greek *logos*. Hebrew wisdom began as a characteristic of practical human wisdom and common shrewdness. It was a quality generalized from man's dealing with man and hence was applicable to man's relationship to God. It was seldom, if ever, descriptive of man's relationship with nature, and was never, in early Hebrew thought, concerned with abstract relationships. *Logos*, in contrast, had initial meanings of *counting, reckoning, explaining,* and although later identified with man's ability to think and reason, never had meanings associated with it exclusively involving personal relationships as did Hebrew wisdom. As associated with mathematics formulated within a Euclidean perspective, *logos* represented a systematic, structured mathematical *all* that was ubiquitous (in, say, characterizing spatial relationships) in another sense than Hebrew wisdom, and it differed further from Hebrew wisdom in that, mathematically, it could be known *without either a religious orientation or an other-person existential commitment.*

The early church had an even more difficult time reconciling the historic Christian faith with the claims of Greek *logos* than the Hebrews did with their historic religion and the apparent ubiquity of Wisdom. But its *means* of solution were essentially the same. It was God's wisdom peculiarly given historically to

[28] Augustine, *The City of God,* Book XVII, 20. Trans. George Wilson, *The City of God* (New York: Modern Library, 1950), p. 604.

the Hebrew and Christian communities that was shed abroad to other cultures and that allowed them what actual truth they may have discovered; although in the Christian community through an identification of Logos-Wisdom with Incarnate Son, it was *He* who "was in the beginning with God" who allowed true knowledge to the heathen. Justin, for example, claims that since Christ is the "firstborn of God . . . and the Word of whom every race of men are but partakers," then "those who live reasonably (*meta logou*) are Christians even though they have been thought atheists; as, among the Greeks, Socrates and Heraclitus, and men like them."[29] Justin's statement is unusually inclusive and, perhaps, untowardly gracious, since it includes within the fold of Christians, as he acknowledges, many who would have been thought pagan, atheistic philosophers. Tertullian, who had little sympathy for Greek philosophers, would not have accepted Justin's statement. But even Tertullian, who used his great powers to oppose the philosophers and who, among all the early theologians, most clearly and radically separated the functions of faith and reason with a clear priority on faith, acknowledges that "it is abundantly plain that your philosophers, too, regard the Logos—that is, the Word and Reason (*rationem*)—as the Creator of the universe."[30] In this quotation Logos is written by Tertullian in Greek and was described, or identified with, as was his custom to write in Latin, the word *ratio*. On the authority of Holy Scripture, Tertullian accepted the *logos* description of Christ as divinely revealed and used *logos* Christology to oppose the rationalizing tendencies of Greek philosophy and Hellenized religions as they perverted Christian doctrine—not realizing the extent to which his own conception of Christ (and hence of God) had been rationalized by the use of *logos* and its contact with Greek philosophy and mathematics.

It appears that the Christian problem of faith and reason is

[29] *First Apology of Justin,* chap. XLVI. From *The Ante-Nicene Fathers,* ed. Roberts and Donaldson (Grand Rapids, Wm. B. Eerdmans), 1: 178.
[30] *Apology,* chap. XXI. *The Ante-Nicene Fathers,* 3: 34.

a significant result of that quality of Greek mathematics understood in its natural unity which provided an example of *a structured all that could be apprehended without mythological, religious* or, from our perspective, *philosophical involvement.* All other world-encompassing views, or views that possessed any understanding of a structured all, previous to, contemporary with, or independent of Greek mathematics, necessarily required some cultic, political, mythic, or religious participation in order to truly understand them. One could not participate in Jewish Christianity without a deep, personal commitment. One could not *understand* unless he believed, but this procedure of belief was essentially different from the procedures necessary in order to understand mathematical structure.

Augustine, Mathematics, and the Problem of Faith and Reason

Augustine was not unique among early Christian theologians in opposing heresy. It seems that the dominant motivation, or at least the specific occasion, for the writing of a majority of his tracts was his intense desire, in order to protect the health of the Christian community, to expose errors in thought and doctrine among ostensible Christians or near religions that were threatening the faith. It seems quite ironical to our age that so much of philosophical content, technique, and procedure was introduced into Christian theology, primarily, at first, simply to make distinctions (or create them) in order to pry loose the offending heretical propositions from Christian doctrine. But this technique of separating by philosophical distinction the wayward Christian or contiguous non-Christian cult and their associated "perverse" doctrines has been endemic to Christian procedure. Far more philosophical content and procedures have been introduced into Christian theology through this device than through any sustained attempt to create a natural theology!

It would seem that the natural base for settling doctrinal arguments would be the standard of Holy Scripture. "What does the Bible say?" ought, perhaps, to be the first (and last) question asked. But in actual situations of claimed heresy, things do not work this way. The Devil quotes Scripture and as "minister of light" influences others to do so also. In practical confrontations of heresy, the church was often faced with two claimants to different doctrinal truths—each quoting the same Scripture as authority. In this case one might use "spiritual distinction" to decide the issue, but inevitably, whatever intellectual distinctions were available were brought to the discussion and were used to justify the conclusion. Philosophy, with its myriads of distinctions honed to a peculiar perfection by logic (as informed by mathematics), has been, and still is, the most useful tool in this regard.

Augustine's earlier doctrinal conflicts were aimed against the Manichean sect, a religious group from which he himself was converted to the Christian faith. They believed, following Manes, that Good and Evil were essentially cosmic, eternal powers, the forces of Darkness and Light, that were locked in irreconcilable conflict. Man's soul was understood by them to be a microcosm of the larger conflict and, since he could not modify the eternal forces, he was not held responsible for his own immoral actions. Augustine saw that any justification of man's sin that did not hold man responsible necessarily placed the blame for evil, in a monotheistic context, on God himself.

Thus Augustine, in a dual attempt to justify God's essential goodness and place the responsibility for man's evil where it justly lay, argued for the necessity of free will in man. His very arguments were later claimed by Pelagius as supporting Pelagius's position that, since man could freely choose the good, his salvation was a result of his own action. Augustine actively opposed the Pelagian doctrine, declaring, as he understood Scripture to plainly state, that man could in no way merit salvation. If salvation occurred, it was the gift of God. Augustine, accordingly, in this second major theological conflict of his life, established what became orthodoxy, namely, the dual emphasis of free will *and* God's grace, which in its very possibility of intelligibility is a theological and intellectual problem of considerable magnitude. Augustine firmly believed that his earlier positions concerning grace in *The Free Choice of the Will* were quite consistent with his later ones and, hence, that his total doctrinal picture over the years concerning the problems of grace and free will was of one piece. In his *Retractions,* that work in which he examined his earlier positions often in some detail, Augustine focused so intently on the relationship of the work to his recent controversy with the Pelagians that he did not even examine his explicit identification of Wisdom, which he understood to be also the Incarnate Word, with an essential part of mathematics itself.

The argument follows in *The Free Choice of the Will* as Augustine states that it should according to the order: "What evidence is there that God exists; next do all things, insofar as they are good, come from God; lastly, should free will be numbered among things good."[31] Augustine's argument for the existence of God is essentially an argument for the existence of Truth. Once the existence of Truth has been demonstrated, then "if there is anything more excellent, then this is God; if not then truth itself is God."[32] In either case, as Augustine asserts, the existence of God is assured. Augustine's goal is to show that there is One truth, one wisdom "higher than our mind and reason,"[33] and this wisdom turns out to be dependent, primarily epistemologically but also in considerable measure ontologically, upon the existence and nature of mathematical content.

To the question "whether anything can be found which all thinking men perceive in common, each one making use of his own mind and reason," Evodius replies to Augustine that it is necessary to single out only one example, "the nature and truth of number, which are present to all who make use of reason."[34] We notice that Evodius's reply, which Augustine accepts without

[31] *De libero arbitrio,* Chap. 3: 7. From *The Fathers of the Church,* trans. Robert P. Russell (Washington, D.C.: The Catholic University of America Press, 1968), 59: 113–14.
[32] *Ibid.,* chap. 15, 39: 148.
[33] *Ibid.,* chap. 13, 35: 144.
[34] *Ibid.,* chap. 8, 20: 129.

question, entails that anyone who possesses appropriate (natural) rational gifts can understand and grasp these number relationships.

Everyone engaged in computing them strives to grasp their nature with his own reason and intelligence. Some do this rather easily, others with more difficulty, while others cannot do it at all, though the truth makes itself equally available to all who can grasp it.[35]

The knowledge of these mathematical relationships is not dependent upon commitment to the Christian faith, but upon another kind of natural endowment. If we identify number structures with Holy Wisdom and especially with the Incarnate Word, does this natural rational gift allow acquisition of the truth of God independently of Christian faith? Augustine would never agree to any such position involving faith and reason. The work presently under consideration, though written early in his life and not dealing in any detail with the weighty issues of faith and reason, abound with illustrations confirming what became Augustine's more mature position. For example, after claiming that freedom is found in submission to the one truth that is under examination and quite thoroughly tied to mathematics, Augustine asserts:

And it is God Himself who frees us. . . . It is the Truth Himself, speaking also as a man with men, who says . . .: "If you remain in my word . . . you shall know the truth and the truth shall make you free."[36]

In his overall epistemological position, Augustine chose to integrate what he considered the best of known knowledge, including philosophy and mathematics, with the Christian faith. This integration was done as ultimately dependent upon faith and not upon reason. One believes in order to know, that is, to know the significant issues of faith and their relationship to other kinds of knowledge. His most pointed and well-remembered distinction, perhaps, is that of knowledge of God as "I Am" and as "the

[35] *Ibid.*
[36] *Ibid.*, chap. 13, 37: 146.

Father of Abraham, Isaac and Jacob," or the distinction between "In the beginning was the Word, and the Word was with God, and the Word was God" and "The Word became flesh and dwelt among us."[37] In each case the philosophers could have known the former, but only by faith and the revelatory initiative of God could we have known the latter. Correspondingly, all personal and cultic matters of salvation, including most doctrine about God and especially his revelatory event in Christ Jesus, the Incarnate Word, are known through the acceptance first of revelation. Once we have received the salvific word of God, and had our conscience and consciousness seared by grace, only then can we appropriately understand Truth. But as Christians, once this has happened, we do have the obligation to effect a wide ranging correlation of all truth, whatever its source, since we then, ostensibly, can integrate it with the whole of knowledge.

But what about mathematics and its relationship to the true Christian knowledge of revelation? What about mathematics in its mode of knowing as contrasted with the knowledge of faith? Augustine never really examined the problem. In an attempt to extend Augustine's general position on faith and reason in regard to mathematics, we might say that although mathematics itself may be known through solely rational means, its relationship on the whole to the Truth of God can be known only through faith, that is, a willingness to accept what is given in revelation, primarily in the Holy Scriptures, by God. If the Scriptures do not make specific allegations concerning the problem, we use our minds, which we hope can themselves be grasped and enlightened by the Holy Spirit, in order to make what knowledge we have consistent with that given in Scripture.

Consider the problem, however, of more closely identifying mathematics with Wisdom, as this identification proceeds in *The Free Choice of the Will*. That it proceeds is clear. Augustine quotes sacred Scriptures to show that the consideration of the relationship of number and wisdom is a legitimate one.[38] Then

[37] *The Confessions*, chap. 9; *The Seventh Sermon*, chap 7.
[38] *De libero arbitrio*, chap. 8, 24: 133.

he proceeds to show that it is not the case that there "are as many wisdoms as there are men capable of becoming wise."[39] Wisdom is obviously one. This is justified by the unity and objectivity of mathematics.

> Just as there are true and changeless rules governing numbers whose laws and truth are as you said, unalterably present, and common to all who see them, so, too, are the rules of wisdom likewise true and changeless.[40]

Evodius asks the question, without any chastisement from Augustine, since number and wisdom are placed together in sacred Scriptures "whether number is derived from wisdom or contained in wisdom," or conversely whether "wisdom is derived from number and is contained in it."[41] Both Augustine and Evodius are hesitant to make a strict and exact ontological identification between mathematics and wisdom—although they are very close. Their conclusion regarding the relationship of wisdom and number is:

> Though we are unable to see clearly whether number is contained in wisdom, or derived from it, or whether wisdom itself derives from number, and is contained in it, or whether it can be shown that both are names of the same thing, this much at least is clear, that both are true and are unchangeably true.[42]

That we are not merely dealing with some minute part of abstract wisdom, but with a wisdom that is at the heart of the Christian faith, is clear from the discussion. After showing the existence of a transcendent number-wisdom or wisdom-number, and using this as evidence for the existence of God, Augustine reverts to the authority of faith, that we know God to exist primarily through faith and only secondarily through this "sure,

[39] *Ibid.,* chap 9, 27: 135.
[40] *Ibid.,* chap. 10, 29: 139.
[41] *Ibid.,* chap. 11, 30: 139.
[42] *Ibid.,* chap. 11, 32: 142.

though, as yet, very inadequate form of knowledge."[43] Continuing the emphasis on knowledge by faith, Augustine affirms:

> If you are uneasy because of what we have received on faith through the hallowed teaching of Christ, namely, that there is a Father of Wisdom, then remember that we have accepted this also on faith, namely, that the Wisdom begotten of the eternal Father is equal to Him [Christ].[44]

Granted that, according to Augustine, God's Wisdom, which is a wisdom associated with transcendent number relationships, is Christ, the incarnate Son and Word, how do we handle the central problem that is, according to my thesis, at the heart of the traditional faith-reason discussion, namely, that these number relationships are available to natural reason? How can the "indestructible truth of number" that is "common to me and to anyone at all who uses his reason"[45] tell us of Christ? One does not know mathematics by Christian faith, and conversely, one does not know God by mathematical procedures, so how, in their intimate relationship in incarnate Wisdom, can the two methods of knowing be reconciled? Augustine simply can not tell us, not because he has not examined the problem of faith and reason in some detail, but because he does not examine it in regard to mathematics itself—that root system and only true science of the day that had within its procedures a pure method of knowing that was the standard and epitome of rational knowledge. What is needed from Augustine is a full-fledged theology of mathematics. What we need today, as I shall try to indicate later, is a good theological analysis of mathematics, and for the same reasons. To a degree we have this for Augustine in the philosophy of Plato and the Neoplatonists, to whom he was indebted. Two factors, however, combined to cripple Augustine's conception of a mathematized Logos-Wisdom: the first, that he did not examine in detail the relationship of mathematics as a discipline to theology,

[43] *Ibid.*, chap. 15, 39: 149.
[44] *Ibid.*
[45] *Ibid.*, chap. 8, 21: 130.

and the second, that he was heir to Euclidean presuppositions concerning mathematics itself. Even if he had made the kind of analysis of mathematics that we desire, the end result would probably have entailed similar difficulties as outlined above in regard to faith and reason. In the next section I want to isolate the mathematical assumptions that gave Augustine trouble in his Christology and see how, with their revision, we may create a more adequate Christology from a modern perspective.

Christology from a Modern Perspective

Let us see whether from a particular perspective concerning the nature of mathematics[46] as informed by contemporary mathematical developments, we can create an outline of a Christology that does justice to the intentions of the early fathers' identification of God's Word-Wisdom with Christ, without involving ourselves in the contradictions and anomalies of the faith-reason paradox as held by Augustine.

From an orthodox Christian perspective, in interpreting Christ as truly man and also as somehow truly God, we need not, and indeed cannot, claim that God Himself, alone, single, and without existence elsewhere, was incarnate and lived in Israel as a man. Such a position is contrary to Scriptural warrant and declared formally heretical. We may claim, however, in continuity with Christian orthodoxy, that Christ was uniquely divine and was in some authoritative way acting *as* or acting *for* the transcendent Father. The adequate description of Christ's divine uniqueness associated with his recognized full manhood constitutes the heart of the traditional problem of Christology. Christological positions have come in many varieties, but basically of two sorts. As indicated above, Christ was understood to be the Word-Wisdom of the Father. And he was understood to have an ontological identity, *homoousios*, with the Father. The two doctrines effectively coalesced at the two Councils, Nicea and Chalcedon. In con-

---

[46] This is the perspective outlined in the Introduction, section "The Underlying Mathesis."

tinuity with the previous discussion I shall examine the former and mention only briefly the latter.

The church fathers and early theologians fiercely resisted, as best they knew how, a strict identification of Christ with the abstract, mathematical, philosophical *logos*-reason of Greek philosophy. Christ did not come to impart just theoretical reason, much less a philosophical system. The salvation he brought was of a much deeper sort, dependent upon some apparently non-rational relationship with him and the Father. But they had no effective way of distinguishing Greek logos from Hebrew wisdom, and as time progressed the concept of the Incarnate Word became more thoroughly rationalized. Indeed, the early fathers were in no position to deny that Christ possessed (or was in fact ontologically also) abstract mathematical wisdom. Their basic problem was the accepted understanding that *logos*-wisdom was inviolable. It was understood to be of one piece. The wise man was not wise simply because he knew only a minuscule part of wisdom, but because he had a comprehensive grasp of the whole. The *true* mathematician knew mathematics *because* he knew the system. His very grasp on number or spatial relationships existed because he knew their systematic dependence on, that is, he knew their relationship to, the integrated whole of mathematics. As Augustine claims, there is one wisdom and only one.[47] A man is wise to the degree that he participates in the one wisdom. Surely then, Christ, who was understood *to be* incarnate Word-Wisdom, either possessed as a whole the wisdom of God, or participated in it to a degree that made him, as claimed, absolutely unique. In regard to the distinction between Christ's *being* Word-Wisdom or *participating* in Word-Wisdom, Christian Orthodoxy championed the former.

It is at the point of assessing Christ's knowledge that Scripture challenges his ontological identity with, or possession of, the full, unified wisdom of the Father. Especially in the light of recent research, it is quite evident that Jesus made no claim to possess the full panoply of theoretical knowledge and indeed made errors

[47] *De libero arbitrio,* chaps. 9, 10.

of misstatement commensurate with the general knowledge, and error, of his day. Jesus' theoretical knowledge was probably no greater than that of any other intelligent, and for his day, well-educated Hebrew. Such a position concerning Jesus is, of course, consistent with the kenosis theory of the incarnation that he "who being in the form of God . . . took upon himself the form of a servant, and was made in the likeness of men."[48] The renunciation of godhead included a renunciation of complete knowledge. If this be the case, what then is the true sense of Word-Wisdom incarnate?

I think that there are essentially two options for consideration. First, we could make a distinction between Hebrew practical wisdom, a wisdom that dealt with personal relationships and especially the relationship of man with God, and Greek theoretical reason, a reason that included and was influenced by abstract mathematical thought. We could eschew the latter as much as possible for an interpretation of Logos-Christology, as has been the direction of contemporary New Testament scholarship, and affirm the former as the primary wisdom of the incarnate Christ, and finally, proclaim him to be the creative Word of Power in an Old Testament sense. This distinction is possible phenomenologically and fruitful for a consideration of the meaning of redemption. We may feel that this is what, in fact, the church fathers desired to do but were prevented from doing by their own ever-progressive Greek, and subsequent Latin, conceptuality. Second, we could try to interpret Christ in some way as *being* the Word-Wisdom of the Father, even in some abstract mathematical sense, without his possessing the full *knowledge* of abstract relationships. This second position will require an analysis of presuppositions concerning mathematics and its relationship to the world before, perhaps, the position can even become intelligible.

I find difficulty with the first position, a difficulty that is patterned after the difficulty of the fathers. No matter how one is able to isolate a spiritual, religious wisdom, the kind, say, which

[48] Phil. 2: 6, 7.

prefers the mystery of "Christ crucified" to the philosophical wisdom of the Greeks, it is impossible to see it as other than shot through with theoretical considerations, mathematical relationships of vast and various sorts, and an engagement at many points with abstract scientific theory. I agree with Paul that the Good News should not be put (exclusively) "in the terms of philosophy (wisdom), in which the crucifixion of Christ cannot be expressed."[49] But the crucifixion of Christ, or any other paradoxical but meaningful religious doctrine, has extensive philosophical entanglements and possesses as a doctrine, in terms of the structures of thought, or the relationship of propositions, or as the reality itself—in terms of its spatio-temporal, scientific, or in terms of its trans-temporal, relationships with the cosmos past and future—a definite but highly complex structure of mathematical connections. One may strain to isolate mentally or in concept, by phenomenological means, the peculiar wisdom of God, or the wisdom of the Incarnate Lord, as isolated from its apparently less essential but ever-present philosophical and mathematical accessories. But this is, in fact, a theoretical device, or a spiritual exercise, designed, in an exemplary way, to get at a central meaning or essential reality. The central meaning does not, however, and apparently can not exclude as a reality the ubiquitous abstract and theoretical considerations. At least I know of no way clearly to dichotomize the two. The domain of mathematical characterization is much too general to be banished altogether from any complex of reality—spiritual or physical.

It is much less difficult, and I think more in accord with scriptural honesty and our knowledge of mathematics, to question and attack certain central mathematical assumptions that prompted Augustine, and many church fathers before him, to attribute the whole wisdom of God, including the knowledge of the unity and system of mathematical connections, to the Incarnate Logos. One of the major assumptions, really unquestioned until this century, when it was proved otherwise, attendant on a Euclidean perspective (to which Augustine was heir), is that mathematics itself is unified by one axiomatic system in terms of one content. We can agree

[49] I Cor. 17, Jerusalem Bible.

with Augustine that mathematically there are "true and change-less rules governing numbers" that are "unalterably present, and common to all who see them."[50] Whether we can agree with him also that the "rules of wisdom" are "likewise true and changeless" is another matter, dependent upon our view of wisdom and its differences from mathematics. But we know something of profound importance that Augustine did not know about mathematics and, perhaps, in an indirect way, about wisdom also, if we make a connection between wisdom and mathematics similar to that made by Augustine. There is no set of rules, no matter how large a (finite) number considered, that are appropriately formalized and axiomatized, that can give us *all* of the properties of number. The properties of arithmetic in their totality somehow transcend any one system. There is an intuitive presentation of the structures of number that cannot be mechanized by rules.

In fairness, these deep results by Gödel and others do not mean that mathematicians have lost interest in encompassing ever-larger areas of mathematical content within the fixed restrictions of a small group of axioms. Mathematicians have been amazingly successful in extending and interrelating vast domains of mathematics within the confines of appropriate axiomatization. They do mean that at the outer edges of the totality of mathematical theory, no one axiomatization is possible and, indeed, not even possible for arithmetic. These results, however, have focused interest on how we know *individual* mathematical relationships. Since we cannot know them *all* by one system, in terms of their ultimate systematic relationship, what does it mean to know them individually? Answers to the question have been given by major philosophers such as Husserl, Whitehead, and Wittgenstein, and we shall look into their answers in more detail in a later section, since these answers affect contemporary theology. A position consistent with each philosopher (though, of course, not in the language of each) is that it is possible to bring to consciousness an individual, isolated mathematical relationship or structure, but if we attend to this relationship or structure there is an ever-

[50] *De libero arbitrio,* chap. 10, 29: 139.

widening horizon (to use phenomenological terminology) of others that are engaged with it that ultimately includes an infinite concatenation approaching, but never reaching, the whole of mathematical relationships or structures. This viewpoint is in stark contrast to a Euclidean one, that mathematics can be mastered and understood through appropriate extensions of one compact system. Within a Euclidean perspective concerning mathematics, if Jesus did not understand mathematics, especially since designated as incarnate *logos*, then he would have been far less than the best in human rationality. The kenosis theory of incarnation has never meant a descent to maximal *human* ignorance. Within a more contemporary perspective concerning mathematics, the fact that Jesus did not know *all* mathematical content and its interrelationships simply means that as human he was limited to the epistemological and logical boundaries of the *best* of human intellect. Within this newer perspective, it seems far less important that Jesus knew *any* mathematics.

If we do not require any *knowledge* of mathematics by Jesus in order for him to be incarnate logos, is there any appropriate sense in which we can, and ought, to capture the traditional mathematical associations of *logos* for Christian doctrine? Let us consider any event or particular situation in the life of Jesus. Whatever bodily activity was involved was related geometrically in terms of space-time characteristics and the host of other presently known scientific mathematical structures. Whatever mental, psychic, or social activity that was present can also be related internally and externally to other activities by a vast multiplicity of mathematical connections. No one mathematical system is capable of presenting and interrelating *all* or even a significant portion of the mathematical connections so involved. Jesus never had theoretical or actual knowledge of all mathematical characterizations in which he participated—this is clearly an epistemological impossibility—and he probably only seldom had consciousness of *any* such considerations.

From our perspective in time, that is, as we look *back* on Jesus' life, we can see that there were for him always certain potential actions for him to take, certain potential relationships, even geometrical ones, that were for him possibilities. Death on a cross became for him a possibility, and here geometrical characterizations of "cross" are significant, for they are relevant to the then dominant forms of punishment and death. The geometrical and mathematical figure of a cross as a religious symbol has associated with it a multiplicity of genuinely religious meanings that today, because of Jesus' death, are different from those of Jesus' time. But potentially even these meanings were associated with his potential death on the cross. On a more mundane level, any intentional act of Jesus, no matter how apparently insignificant, meant fulfilling or instantiating some complex set of mathematical relationships in the physical world that could in their *mathematical capacity* be viewed as potential. I have said nothing philosophically about Jesus that could not be said about any other person or entity. I have utilized an assumption, discussed explicitly in the Introduction, that mathematical structures are pure potentials for matters of fact. Some of these mathematical structures may be actualized by actual entities and in our particular case under consideration, by a person involved with other persons, cultural structures, and individual entities.

I have also said little about Jesus in terms of the examples chosen that could not have been said from an earlier mathematical context of the *Elements*. Jesus could have, and indeed did conform to geometrical patterns of existence. He lived in a geometrically extended body that had geometrical relationships with other bodies. And he did this as a man without conscious theoretical knowledge of his continuous geometrical existence. The differences mathematically in this regard between then and now is a matter of difference in both degree and kind. The difference in degree is that we have extended mathematical knowledge to apply to almost every conceivable kind of actual relationship. Geometry was little thought of in Greek times as a tool for actually describing the physical world, although there are some uses of it in this regard.[51] It concerned primarily the more stable properties of the abstract

[51]Plato's attempt to develop a mathematical cosmology in the *Timaeus* is an example, although there was very little actual description by means of mathematics.

figures themselves. In our time, of course, with the development of the full range of the sciences with their ever-more-thorough mathematization, it is possible to consider any particular event as structured in its relationships by a fantastic domain of infinitely connected finite and infinite mathematical structures. And the new uses of mathematics in the sciences are more often than not quite thoroughly nongeometrical.[52] The difference in kind, that is, the basic changes in an understanding of mathematics and its relationship to the world, is the result of a number of factors, of which in continuity with the previous discussion, I continue to emphasize only one, the breakdown of the traditional unity of mathematics. In a Euclidean perspective, whatever mathematics that was used to describe the world was thought to be part of the one system. Because of this, something described mathematically could not be, both at the same time and in the same way, triangular and square, since both characteristics are geometrical. It is possible, however, with a multiplicity of different systems, especially if we understand that the different systems may describe different aspects of the same event, to have complementary mathematical descriptions which, if forced into one axiomatized system, would be incompatible. For example, a person's motion and position may be described in a rough way by Newtonian mechanics, whereas his propositional utterances as they are "logical" may be characterized by Boolean algebras. I do not mean to say here that Boolean algebras and a mathematized Newtonian mechanics are not related mathematically. Of course they are, and in many ways. The breakdown of the Euclidean perspective, however, has allowed us, when focusing on any one event, to bring to it a vast variety of mathematical structures, which may be used to describe it in its many facets, without feeling compelled to weld these structures into one systematic whole.

We may now extend our consideration of the mathematical connections of any one event in Jesus' life, which would involve an almost infinitely complex analysis, to the mathematical con-

[52] The uses of statistics and probability, Boolean algebras, groups, and so on.

nections of the events themselves. Thus we could consider the
total mathematical configurations of his complete life. This would
be, if it were possible to amass and conserve this kind of information, a complete scientific record, complete in the sense that it
would contain all actual mathematical relationships, ranging from
the minutest mathematical status of the atoms of the brain (as far
as mathematical theory can describe this) to the vast interrelationships that we would term, perhaps, psychical, which do have, as
they exist, certain mathematical connections, say, for example,
if nothing else, the recognition by Jesus of the bodily reactions
of Nicodemus when Jesus told him he must be born again. It is
possible to obtain a great deal of mathematical information about
a particular event or sequence of events. Any space shot, for
example, not only has been preplanned, where trajectories in their
relationship to power of rocket blast, and so on, are minutely
calculated and examined on computer models, but also is monitored by the receipt of extensive information during the actual
flight itself. Even here, however, only certain parameters are
considered important and monitored. The total complete multiplicity of mathematical considerations is impossible to grasp and
impossible to record in any known human way.

Thus, in order to consider the total mathematical structures of
any one complex sequence of events, as in this case the life of
Jesus, we must presuppose, as one of our basic assumptions
mentioned earlier, that God knows mathematics and knows it in
its infinite detail and connections. Although we do not require,
or see as scripturally warranted, any theoretical comprehension
or conscious awareness of mathematical relationships by Jesus
for our present discussion of Christology, we do require this of
God himself.

As we attempt to capture the initial mathematical character
of the word *logos,* and not avoid it, for Christology, we may
understand Logos, the hypostatized Wisdom of God, to be (only
in part) the vast set of mathematical interconnections that can be
associated with the man Jesus in his total function—a function
that not only includes the events of his day but one that reaches

into our time as a result of his crucifixion and resurrection. As we focus on the mathematical aspects of Logos, we may also consider the internal nature of Logos as pre-existent to the Incarnate Christ, as the set of mathematical possibilities associated with what God would consider as fulfilling His will. This would be a vastly complicated structure that would allow mathematical structures to be associated with God's criterion of obedience for any time and any place. God, by ordering these structures, would determine the potentials, which could become actual, of all things and events in a manner according to His good will.

In attempting to view Jesus Christ as the Incarnate Logos of the Father, I understand the Logos-Wisdom pre-incarnate as that array of potentials, intimately connected in their mathematical and logical relations and involving all aspects of relative contingencies, that is, not bound by a rigid determinism. I of course do not intend to limit our understanding of Logos to exclusively mathematical potential relationships. Though obedience in a particular circumstance, in particular times and places, and in the context of particular provocations, would necessarily have a vast intertwining and complex set of mathematical structures, especially as made definite by particular actions, and in certain cases *might* be identifiable by the mathematical connections alone, but in general, or at least from the perspective of our present knowledge, this would not be so. What I am recognizing is that the present content of scientific knowledge, especially as presented in its "purest" form mathematically, seems in large part isolated from human values. Any kind of scientific theory employing mathematics requires some kind of a standard of *measure* for physical or other quantities being structured. We have a measure of mass, of energy, etcetera, but no measure, at least at present, for justice. Justice itself is not quantifiable. But to say this does not mean that "justice" as a goal or potential is not related to mathematical characterizations. Justice, for example, may be very much related to "equality before the law," which statistically, at least in part, can be analyzed mathematically in terms of cases and their dispositions as related to class and race categories. In terms of the example of population increase that began this book, is not justice related to the ethical questions of who shall live, which is intimately involved in the statistical models of food resource and population increase?

In my description I am assuming that the complex of mathematical relationships that may describe an event, no matter how complete scientifically, can never completely determine it or characterize it altogether. There are probably degrees of sufficiency here. An adequate mathematical theory more nearly describes an electron than a pet cat; and the pet cat can be more nearly described mathematically than men in religious involvement. But even in the deepest throes of religious existence there are hosts of mathematical connections characterizing some range of potential actions. One of the really important problems in the philosophy of science is to decide how in general nonmathematical characteristics of an event are related to mathematical ones. As science and mathematics continue to develop, I think we will know more about this relationship.

I am maintaining that God, conceived in terms of the combination of insights that were precipitated by the Hebrew-Christian tradition as interpreted by Greek and presently scientific rationality, does have an understanding of the relationships of mathematical combinations and potentials to the genuinely religious ones. He would know what obedience to His "will" might be in certain circumstances and this might not take rigid form. Due to the particular evolution of the world and culture, in individual circumstances as precipitated and conditioned by such and such events, obedience might include a range of options. These options would be conditioned by actual possibilities, determined *by* the past history of the world and cosmos, with each possible past history included in the totality of eternal Logos. As potentials, however, religious, psychological, social, physical, and mathematical feelings and constructs could be structured by God into a vast complex, similar in many respects (mathematically) to the quantified applications of a computer program that analyzes and handles quantitative contingencies—if such and such a "number" results, then such and such a computer action is appropriate. Even though vast and intricately organized, and not representable by any one mathematical system but having the complexities and potentialities attendant on particular actions, the structure could itself be seen by God as one structure, the Logos of God, having to do with potentials and relevant actions concerning any event, and thus could be considered as the word or message of God to man.

Jesus, in fulfilling, that is, by maximizing, the qualities and responses desired by God in terms of some measure or standard probably known only to God, particularized the Word, not by knowing it but by *being it*. In prehending God in an awareness peculiarly personal to him, he accepted and accomplished the individual potentials given to him as initial aims in such a way that he was the Word, and, because he was a particular incarnation, became the Word in a way that the abstract or potential word could not be. A possibility is always less definite than its actualization.[53] The actualization always limits by decision (a cutting down) the range of possibilities. The Incarnate Christ, by being just who he was in a particular circumstance or in coming in the century that he did, eliminates as well as fulfills certain possibilities in the Eternal Word. Although it might be possible in terms of the overlay of potential upon potential for it to be decided when, say, the Incarnate Word was to be manifest, the time and place were probably determined by the past decisions of men (to a degree freely exercised) and by God Himself in response to these historical actions of men. So shall it likely be for the grand consummation, the Second Coming, Teilhard's Omega Point, whose time will be determined by the combined decisions of God and man. At that time the ultimate decisions of God may make definite many past values and historical ambiguities.

The essential difficulty of any mathematization of Logos is

---

[53] See Charles Hartshorne, "Ontological Primacy; A Reply to Buchler," *The Journal of Philosophy* 67, no. 23 (December 10, 1970): 981.

that associated with the feeling that we are returning theologically to a cosmic monism rather than to the historical existence of the Hebrews. If the Logos is the structure of possibilities as ordered by God, was not then Jesus simply acting out, apart from any historical ambiguity, the will of the Father that was predetermined by Him and is and always has been statically existing? My point here, as in other places in this section, is that, within the older Euclidean perspective, this conclusion is hardly to be avoided, whereas in a newer perspective concerning mathematics, the conclusion is hard to justify. The structure and order of Logos require the decision and appropriate envisionment of potentials by God Himself. A particular act by man may require a particular response by God. In this sense, the crucifixion of Christ has elicited responses by God that condition the meaning of Word for us today.

In regard to my discussion of an Augustinian posture on faith and reason, there is no need to affirm, as I criticized Augustine for doing, that rational mathematical knowledge apart from faith gives us any clear knowledge of Logos-Wisdom. Augustine knew mathematics, in his case number and magnitude, from the rules of the system, but no system in either Augustine's time or ours can allow us to specify the particular mathematical characteristics that would attend Logos. Any particular event, especially a complex human one, cuts across the vast variety of systems, employing mathematical relationships from many of them with consistency but without assuming any strict determinacy from the systems. We might try to build up an ethical mathematical model (of the simplest sort, of course) that outlined contingencies of action —what one should do in a particular situation—and try to write a computer program that would compare in some minute aspect to what we might think some small part of Logos would be. But we would probably be wrong, even in A.D. 1975, twenty centuries after Christ's incarnation. Our program would probably be modeled after the traditional legal statements of the Old and New Testaments, informed by our tradition of common law, and modified in terms of recent social, environmental, and ecological problems. But on a morally complicated matter like abortion, or decisions of *who* shall receive an organ transplant and life, or the approaching possibility of whether anyone, and who, shall be reproduced (identically) by artificial cloning—these all require an input other than legal considerations. We cannot live, according to the New Testament, exclusively by the law. The Logos cannot be known (either in its entirety or for appropriate personal action) by legal or mathematical means. Even though the Logos is constituted in part by abstract potentials, we can not know them in any detail by natural means because they do not correspond to any particular or any precise combination of human disciplines.

We know Logos, and this is a very traditional Christian doctrine, by prehending our possibilities in God. This includes, as Christians, prehending those possibilities in relationship to the historical Logos-Christ, who fulfilled them. The very structures of our existence are changed by his event. He and the possibilities inherent in him are a necessary part of our possibilities. We know this by direct experience of God, in terms of our immediate, possible, though not necessarily conscious, actions. Conversely, we know who God is and something about His nature in terms of Jesus' response to God. Who would have guessed that the most appropriate response to intimidation, prejudice, and gross injustice was death on a cross? Who would have known that these possibilities hierarchically ordered in Logos were of paramount importance for true obedience to God? Who would have guessed that Christ's death on the cross and subsequent resurrection include and determine as possibilities for our existence a new structure for joy and relationship to others? We learn this by faith (not by propositions), through actions of obedience, prehending and fulfilling (with God's help) His intentions for us. We experience Christ's death *for us* by recognizing that most of our actions are not fulfillments of Logos potentials but modifications of them, perversions of the good that obscure even the good that we know.

In order to secure true Christian faith from destruction by

means of (merely) rational categories, I have attempted to use rational categories and philosophical structures, in this case a particular viewpoint of mathematics and its relationship to the world. I do use *logos,* reason, in its general character to secure a knowledge that Logos, word of God, exists in a particular way, which in itself *cannot be known* by rational categories. I know rationally how it is possible to obtain knowledge not rationally expressible of the Christian faith. I am motivated to do this by Christian belief. The danger is, of course, that the rational structures that allow me to see my own possibilities of faith may, in fact, obscure or limit actualities of the faith. One must remember that the Augustinian maxim "I believe in order to understand" is first of all a rule of safety. It allows one to accept the changing nature of rational knowledge. Viewpoints concerning mathematics, which I claim affect Christology, have changed from Augustine's time to ours, and constitute the basis for my revisions of his doctrine. These viewpoints, of course, could change radically in the future. Should this be, and from the present state and flux in the foundations of mathematics, it probably will be, we do not want to have enshrined a particular doctrine of mathematics on the authority of faith. But we do, I think, have an obligation to attempt to reconcile Christian faith with the best of contemporary scientific knowledge. With the rapidly changing state of the sciences, such revaluation of the relationship of science to religion will have to occur more frequently than in the past.

The above beginning doctrine of Logos will be reinforced if I can make intelligible, from a modern mathematical context, the orthodox claim of Nicean Christology that Christ is of *one substance* with the Father. The most pointed traditional philosophical difficulty associated with this theological doctrine was the disbelief that, and inability philosophically to express how, any one substance could be included in another. Such difficulties were the result of, at least in part, the rigidly held belief that mathematical units were indivisible. Revised philosophical positions of our day, in particular those dependent upon a Whiteheadian perspective, which itself was initially formulated in response to problems in the foundations of mathematics,[54] allow an intelligible and persuasive account of how one substance may be genuinely included in another. A Christology based upon Whiteheadian presuppositions has been formulated by John Cobb and others in which traditional *homoousios* claims make sense.[55] I refer the reader to these works in the hope that he can see the consistency of my exposition of Logos-Wisdom above in the larger and more comprehensive theological context as expressed by Cobb and others writing from the vantage point of process theology.

In the above section, I have attempted to outline how contemporary mathematical revisions of the Euclidean perspective may result in a revised understanding of Logos that does conform to the intentions of the church fathers and may specifically result in a doctrine that emphasizes "faith" in contrast with "reason," even more so than Augustine's position. I must have left the reader at least somewhat dissatisfied, however, with the presentation, or lack of it, of the actual scope of Christ's wisdom. More important, I have not dealt with the issue of the *unity* of divine wisdom at all. Such discussion, in the light of the plurality of axiomatic systems and the now known inability to characterize completely the content and relationships of known complex domains, for example, arithmetic, by any axiomatic system, is crucial if one is to maintain belief in a unified divine Logos. The reasons for the omission of such discussion are twofold.

First, there are recent mathematical developments, specifically the formulation and discovery of nonstandard models of the natural and real numbers that pose really new questions concerning the nature of potentials. For example, it may be appropriate to understand the realm (however understood) of mathematical relationships, and hence of potential relationships, as *evolving* —a rather radical departure from modal Western philosophy or at least from its Christian adaptation. Such understanding further

[54] See chap. 5.
[55] John B. Cobb, Jr., "A Whiteheadian Christology," *Process Philosophy and Christian Thought,* ed. Delwin Brown, Ralph E. James, Jr., and Gene Reeves (Indianapolis: Bobbs-Merrill Co., 1971), pp. 382–98.

"loosens" any natural understanding of the unity that mathematical-logos structures might have had and presents additional problems for a traditional understanding of such unity. It may, however, also provide an opportunity for theological revision, not only in regard to the questions of divine unity but also in regard to the issues of the relationship of divine wisdom to the actual world. I prefer to present the problem of the unity of Logos after some attempted careful exposition of the nature of nonstandard models, which I give in the last chapter. Second, there are many factors that bear on the unity of Logos, or for that matter the unity of God, that have not been discussed at all. One of these is the history of the understanding of *unity* as it relates to theology, which is, after all, in significant part mathematical history. This is the content of chapter 2. Other issues are the relevance of mathematics to the use of phenomenological tools (in chapter 3), the relevance of mathematics to an understanding of causality (chapter 4), and the relevance of mathematics to epistemological matters, especially those of skepticism (chapter 6).

If I maintain that Logos-Wisdom includes the vast and hierarchical infinities of mathematical possibilities that describe in some way what it means to be obedient to God, and if I maintain that Jesus in being this Word has historically affected the Word for us, that is, engaged us in what is our appropriate response to God, then surely the population crisis (and its associated resource and pollution crises) as expressed mathematically with its human historical tragedy is part of the Word and has a claim on us individually and as a church. If the microscopic intricacies of the functioning of the human brain with the associated emotions of love and hate, dread and joy, are known mathematically to God and form a part of the structures of the Word, then surely the simpler properties of exponential functions that apply macroscopically to living populations are known to God and form a part of the Word. God knows the "surprise factor" of an exponential growth function—that throughout recorded time, through a large number of doubling periods, growth has been seen to be well within bounds, whereas in one doubling period alone, the critical barriers of creation of pollution and depletion of general resources can be broken with disastrous results, while growth still obeys the same familiar law that previously assured security and prosperity. I say this simply to emphasize that a Christian's appropriate understanding of Word-Wisdom incarnate in Jesus Christ is relevant to the approaching human crisis of our times. As conceived in mathematical terms, which show the magnitude but cannot express the human anguish, the crisis ought to drive the Christian community to those modes of understanding peculiar to itself, modes that involve faith, prayer, worship, and experiential authority, in conjunction with the best of scientific theoretical analyses available, in order both to act for the common good of man and to fulfill its unique devotion to Christ. I say also, in passing, that the doctrine of Logos presented above allows the possibility of, through prayer, grasping content, even that of mathematical structure relevant to historical action. Mathematical *logos* can be revealed—by God's revelation. This would occur, probably, only in the obedience structures, fulfilled by historical action, that are the very essence of Christian Logos.

Of course, if my position on faith and reason is correct, the church cannot know what it ought to do based on mathematical and scientific analyses alone. Nor can its leaders attempt to lead the Christian community by an authority based on demographic mathematical projections. One of the means of calling attention to the problem for the church at large, however, is to present responsible scientific analyses as it is possible to determine them. One cannot presume that the church, or even a major faction thereof, will respond to the Word as called by God. Indeed, it is discouraging to see an apparent lethargy in regard to the problem, and actions by some segments of the church that appear to intensify it. But the resources of devotion and worship are there, if only in part. As in the past, the true solution, that is, the nature of the true response to the will of God, may come as a surprise. It will, however, probably involve the traditional Christian virtues of sacrifice and the willingness to give oneself individually and communally for others. The solution is there, available in the Word, whether it is acted upon or not.

2
God and Soul
as Unchanging

Concepts of God change even within religious communities that maintain close continuity with their past. Changes in a Christian doctrine of God have often paralleled changes in an understanding of the nature of the soul. The understanding of both underwent significant change between the end of the New Testament period and the culmination of the theology of the early church in Augustine. This change was basically toward emphasizing an understanding of the soul as eternal and of God as unchanging, as contrasted with an understanding of the soul (or spirit) that decays or dissolves at death to be resurrected by the power of God and of a God who is active and involved in the affairs of men and hence who changes. Both of these latter positions are nearer biblical emphases than the former. The God of the Bible is never presented as absolutely immutable and static ontologically. He loves, wills, acts in history, becomes incarnate, changes his mind, and knows particular changing and quite mutable men. If one accepts a *real knowledge* by God of a changing world, then such understanding would indicate that there is some change, perhaps minor, in God himself.

115

This movement within Christian theology is generally recognized to have resulted from a contribution of Greek philosophy and religion. The Greek contribution, however, was not seen by the church to be incompatible with Scripture or orthodox doctrine. For centuries, theologians have seen the traditional scriptural accounts of creation, of covenant, of historical deliverance, of Incarnation, and of Atonement as confirming a doctrine of God Who is best understood as absolute and unchanging, while they did not appreciate the anomaly of this doctrine with God's activity witnessed in each scriptural account.

Let us define religion as a concern for ultimate invariableness. The religious search is for that which is ultimately not subject to decay and destructive change, which ultimately maintains a set of values that can give meaning to and save a cult, people, or nation. Only a god or being that "is" and suffers no danger of "not being," only a god or existence who can remain through historical and cosmic disaster, only a god or presence who either is guaranteeing eternal values or has eternality of person can give meaning in the face of ultimate destruction through death. The fear of personal nonbeing and the hope for alternatives to it condition a search for an ultimate ground that assures some moral quality and meaning in life.

Both science and mathematics can be seen to have a religious dimension in terms of this definition. The essence of pure science, and its appropriate goal, are a seeking out of invariablenesses among change—the more comprehensive the invariableness the higher the order of scientific "truth" obtained. "Invariance" within science is presented primarily in mathematical terms. That which may remain unvarying under change, for example, the quantity of energy in a closed system, is represented by a mathematical structure that equates relationships between changes as characterized by mathematical magnitudes. We see invariance in science as dependent upon the understood static nature of mathematical relationships themselves. Mathematical figures, structures and equations, as themselves static, allow the representation of unvarying aspects of the world. Can the static nature of mathematical relationships provide an example of a quality of immutability in God and the soul? Did mathematics in the early history of theology have some bearing on the doctrine of God and the soul in this manner? I think that it did.

Within Judaism and Christianity, there is serious concern for an understanding of God Who exists in His own right, Who is not dependent upon the flux and the changing conditions of the world and Who does not change in ultimate character. He is the "I Am" Who makes everything else relative, the One who "causes to be" everything other than Himself. He is the One as presented by Christian New Testament theology Who has the power to guarantee the nondestruction of the human person at death.

Notice the asymmetric relation here; it is the adequacy and invariability of the *power of God*, the assurance of his unchanging character, that insures the possibility of resurrection of the soul and its eternal life, and not *vice versa*. In a study of the relationship of the invariability of mathematics to God and the soul, we would expect a similar asymmetric relation to hold; namely, that the nature of mathematics as invariable Truth or as a static part of the Divine Nature assures an aspect of invariability and hence immortality of the soul. Such an asymmetric relationship appears to hold in all cases where mathematics is used and indicates a priority of examination; we should examine the ontological relationship of mathematics to God first and then see how this applies to the soul. Among Christian writers, however, there is a more intelligible discussion of mathematics' relationship to the soul than to God. The latter is somehow assumed. For this reason I begin my analysis with the topic of the soul.

Corporeal and Incorporeal Soul: Tertullian and Augustine[1]

In continuity with the other Christian writers before him, Augustine believed and taught that the Christian religion affirmed

[1] See Granville C. Henry, Jr., "Nonstandard Mathematics and a Doctrine of God," *Process Studies* 3, no. 1 (Spring 1973).

the immortality of the soul. He considered this belief to be a direct message from the Holy Scriptures. Although affirming the immortality of the soul, Augustine could not consent to its immortality as a natural right guaranteed independently of the grace of God. Immortality was given to man only because of the unmerited favor of God and, according to Augustine, must always be understood to be radically dependent upon God's grace. With such a Christian reinterpretation of the Platonic position that souls are immortal, Augustine could then use neoplatonic arguments to show immortality, and thereby confirm what the Christian ostensibly knows through Scripture and tradition.

In his treatise *On the Immortality of the Soul,* Augustine's argument proceeds from the unchangeable nature of mathematics to the eternal nature of the soul.

> Whoever admits that it is impossible that a line drawn through the midpoint of a circle is not greater than all lines which are not drawn through the midpoint, and admits that this is a part of science, does not deny that science is unchangeable.[2]

The argument (simplified) is as follows. Anything that contains something eternal, that is, unchanging, can not itself be noneternal. The soul or mind contains something eternal, namely science, which in turn contains the mathematical relationship mentioned above, and hence is eternal itself.

The critical relation on which the argument hangs is inclusion. The soul A includes (contains) science B, which contains an eternal truth of mathematics C. Put in set theoretic symbolism, we have A⊃B⊃C, or presented geometrically:

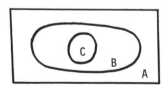

[2] *On the Immortality of the Soul,* chap. 1, trans. George G. Leckie, *Basic Writings of Saint Augustine,* ed. Whitney J. Oates (New York: Random House, 1948), p. 301.

A cannot be totally destroyed or eliminated without eliminating both the subsets B and C. Thus, the guaranteed or eternal existence of C entails the conclusion that the soul can never be ultimately or completely destroyed. The argument rests upon an assumed unity of the soul, that is, that the soul is one and cannot be divided. For if the soul is composed of parts, the eternal existence of C may only guarantee the existence of that part of the soul which is C. This would entail that that which truly continues to live is mathematically pure form, which would be too much of a Platonic realism even for Augustine.

In his later life Augustine was not altogether happy about this argument for an eternal soul based upon mathematics. His chief complaint was that he could not understand the argument that he had at one time made![3] But Augustine in no way criticizes his use of mathematics or his assumptions concerning it. During the general period of writing *On the Immortality of the Soul,* he was in process of writing books on geometry, arithmetic, and philosophy as well as on dialectic, rhetoric, and music, but only beginnings were made on the mathematical subjects and these were subsequently lost. His purpose in writing the books on the liberal arts was to show how one proceeds from things corporeal to things incorporeal in order to have some knowledge of the invisible things of God. Mathematics was essential to him for this endeavor.

Augustine believed that anything eternal and unchanging had to be noncorporeal. Tertullian had stated, on the contrary, that there was something eternal and yet corporeal—namely the soul! In his search of Scripture Tertullian found no evidence that the soul was noncorporeal; if it were incorporeal, how could the rich man in hell, for example, implore "from the *finger* of a happier soul for his *tongue,* the solace of a drop of water."[4] The source of the doctrine of an incorporeal soul, according to Tertullian, is the unnecessary impugning of the senses. If we deny the legitimacy of the senses, then we may affirm an incorporeal soul—but only

[3] *Retractions,* chap. 5.
[4] *A Treatise on the Soul,* chap. 8, *The Ante-Nicene Fathers,* 3: 187.

then. But such denial casts doubt on Christ's sensory experience, of which we are plainly told in the Scriptures.[5]

It was the philosophers, those "patriarchs of heretics," and the chief among them Plato himself, who, according to Tertullian, have led us astray to suppose that the soul is not bodily in existence.[6] The fault lies squarely in Plato's doctrine of forms which, in separating intellectual faculties from bodily functions, make claim to a kind of truth "whose realities are not palpable, nor open to the senses."[7] Tertullian complained that the Platonic dichotomy of reality into eternal forms and transient, inferior sensory experience had allowed heresy to run rampant. Christ himself had been denied bodily existence and some thought thereby that he was a mere phantom.[8] Tertullian fought such heresy with detailed scriptural analysis and scathing ridicule of Platonic forms.

Is it true that Plato's doctrine of forms is the chief source, as Tertullian maintained, of the error, as he believed, of an incorporeal soul? Not only did Platonic form condition the view of an incorporeal soul, as Tertullian showed, but it affected the understanding both of the soul as eternal and of God as immutable. The last two doctrines Tertullian believed implicitly on the authority, as he thought, of Holy Scripture.

Regarding Augustine's argument for an eternal soul, I claimed that it made sense only if one assumes the indivisible unity of the soul. Further, it is the assumption of the unity of God, either by itself or in conjunction with Platonic forms, in association, of course, with religious motivations, that has allowed the claim of the immutability of God. Both Platonic forms and an understanding of the One have a close association with mathematics.

Mathematics, Platonic Form, and Unity

I am affirming that the two main contributions of mathematics

[5] *Ibid.,* chap. 17, p. 197.
[6] *Ibid.,* chap. 3, p. 183.
[7] *Ibid.*
[8] *Ibid.,* chap. 17, p. 197.

toward a Christian understanding of an immutable God are those mathematical developments that influenced an understanding of Platonic ideas and the mathematical understanding that prohibited any division of unity.

There is excellent evidence for believing that Plato's doctrine of forms was precipitated by his mathematical involvement and that he modeled his understanding of forms after an understanding of mathematical figures that was then held by the burgeoning mathematical community. Aristotle claims that Plato's ideas had ontologically the same status as Pythagorean numbers and were used by Plato the way the mathematical society used their numbers.[9] Plato himself frequently used examples from geometry to show what the nature of a form is.[10] A. E. Taylor in *Varia Socratica* made a comprehensive study of the usages of *idea* and *eidos* in Greek literature prior to and contemporary with the Platonic dialogues.[11] He actually lists each use of these words. His conclusion from the study was that the term *idea* itself came from a technical Pythagorean use that meant geometrical pattern or figure. Since the publication of his study, the main thrust of argument against it has been, not that there is close ontological identification between the true nature of mathematical existence and the other ideas, but that the concept of Platonic form *could have* arisen from sources historically independent of mathematics.[12] Even if the concept of *idea* did arise independently, it was quickly welded to mathematical examples, identified with them, and influenced by them.

A mathematical example is never far from any philosophical example in the Platonic corpus. Socrates gives an example of an idea in *Phaedo* that is eternal, transcendent, real in itself, and by which we interpret ordinary experience—namely, the idea of equality.

---

[9] *Meta.* 987b9–13.

[10] For example, *The Republic,* chap. 7.

[11] A. E. Taylor, *Varia Socratica* (Oxford: James Parker & Co., 1911), pp. 187f.

[12] See Sir David Ross, *Plato's Theory of Ideas* (Oxford: Clarendon Press, 1951), p. 13.

... there is something we call equal, not as block to block, or stone to stone, or anything like that, but something other than all these, a thing distinct, equality itself.[13]

The equality of which Socrates speaks is clearly a mathematical one. Only in mathematics had, at this time, an isolation of qualities taken place, for example, the properties of triangles, that would allow an "absolute equality" to be seen. Any other things, especially physical ones, always possessed some aspect of inequality, and hence could in no way exemplify "pure" equality. Equality was in some way above and outside of all particular things and was the means by which any particular equal things were known.

The mathematical nature of equality as used by Plato in this case is not in any way so fully objectified as we are capable of doing today. It is not a technical mathematical object like a geometrical figure or number. It is a semi-intuitive and partially objectified relation that functions in a meta-mathematical or logical capacity rather than as object to be manipulated. It is clear that "equality" seems different in mathematical function from "line" or "number." My point here, in continuity with my discussion in the introduction, is that "equality" as used mathematically as an overarching relation in which the mathematician participates, is much more likely to be involved in religious and theological matters than the more objectified entities. It is, however, no less mathematical because of its less mathematically objectifiable status. Its very meaning is derived from these objectified entities. We can understand almost all—though not all—aspects of a use of mathematical equality as itself an objectified set, a set of ordered pairs of "equal" things satisfying the characteristics of an equivalence relation, namely, the properties of being symmetric, reflexive, and transitive.[14] As such, and in

---

[13] *Phaedo,* 74 a, b., trans. Lane Cooper, *Plato: On the Trial and Death of Socrates* (Ithaca, N.Y.: Cornell University Press, 1941), p. 133.

[14] It is important to notice that even today we cannot objectify a concept of equality understood as identity by exclusively formal

such understanding, equality would be much less likely to be identified with some psychological or religious function. *We* would never think to use it as some indication of a property of the soul. But when it is understood in its initial usage as an overarching cosmic connective, one sees how tempting it must have been to appropriate for personal, religious use that which was already known in authoritative mathematics. The one dominant impression concerning equality was its unchanging stability. Such stability, and the immutability associated with it, could easily be applied to God.

Greek mathematicians consistently insisted that the true mathematical *one* could not be divided. In the introduction, above, I examined the elaborate system of ratio developed by Euclidean mathematics in order to maintain an inviolate *one*. Seldom was *one* listed as a number. The first number was *two*. The chief reason for this, aside from extraneous metaphysical or religious concerns, was that the unit was the *standard* of measure, the means by which number was determined, and hence in itself of a different order of reality than other numbers. One, according to Aristotle, who is attempting to relate the essentially mathematical tradition, is to the other numbers as is the measure to the measurable.[15] By virtue of its use as a standard, it both transcends and gives meaning to other measurements. It is the number one, however, as contrasted with the geometrical measure of one, that is, according to Aristotle, in every way indivisible. It is interesting to note the qualities given to Aristotle's prime mover in the *Physics*—"indivisible, possesses no parts, and is not dimensional [i.e., has no magni-

means without intuitive remainder and still possess the rigorous mechanical deductive powers of the first order predicate calculus. The formalizations of symmetry, reflexivity, and transitivity insure a partition of a domain into equivalence classes but not necessarily into identical entities. An adequate formal definition of the identity relation may be given in a second or higher order logic, but in such logic there is no universal effective procedure for identifying valid inferences.

[15] *Meta.* 1056b35. See Leo Elder, *Aristotle's Theory of the One ; A Commentary on Book X of the Metaphysics* (The Netherlands: Van Gorcum, 1961).

tude]."[16] These are the characteristics of the true number one, which is not divisible, has no parts, and, as the standard for magnitude, does not itself possess magnitude.

Platonic Form and Immutable God

One may immediately object to the position that Platonic forms somehow entail or make reasonable an immutable God and point out that Plato accepted neither an exclusively immutable soul nor an exclusively immutable God. In the earlier works of *Phaedo, Republic,* and *Parmenides,* the deity and at times the soul are supreme example of fixity and immutability, whereas in the *Phaedrus* and the *Laws,* the deity is freely mobile. In the *Timaeus* the eternal God is immutable and the world soul is self-moving. Plato ultimately appears to have created for himself an outright contradiction. How can god and the soul be fixed, eternal, unchanging, immutable and yet, as Plato would also have it, quite thoroughly mobile? There is value, of course, in not letting mere consistency eliminate theological or philosophical realities that seem important, and in this matter Plato had a marvelous genius. But some theological resolution must be made between the conflicting and contradictory attributes of God if the value of consistency itself becomes of high importance.

It was Aristotle who, in revising a Platonic understanding of form, championed an exclusively immutable god. He understood Platonic forms to be immanent within physical things and not in a realm transcendent over them. In ordinary substances each sensible thing was seen to be a composite of matter and form possessing a combination of fixity, the form, and potentiality for change, the matter. All such substances, according to Aristotle, are in motion, that is, changing from one form to another. The reason for change from potential to actual in the individual substances is ultimately pure form itself, that is, God (as much as Aristotle has a god), who attracts, as it were, by virtue of being a final cause or goal, all things unto himself. The unmoved mover, or pure form, is absolutely immutable. He possesses only actuality

[16] *Physics,* 267b25.

and has no trace of potentiality. Thus the logical problem of Plato's philosophy concerning the relationship among the forms is given an attempted solution by Aristotle, who makes all finite form dependent upon the one pure form by categories of causality. Although Aristotle differs markedly from Plato in the *use* of forms, the forms themselves, which constitute that which is most real in any particular substance and is reality itself in God, are essentially Platonic in nature, possessing Platonic characteristics of eternity, fixity, abstractness, and logical relatedness. In Aristotle's view of God as pure form, we can see a direct continuity with the philosophy of Plato, whereby Aristotle chose the one polarity of immutability of God over his claimed mobility and fashioned his concept of mutable substance to be consistent with this emphasis.

If we look at an argument for the eternality of the soul in Plato's *Phaedo,* we see a structure of argument similar to that as presented by Augustine. Socrates divides existing things into two sets, the first consisting of all that is invisible, unchanging, and indivisible, namely the essences or ideas, and the second consisting of that which is changeable, visible, particular, and made up of parts, namely, all that which participates in the ideas. We should not take too seriously any specific bipartite division of reality in Plato's thought, for almost inevitably, after such a division is made, some exception is presented. In this case it is the soul that does not quite fit into either category. The soul, however, is declared to be in its moments of true authenticity much more like the invisible than the visible.

> When the soul inquires alone by itself, it departs into the realm of the pure, the everlasting, the immortal and the changeless, and being akin to these it dwells always with them whenever it is by itself, and it has rest from its wanderings and remains always the same and unchanging with the changeless.[17]

It is the soul's participation in, and its natural propensity to be identified with, the eternal and the changeless, that gives Socrates

---

[17] *Phaedo,* 79d. trans. H. N. Fowler, *Loeb Classical Library* (Cambridge, Mass.: Harvard University Press, 1958).

justification for finally asserting its natural immortality. When the soul participates in the realm of eternality and the unchanging ideas, it is itself in communion with the unchanging and is itself unchanging.

If the soul is capable of immutability as it participates in the eternal realm of ideas, so then, of course, ought the divine—the gods, or if affirmed, the one God—be immutable as it participates in the ideas or is identified with them. As mentioned earlier, Plato had no consistent position in this regard. He recognizes in *Parmenides* that were God identified exclusively with the ideas, he would be completely impassible, immobile, and fixed, with no knowledge of or communication with men, a position that Plato appeared to dislike. In the same section of *Phaedo* as quoted above, however, he likens the eternal realm of ideas to the divine and gives it qualities appropriate to divinity.[18]

In the two basic philosophical positions the church had available to it to use for its own purposes, the Platonic and the Aristotelian, the choice of an Aristotelian emphasis led quickly and easily to an immutable God. God as pure form did not change. In a Platonic emphasis adapted to Jewish and Christian monotheism, if one considers the realms of Platonic ideas to be part of the thought of God—as did Philo, who more than any other is the founder of classical theism and who influenced most of the Christian theists to accept his position in regard to the Ideas—we can understand how God, Who possesses these ideas, is necessarily, at least in part, immutable. We can make sense of Augustine's statement:

> For He does not pass from this to that by transition of thought, but beholds all things with absolute unchangeableness; so that of those things which emerge in time, the future, indeed, are not yet, and the present are now, and the past no longer are; but all of these are by Him comprehended in His stable and eternal presence.[19]

18 *Ibid.*, 80b.
19 *The City of God*, chap. 21, *Basic Writings of Saint Augustine*, 2: 162.

Possession of these ideas by God, however, is no true authority for the claim that He is altogether immutable; something else is required, namely that God is One, and not just the one and only God, but One in the then understood mathematical sense that unity is not divisible. As Aquinas states, "*one* means undivided being," and this is his authority for affirming "*one* is convertible with being."[20] Now Aquinas, in his awareness of the mathematical developments that allow *one* to be part of the "genus of mathematicals," that is, of the same *kind* as other numbers, does not allow this more refined numerical *one* to apply to God. It is the metaphysical one that so applies.[21] At some point in history the metaphysical one was separated from the numerical one and applied to God. The metaphysical one then became a presupposition for subsequent philosophers and theologians though not always surfacing explicitly in their arguments for an immutable God. Augustine, for example, seldom mentions the One in his discussions of God, although his assumption of it is clear. When did the metaphysical One arise historically, and how was it related to mathematics?

The Pythagorean and Parmenidean One[22]

Parmenides was the first Greek philosopher to associate a metaphysical One with the strict immutability of Being itself. He may have been indebted to the Milesians, who affirmed a generalized divine substance, the *arche,* as the foundation of all things, or to Xenophanes, who in reaction to anthropomorphic Homeric polytheism described God as motionless though not strictly immutable. But it was Parmenides who, in reacting to his mathematical training with the Pythagoreans, affected decisively Western philosophical and theological tradition by insisting that Being is one; it was he who introduced that presupposition, which was later to guide Christian theologians to affirm the Christian God

[20] *The Summa Theologica,* Question XI, First Article.
[21] *Ibid.,* Third Article.
[22] See Granville C. Henry, Jr., "Nonstandard Mathematics and a Doctrine of God," *Process Studies* 3, no. 1 (Spring 1973).

to be immutable. In order to see Parmenides' relation to mathematics, we have to examine briefly that mathematical tradition from which he came.

Aristotle, in his general summary of the Pythagoreans, points out that their general metaphysical dualism can be characterized in terms of two opposing sets of contrarieties.

> Evidently, then, these thinkers also consider that number is the principle both as matter for things and as forming their modifications and their permanent states, and hold that the elements of number are the even and the odd, and of these the former is unlimited, and the latter limited; and the 1 proceeds from both of these (for it is both even and odd) and number from the 1; and the whole heaven, as has been said, is numbers. Other members of this same school say there are ten principles, which they arrange in two columns of cognates—

limit	and	unlimited
odd	and	even
one	and	plurality
right	and	left
male	and	female
resting	and	moving
straight	and	curved
light	and	darkness
good	and	bad
square	and	oblong.[23]

The ten contraries of the Pythagoreans represent ten different manifestations of two primary opposites, which may be classified in terms of the headings of the two columns, the limit and the unlimited, the *peiros* and the *apeiron*. The limit, *peiros*, is that which can be objectified, made finite and bounded in some way. The *apeiron* is that which cannot. The Pythagoreans are expressing what became a natural Western rational inclination, as opposed to a general Eastern one, namely, that which we can understand and *grasp* as objectified is superior in knowledge to that which we cannot. The limited is associated with good as opposed to bad,

---

[23] *Meta.*, 986a15, trans. Kirk and Raven.

light as opposed to darkness. A resting object is more self contained, visually distinct, and exactly characterized than a moving one. Something moving may move we know not where, and accordingly will change we know not how. The straight is characterized by exactness of concept, the curving has unlimited varieties of possibilities and cannot be contained as a precise and fixed structure. The number one is the epitome of exact objectification. As understood by the Pythagoreans, it was essentially a unit point and was that out of which the unlimited plurality of numbers and, as Aristotle indicates, the whole heaven itself, was constructed.

The contraries odd and even, square and oblong, however, need some explanation, some key, to associate them with the general opposites of limit and unlimited. Neither contrary seems naturally to fall into the basic dualism that was so fundamental to Pythagoreanism. We see from a contemporary perspective no particular reason why oddness should be involved in more precise objectification than evenness. They seem to be similar ontologically. The even numbers and the odd numbers are sets, respectively, and each is a subset of the natural numbers. The even numbers can always be divided by 2, whereas the odds cannot be so divided. But most odds can be divided by some number; only the prime (odd) numbers cannot. The distinction, however, is not between prime and nonprime, but between odd and even.

The clue is in the Pythagorean representation of numbers themselves. The Pythagoreans had no adequate form of numerical notation. Numbers were expressed in terms of patterns of dots, which allowed them to associate numbers with geometrical figures. If odd numbers are portrayed in Pythagorean form as gnomons grouped around the number one, the figure representing odd (or oddness, but not necessarily an odd number, since the total number of dots may be even), no matter what successive additions of odd numbers we make, is always a square; whereas if we portray the even numbers in the same manner, by grouping in gnomons around the number two as represented by two dots, we see that the figure on the addition of any successive even number changes its shape, specifically the ratio of its length to its height.

odd   even

We may object that both odd and even are getting larger with the successive addition of odd and even numbers (of points), and hence the odd is changing as well as the even. But if we focus on *ratio,* the odd has sides in fixed ratio of unity, whereas the even changes in ratio of sides upon each addition of an even number. The resulting *form* for odd is fixed, exactly determined, and precisely a square. Even is not objectifiable as an exact form or shape, but is unlimited in the sense that it is necessarily always changing upon any addition of even numbers. The opposites square and oblong, the last of the contraries, are also generally thought to refer to the two diagrams for odd and even.

In the quotation, Aristotle tells us that the number one proceeded from both the even and the odd. Other fragmental evidence indicates that the Pythagoreans were perhaps describing a cosmogonal impregnation of the even by the limit (the finite odd) itself, which resulted in the birth of the number one. Perhaps a more accurate interpretation, one concerning the mythological beginnings of the world, is that the even as unlimited, representing the forces of chaos, had combat with the odd, that is, the limit, and the victory of the limit wrested from it the contamination of the unlimited, and resulted in the pure limit, namely, the one. But ultimately this is speculation based on very fragmental evidence. To confound matters, Aristotle tells us in another place that the Pythagoreans seemed at a loss to describe how the first unit was formed.[24] In any case, whatever was the true Pythagorean

[24] *Meta.,* 1080b20.

interpretation of the evolution of the one, once it was gotten, the one, by some cosmogonal process in which it "drew in the nearest part of the unlimited and began limiting it by the limit itself"[25] produced the other numbers, and, according to Pythagorean cosmology, from there the cosmos itself.

The crucial mathematical-philosophical error of the Pythagoreans was an identification of the number one with the unit point of geometry. For us a distinction between the two is evident. They are simply different things. A spatial point, for example, has a spatial relationship in respect to other points, which themselves were identified by the Pythagoreans as a number one. The number one, in contrast, has a numerical relationship to other numbers, none of which is the number one. Their mistake, however, is understandable. Just as any number is made up of units, so also any geometrical figure: line, triangle, sphere, etcetera, is made up of points. The Pythagoreans had no intellectual means for grasping the truly abstract nature of mathematics or its transcendence over physical things. For them the process of objectification that allowed any *thing* to be grasped mathematically as one thing was the same process that allowed the geometrical point to be understood as one; and the point, as was their custom of writing numbers, became not only the symbol of one, but in some mysterious confusion, one itself.

One, so understood as a geometrical point, could not be divided. It, evidently, was an ultimate indivisible atom, out of which, in the finite multiplicity of such atoms, all things were created.

Two characteristics of Pythagoreanism, brought out by Aristotle and confirmed by other evidence, are (1) the ontologizing of mathematics itself and (2) a basic dualism as represented by the two sets of contraries. The dualism, however, though represented by the Pythagoreans mythologically, can be seen when viewed epistemologically as a championing of the newly arising processes of mathematical objectification. The objects of mathematics were seen to be the basic substrate and substance of the universe; also,

[25] *Meta.*, 1091a12.

the basic procedures of consciousness that *gave* mathematical awareness were elevated to be of primary religious and salvific efficacy.

Parmenides, though trained as a Pythagorean, rebelled against Pythagorean thought by intensifying the importance of objectification, by identifying the properties in the left-hand column of the Pythagorean dichotomies as the true and only properties of Being, and by rejecting altogether the properties in the right-hand column as having no existential import whatsoever. As such, his project may be viewed as an attempt to make Pythagoreanism consistent by *really* taking seriously the Pythagorean identification of being with that which is objectified. Parmenides, however, in his movement toward objectifying the whole, culminating in his ecstatic and religious revelation, came to the view that, upon grasping Being, that which is as a unified whole, all internal structure —time, space, multiplicity, sense experience, etcetera—must be denied as truly real. Essentially Parmenides saw everything, the whole, as the one, but having the then understood qualities of the number one—namely, *no internal divisions whatsoever.*

As brought out explicitly by his student Zeno, if one experiences Being as it is the whole, then Pythagorean mathematical multiplicities must be quite contradictory. For example, if we accept a multiplicity of objects, say two of them, then we have two choices, according to Zeno—either to ascribe to the objects no physical existence or dimension, or to allow them some physical dimension. If we accept the former, the object itself could not even be, for if added to another it would not increase its size at all. Obviously, things that have no size, when added to each other, result in nothing. If we accept the latter conclusion, then the object must have some size and one part of it must be at a distance from another. But the same argument applies to that part which is at a distance; it too must have some size and some part of it will be in front. To say this once is to say it indefinitely. Thus, no part of the object will be the last, and the original object will be indefinite in extent. Thus, if there is a plurality, things will be so small as to have no size at all or so great as to be infinite. This is but one of a number of arguments by Zeno, each designed to frustrate Pythagorean ontology and confirm his master Parmenides' affirmation that being is single, homogenous, indivisible, and without change, time, or internal dimension. Being is perceived as the One—without internal division at all.

Parmenides came out of a mathematical tradition in which the problems of objectification of numbers and their relationships were of paramount importance. Although repudiating many of the major tenets of his Pythagorean teachers, he and especially his student Zeno used, at times, the tools and devices of argumentation that were developed in the Pythagorean society. He, like many another Western philosopher or theologian who reacted against a contemporary mathematical perspective, inevitably found himself using those modes of objectification and rational categories that were a part of the mathematical tradition.

Unchanging God: East and West

In the Upanishads, which were being written at about the same time as the development of mathematics by the Pythagoreans, God or Brahma is understood to be totally set apart from the flux of the physical world. He is without time and space, without motion and change, the great void of being but also its plenum, and immanent within the smallest cut part of a fig seed. Although we can recognize Parmenides as the first in Western thought to recognize an absolutely immutable Being, we cannot claim that an understanding of the immutability of God in Western thought is unique, or dependent exclusively on a unique mathematics, for we know that a civilization of similar ethnic and religious background did independently, through a most radical objectification of sense experience itself, understand God to be wholly and completely immutable and transcendent. What appears to be a legitimate claim, however, is that similar developments toward an objectification of God that were maturing among the Greeks (and independently among the Hebrews also) occurred in an intimate relationship with the development of mathematics, and thus acquired a characterization that distinguished them from doctrines of God that arose in India.

There seems to be a general agreement that what happened in at least five different cultures during the sixth and seventh centuries before Christ constituted an intellectual revolution of the highest order. The decisive break with the mythological age occurred in apparent independence among the different cultures: in India among the writers of the Upanishads and in the person of Gautama the Buddha, in China through communities associated with Confucius and Lao-tzu, in Persia through Zoroaster, in Israel as reflected in the explicit monotheism of Second Isaiah, and in Greece among the philosophical and mathematical communities associated with the Milesians and Pythagoreans. It is very difficult to answer the pressing question, "Why did this remarkable intellectual development occur at roughly the same time among five disparate cultures?" Perhaps the most attractive answer is to assume, and with considerable evidence, that mankind was undergoing a common psychological and social development that reached a critical stage in the sixth century B.C., resulting in a drastic break with older modes of existence. But it is notoriously difficult to trace changes in human existence, in terms of any contemporary existential stance, prior to the seventh century, because these occurred primarily at a subconscious level. As a result of the axial revolution, *we* are trapped within the confines of certain rational explanations that simply can not do justice to the pre-rational thought and expression.

It would be easier to explain the emergence of more rational modes of thought in each of these five cultures if they had moved to similar positions. There are certain similarities, of course. John Cobb has characterized the basic common change as a shift of the seat of existence from the subconscious to the reflective consciousness in certain influential members of the community.[26] This shift, however, as Cobb maintains, in no way guaranteed control

[26] John B. Cobb, Jr., *The Structure of Christian Existence* (Philadelphia: The Westminster Press, 1967), chap. 5, esp. pp. 54–55.

to the reflective consciousness. Subconscious forces remained as powerful as ever. Often they exercised more power, because they were obscured by the luminosity and precision of new-found rational powers. The growing unity of reflective consciousness set up a dichotomy where the massive inputs of the subconscious were viewed as alien, powerful, and to be overcome. The shift in the seat of existence did, however, allow the emergence of a new kind of freedom associated with an intensification of understanding of man's individuality.

How these cultures understood this new individuality and how they developed structures of reality to handle it varied *markedly*. The Hebrews understood themselves as a community and as individuals within a community in terms of their relationship to a transcendent, personified God. Hindu and Buddhist thought, however, reflecting the pain and isolation of individual autonomy, sought release from such autonomy through an identification with an a-personal God and through psychological means, respectively.

Nowhere, however, have differences been more illuminating and more significant than between the ancient Greek and Hindu communities. The cultures of Greece and the Indus Valley had in ancient times certain similarities, which are almost ready made for comparison. These similarities will allow me to show the fundamental and essential difference in the understanding of human existence brought about through their axial revolution.

Both Hindus and Greeks came from common racial stock, the aggressive and dynamic Aryans who came into Greece around the end of the second millennium B.C. and entered the Indus Valley in successive waves during the middle of the second millennium. The religion of the Aryans in India suffered revision because of their long history of travels across Asia Minor. We may learn something about these travels from the changes in religion itself. But there is no question about similar origins. Both the names and functions of the gods are similar to those in Greece. Major changes occurred after reaching the Indus Valley, with absorption of the dark-skinned Dravidians who were indigenous to the land.

From this source the Aryans received the doctrines of reincarnation and Karma that were to become extremely important aspects of Indian religion.

In Greece, reincarnation had little importance for religious sensitivities. No widespread popular religion was based on it. There is scarcely mention of it in the main-line philosophical tradition. Among the Pythagoreans, however, reincarnation did assume a fundamental importance.

Western religion, even in its mythological roots, has not been significantly associated with any understanding or feeling for reincarnation. With the acceptance of death as the end of personal life, Western religion has focused on how one might have a new life in some eschatological future. Often it is difficult for us to understand what it might mean to "possess" eternal life as many Easterners do through their belief in reincarnation. Far from giving a natural satisfaction or religious peace, the prospect of continued reincarnation poses a major threat to any kind of integrated and significant human existence. Especially as one feels the pain and sorrow of this world does the prospect of unlimited birth and rebirth appear intolerable. Where reincarnation is accepted as the basic fabric of natural life, a concerted religious effort has been made to break its rigid control on man by discovery of kinds of human existence where its power is dissolved. The investigation of how one achieves true reality and thereby may escape the tyranny of continued rebirth was a dominant religious quest of both the writers of the Upanishads and the Pythagoreans.

As sensitive religious representatives of both Indian and Greek cultures began to achieve an autonomy of reflective consciousness and embarked upon a successful process of rationalization, there arose an attendant sense of individuality and a consequent isolation from ancient mythology and the cultic community. In the Greek community the mythical Gods had been projected aesthetically by Homer in a way similar to a process of visual distancing. The Gods were portrayed as idealized men and women whose most consistent attribute was beauty of physical form. The aesthetic distancing allowed escape from the numinous power of the mythological gods, and put in its place idealized human forms that were subject to symbolical manipulation by talented poets. But it also allowed the possibility of radical skepticism and disbelief.

In the East, in order to allow escape from the situation of painful individuality brought about by increased rationalization, a brilliant attempt was made to *objectify consciousness as a_whole* and thereby permit through religious exercise a separation of the individual from it. Among both the writers of the Upanishads and the Pythagorean community, in addition to a common ethnic origin and common cultic gods, we see similarities of belief in reincarnation and a growing rational development that demanded movement to a new kind of existence that would solve the human and religious problems presented. But movement to what kind of existence? The choice of what was to constitute salvation among the Pythagoreans and Hindus effected a crucial division between the communities and may be used as one of the primary criteria in understanding that difference today.

The Pythagoreans found their purification by contemplation of mathematical form. This contemplation provided ecstasy, a standing outside of oneself, and thereby allowed escape from the round of birth and death. We may have some understanding of this ecstasy in terms of our feelings of exhilaration after understanding a proof of a difficult mathematical theorem. There is a sense of power, control, and release at the winning of "possession" of an intricate and at times very beautiful structure in which our being participates.

When we look at the philosophy of the Upanishads, we see an apparent diversity of views. Close to the source of the guiding religious motivation, however, is a restive dissatisfaction with the *structures* of ordinary religion. By utilizing and reforming the Vedas by commenting on their *essential* nature, the authors of the Upanishads began a radical generalizing and grounding process through which the mythological and blossoming rational structures point to and symbolize through appropriate kinds of negation and affirmation an unstructured, all-inclusive, infinite, and self-sufficient reality beyond all sense apprehension, commonly called Brahma.

Brahma is personal and impersonal in the fullest sense. Distinctions in Brahma between subjective and objective are lost religiously through the affirmation of both. The great discovery of the Upanishads is that Reality in its most real and generative sense, true Reality, which is and constitutes all things, is readily available just outside the structures of human consciousness. Thus, in order to approach toward and to participate in this reality, consciousness and its rational facilities must be objectified as a whole in order to be appropriately set aside for participation in the only true and authentic reality.

Western observers have been too much impressed by the negating process involved in the religious and philosophical disciplines of the East. Any objectification requires some negation. The bringing forward to attention of some sense experience requires relegation of the massive amounts of other sensory input to various locations in a penumbral background. The objectification of a mathematical form requires a broad exclusion of other apparently irrelevant and contradictory relationships. The brilliant accomplishment of the Pythagoreans was to devise methods whereby this could be done. Particularly within mathematical objectification, however, does one negate what has been previously successfully objectified. Whatever is rejected as inconsistent must have some determined structural form, that is, must have been objectified itself at some time. The goal of the Pythagoreans (and of mathematics since then) was to achieve as much generality as possible through their precisely objectified forms. How much generality is possible? Can one achieve a complete generality over all conscious sensibilities? The Pythagoreans would say No, precisely because of logical and analytical difficulties in the mathematical relationships that formed their experiential catharsis. Hindus, however, dependent upon the Upanishads, would say that it is possible to objectify consciousness—as a whole. If consciousness can be so objectified through religious or philosophical disciplines, can it not then be rejected, not for the purpose of nihilism, but in order to obtain a universal synthesis? The writers of the Upanishads found that upon rejection of the *objectified* consciousness, what was left was a nonobjectifiable ground of all being, the true source of salvation, and a genuine and complete synthesis. The true Being does not negate or destroy either consciousness or rationality, but fulfills them. But it is clear that one cannot understand truly *that which is* by sheer immersion and identification with the flickering powers of rational consciousness. If the Westerner insists on operating primarily *within* the structures of consciousness, he will see in much of eastern religion only a vague and general negation.

The chief difference between the ultimate reality that allowed release in the Upanishads and that which gave catharsis for the Pythagoreans is that Brahma in its true nature is nonobjectifiable and thus unstructured, whereas mathematical relationships are highly objectified and therefore precisely and exactly structured. The chief similarity is that both Brahma and mathematical reality were interpreted to be unchanging and eternal, the participation in which gave security from the destructive forces of change.

The discovery of deduction by the Pythagoreans and the precision of structure attained thereby insured that mathematics itself would change. The religious conviction that sought eternal truth through mathematics was coupled with the tools that point out paradox and contradiction. The desire to maintain the inviolability of mathematics made paradox the stimulus for further mathematical research. The Pythagoreans hit on paradox very early in their researches through the discovery of incommensurable magnitudes. This and other difficulties provided an intense motivation among the growing community of mathematicians to provide an adequate solution of basic problems, resulting finally in the cumulative synthesis of Euclid's *Elements*. The discipline of mathematics has had from its beginnings in early Greek thought a built-in dynamic for change. Yet this change has occurred within the discipline's cumulative development. Faith in the legitimacy of successfully proved theorems produced conviction that any paradox or contradiction could be overcome. There is great contrast between an understanding of an ultimate reality in which there is no structure or change and of one that is structured and necessitates an orderly and cumulative change in our knowledge of it.

I do not intend to give the impression that Hindu thought has been either static or unified. I have not done justice to the variety of positions within the Upanishads themselves; for example, the dualistic Sankhya position did not affirm an ontologically prior Brahma. Nor have I taken into account the most significant development out of Hinduism, the religion of Gautama the Buddha. Buddhism has further clarified the nature of illegitimate objectifications. One cannot say, according to the teachings of the Buddha, that there is a universal ground of all things, that is, Brahma, but neither can he say that there is not. One cannot say that there exists a human soul or an empirical ego. Neither can he say that it does not exist, for to do so is to foolishly negate and thereby *objectify* a meaningless mode of being. Salvation does not lie in knowledge or devotion but in the control of feeling, especially the abolition of the feeling of desire that is primarily object oriented, that is, requires a religiously damaging process of objectification. Westerners tend to see an even greater degree of negation in Buddhism than in Hinduism, primarily because objectification is more radically limited. But again, we should be careful to keep as open as possible our largely untrained sensitivities to that reality which is positive in Buddhism's basic approach.

Nor do I intend to imply that Western thought has followed step by step with developments in mathematics, that new developments in mathematics, whether in content or perspective, have always found their way into a significant modification of philosophy. Often there have been profound and significant reactions against the modes of mathematization in Western philosophy. One of the earliest, strongest, and most influential was by Parmenides himself. His reality was more than, and different from, that structured existence by the Pythagoreans. It was to him, indeed, One, unified, unstructured by time or place, and simply existing. His position is, of course, similar to that found in the Upanishads —with the crucial difference, however, that he did objectify Being as the One. Though rejecting mathematical structure within the unity of being, the Unity itself reflects clearly the modes of mathematical objectification used by the Pythagoreans.

There is, of course, reference in the Upanishads to Brahma as "the One." But this One cannot truly be understood as the whole, nor that which can be grasped by the understanding, even as rarefied, abstract, mere unity. Such would deny that Brahma is also the essential Atman, the self. That which knows an object cannot be known as an object.

> He is never seen but is the seer. . . . He is never perceived but is the perceiver. . . . There is no other perceiver but he. . . . He is yourself, the inner controller, the immortal.[27]

Even the process of consciousness that can be known in some definiteness presupposes a knower that is itself not known as an object among consciousness. A participation in the basic reality of ourselves gives an immediate intuitive understanding of a reality, as we follow the main thrust of the Upanishads, which must be identified with everything that is experiential and everything that is quantified—yet which itself cannot be grasped by any intensive analysis. The guiding command to understand "that art thou" is an exhortation to understand that ultimate reality is not objectifiable in any sense, even (and perhaps especially) that of an abstract unity. Whether one can "understand" this goal is in question, but the Upanishads do claim that we can approach or experience the ultimate reality, Brahma, for it is closest to us, our most intimate inmost self.

Though similar in feeling and intuition to Vedantic Brahma, which is also ultimately without internal divisions of time, place, or sensible qualities, Parmenidean being ultimately itself has a limit and is capable of objectification as a *well-rounded sphere*! I quote the relevant fragment:

> But since there is a farthest limit, it is bounded on every side, like the bulk of a well-rounded sphere, from the center

[27] *The Principal Upanishads,* ed. and trans. S. Radhakrishnan (New York: Harper & Brothers, 1953), p. 230.

equally balanced in every direction; for it needs must not be somewhat more here or somewhat less there. For neither is there that which is not, which might stop it from meeting its like, nor can what is be more here and less there than what is, since it is all inviolate; for being equal to itself on every side, it rests uniformly within its limits.[28]

This is clearly a major distinction between Eastern ultimate Being and Western Parmenidean Being. The One of Parmenides is objectified. The true Brahma is not.

God as Objectified and Changing Mathematics

In summary, the two primary inputs from Greek philosophy toward an understanding of an immutable God as developed by Philo and the Christian theologians were Platonic form and the metaphysical One. The Hebrews in their axial development had projected and objectified the one personal God as transcendent over the physical world through the asymmetrical relation of creation, but had understood him, however, as involved in history and hence as mutable in some way. The *religious* desire to understand God as essentially different from man, *without* the imperfections of human nature, and *with* the religious invariance of His power and morality, contributed progressively toward understanding Him as invariant. God's eternal wisdom, His will and intentions for men which, according to the *revelation* given to the Hebrews, do not *essentially* change, could be seen as *strictly invariant* when interpreted as Platonic form. His essential difference from man, requiring not the statements of what He *is* but what He *is not*, resulted in a stripping away of human attributes, the famous *via negativa* of Philo and subsequent Christian theologians, and left only His pure *objectified* existence as God, and hence, also as the metaphysical One *without change*.

The mathematical developments that had initially been associated with Platonic form and an understanding of the One were severed from the essentially metaphysical aspects of both.

[28] Fr. 8, 1. 42, Simplicius *Phys.* 146, 15., trans. Kirk and Raven.

Platonic form and the metaphysical One have had their own history independently of the history of mathematics. It is not necessary to point out that the mathematical disciplines today do not require either Platonic form or the indivisibility of the unit. This has been known for a long time and was, of course, suspected even in antiquity. But Platonic considerations on the question of the nature of mathematical existence and philosophical questions concerning the nature of objectification and unity are relevant to an understanding of God today.

As discussed briefly in the section on Christology in the last chapter, even if we understand individual mathematical relationships as fixed, unchanging, and somehow eternal, and allow these relationships to be a part of, or simply known by, God, we do not have to require, as a result of our knowledge of contemporary mathematics today, that the entire body of mathematics be rigidly unified by one system or intuitive content. What contemporary developments in mathematics seem to tell us is the impossibility of such unification. God may have far more freedom to "play" with the ordering of mathematical relationships than we could have understood previously. Put in the language of process theology: the true order of the mathematical eternal objects may be determined by God's envisagement and not vice versa. This is to say that the traditional model of the immutability of mathematics is not a good model for an understanding of God's immutability. The nature of his true religious invariability must be determined by other, essentially religious and philosophical, means. This is not to say that an appropriate understanding of mathematics is not relevant to an understanding of God. As discussions in the foundations of mathematics progress toward some consensus, or some set of proofs that determine the nature of the unity of mathematics in some new way, we may find it easier to understand God's knowledge as ordered by His unchanging will, rather than His will being determined by an unchanging knowledge.

There is a sense in which we can view the nature of unity as inviolate and indivisible. The intentional procedures by which we view an object as object determine that object as unique. Any division or modification of an object is done in terms of *different* intentional activities, which are therefore different unifying processes. The set {a, b, c, d} understood as a unity is different from the set {c, d} which can be understood as part by inclusion in the original set; the former, for that matter, also differs from the set { {a, b, c, d} }, which can be understood to include the original set. (The three sets have different numbers of objects in them, respectively, four, two, and one.) Unity, as I am here using the word, describes a quality of being of an object, established by regarding some multiplicity as a whole. Whatever is unified as a thing can be counted *one*; a multiplicity of things can be counted *one* over and over again to get their number, say, *eleven*. The eleven things, however, are again another kind of objectification, that is, the unification of eleven things as a collection or set of eleven, and we call this set one set. There is a natural tie between the number one and unity. One is the number of that thing which has been unified. The number one can be divided mathematically into fractions. It makes no sense to speak of a division of unity as here defined. The confusion of this sense of unity with the number one afflicted early mathematics and had, as we have seen, its metaphysical and theological consequences.

Mathematics has continued to grow in terms of new kinds of objectifications: the introduction of fractions became possible as they were objectified as entities; the objectification of rates as derivatives established the calculus; the objectifications of new kinds of axiomatic systems, for example, non-Euclidean geometries, revolutionized both algebra and geometry; the definitions of Cantor that allowed an objectification of infinite sets has added a whole new dimension to the body of mathematics. The controversies and questions concerning the existence of an actual infinity are really questions concerning the adequacy of objectification of infinite sets. Have the newer attempts to objectify infinite sets affected theologically the concept of the infinity of God?

Instead of calling God the One, the later Middle Ages more often called Him the Infinite. The Greek prohibition against infinity, which was really at its source their inability to decide what it meant, that is, their inability to objectify it as some unity, was being overcome. Actual progress was made mathematically on concepts of infinity, a progress that seems to us a necessary condition for the later emergence of the calculus. It was a progress, however, that was made in intimate contact with theological speculation. Bonaventura had claimed that infinity could be found only in God and never (even in the understanding) of anything created.[29] In this viewpoint, which was not uncommon for the age, one had to look to the theological nature of God to have any mathematical understanding of infinity. At a later date Father Malebranche actually claimed that one might have a finite ratio among infinites themselves, or even infinite ratios, since God the Father "embraces all the perfections of his Son with an infinite love."[30] Since God may love some more than others, all the infinities, so he argued, may not be equal—an interesting anticipation of Cantor's later mathematical proof. Contemporary understandings of the number one and mathematical infinity, however, seeem to be essentially irrelevant to an understanding of God.

This is the result of the more thorough formalization of the concepts of one and infinity. As the number system was able to include not only the number one, but zero, negative numbers, rational numbers and irrational ones, all as numbers, the peculiarity of the number one (as nonnumerical measure) no longer appeared evident. In an axiomatization of the number system, the number one is a number among numbers whose properties are *characterized by the system.* Although possessing certain unique properties, that of multiplicative identity, for example, it is not of a different kind from the other numbers. As this kind of formalization has

[29] Bonaventure, *Disputed Questions Concerning Christ's Knowledge*, 1 : 22.

[30] *Méditations Chrétiennes,* quoted from Paul Schrecker, "On the Infinite Number of Infinite Orders ; A Chapter of the Pre-history of Transfinite Numbers," *Studies and Essays in the History of Science and Learning in Honor of George Sarton,* ed. M. F. Ashley Montagu (New York: Shuman, 1946).

progressed mathematically, it has been much more difficult to use the more precisely understood mathematics theologically. God does not appear to be in any traditional sense the same kind of one that we characterize by an axiomatic system. Neither is He, in some general sense, a set that can be placed in one-one correspondence with some proper subset of itself—an adequate definition of an infinite set. In spite of the close association of theology with investigations of mathematical infinity in the Middle Ages, contemporary mathematical investigation of infinity has essentially separated it, in any mathematical sense, from concepts of God, except, perhaps, as relevant to God's *contemplation* of mathematical infinities. Here, of course, the word *infinities* refers to mathematical subject matter and not necessarily to the being of God.

A crucial contemporary theological question, and one that has roots as ancient as we can investigate, is whether we can objectify God, that is, consider Him as some entity among other entities. The initial Hebrew objectification of God allowed an identification theologically with the objectified One of Greek thought. Whether God can be objectified, for example, is a clear and fundamental division in the philosophical theology of Tillich and Hartshorne, with Tillich essentially saying No and Hartshorne saying Yes. The true answer can not come from technical mathematics—as is obvious to all—but from some other source. If we can determine that it is appropriate to objectify God, to consider Him as a unity, then we also in a rather superficial manner can call Him one—but, of course, with no mathematical suppositions of indivisibility. Only if we can clearly objectify some aspect of Him, can we refer to Him *mathematically* as infinite, since any contemporary mathematical definition of infinity requires some objects to constitute the infinity. The attribution of being mathematically infinite is a rather trivial knowledge after the more important task of determining that some aspect of His nature fits the categories.

Although we recognize that contemporary mathematical theory is not helpful in determining some central matters concerning God, in particular whether he can be objectified or not, we may be surprised to learn that the problem of objectification in mathematics has, in a rather circuitous way, affected the general theological discussion of the objectification of God. It has done so through the philosophical discipline of phenomenology, a posture of looking at things that was initially developed by Husserl in order to capture the true objectivity of the new mathematics and logic. The phenomenologists as a whole have come to a negative conclusion concerning the objectivity of God. How their conclusions are related to contemporary developments in mathematics will be examined in the next chapter.

PART II

Modern Mathematics
and
Contemporary Theology

3
Theological Tools: Phenomenology and Language Analysis[1]

Any complex mode of expression guided by a dominant perspective that is used for theology ultimately affects its content. For theology as well as art, the tool limits the finished creation. This need not be a major limitation to the art of theology, provided we understand the kinds of restrictions involved. For different kinds of philosophical perspectives have different kinds of restrictive limitations, and the knowledge of these limitations, though, in effect, relativizing each philosophy, allows us to use and appreciate each in its place.

Both phenomenology and language analysis, as is well known, have had a considerable impact on contemporary theology. Phenomenology is the primary descriptive tool of Bultmann and Tillich.[2] Many aspects of Catholic theology are markedly different

[1] See Granville C. Henry, Jr., "Mathematics, Phenomenology, and Language Analysis in Contemporary Theology," *Journal of the American Academy of Religion* 35, no. 4 (Dec. 1967).

[2] Bultmann is in the main stream of influence from Heidegger. His program of demythologization is an attempt to get at the true

today because of phenomenology.[3] The study of world religions has undergone major changes due to the set of disciplines called the phenomenology of religion.[4] Wherever the influence of Heidegger's *Sein und Zeit* is present, the influence of phenomenology is there.[5] Many American and English theologians have concerned themselves with, and picked up the tools of, the early language analysis in its logical positivist form, though primarily in an attempt to dissolve its negative conclusions. The later language analysis is being used in a positive manner by John Hick, Frederick Ferré, and many others. Many of the "radical theologians" of the last decade, for example, William Hamilton, Thomas J. J. Altizer, and Paul M. van Buren, acknowledge their heavy debt to both phenomenology and language analysis.

In our day we are realizing the similarity of function of language analysis and phenomenology in theology. Neither tool can (or should) have a normative function. In their common legitimate use, both can say in an accurate manner what an intentional religious object or belief is and can clarify differences between various faiths and cultures, but neither can judge which, if any, beliefs are true. Why is this the appropriate function of phenomenology and language analysis, and why should we limit them to this function? Primarily because we have sensitivity to what is happening in theology and how the tools are used there. Secondarily, and this is where an examination of mathematics can

objectivities of myth by means of phenomenology. The use of phenomenology by Tillich in his *Systematic Theology* is very extensive ; the beginning of each of the five parts is a phenomenological analysis of the meaning of the ideas that are subsequently asserted.

[3] A number of Husserl's students, e.g., Edith Stein and Dietrich von Hildebrand, were converted to Catholicism through their study of phenomenology. The most important influence continues to occur through the Catholic University of Louvain, which is the center of Husserlian studies and the site of the Husserl Archives.

[4] See the brief history by Joachim Wach, *The Comparative Study of Religions* (New York: Columbia University Press, 1958), pp. 1–6.

[5] In *Sein und Zeit* Heidegger uses the phenomenological tools of Husserl to examine the nature of human existence. Theologians using Heidegger's categories have invariably picked up his phenomenological stance.

have relevance for theology, we should use the tools only in a manner that does not violate their legitimate use in the foundations and philosophy of mathematics as established by those philosophers and mathematicians who gave us the tools.

I can understand the retort of many theologians that we should use these tools in any manner whatsoever that is helpful, irrespective of how they have been used for an analysis of the nature of mathematics. The general assumption among theologians is that mathematics has no integral relationship to theology today, and therefore the use of these tools as they apply to study in the foundations of mathematics is simply irrelevant for theology. And why should we restrict the use of a tool in theology when one of the problems of theology today is its reductionistic nature?

An answer, it appears to me, is on the one hand that mathematics is having an influence on theology today and in the same manner that it has had in the past. It is not the content of mathematics that generally finds its way into theology but mathematical and nonmathematical assumptions that arise out of an immediate mathematical context. In the study of mathematics these assumptions are required to clarify the nature of mathematical existence and the nature of human subjectivity and objectivity as it is related to this existence. In theology these assumptions structure the relationship between human subjectivity and intentional religious objects.

On the other hand, an understanding of the appropriate function of language analysis and phenomenology for studies in the foundations of mathematics, as initially conceived by Husserl and Wittgenstein, and a limitation by theologians to a similar function in theology, relaxes restrictions that have tended to be reductionistic and allows a more open appreciation of the positivistic content of religion. Both these points need clarification and the burden of this chapter is concerned with this task.

The study of how the tools of phenomenology and language analysis have been used for an analysis of the nature of mathematics is relevant for contemporary theology because both phenomenology and the later language analysis in their mature

Husserlian or Wittgensteinian form had their origin in the study of certain problems in the foundations of mathematics.[6]

Before I proceed with an analysis of the mathematical development of Husserl and Wittgenstein, however, we need a brief survey of selected mathematical developments in the nineteenth century that signaled a transition from classical to modern mathematics.

The Breakdown of the Euclidean Perspective in the Nineteenth Century

The transition from the old Newtonian and Euclidean presuppositions on which Kant relied so heavily—a homogenous geometrical mathematics unified by one content and one axiomatic system—to that of the new can be seen in the work of Joseph Louis Lagrange. Lagrange had a love for and loyalty to the old mathematics and led the way to solid accomplishments in the new mathematics. Newton was to him "the man of genius par excellence."[7] Lagrange's masterpiece, *Mécanique analytique,* published in Paris in 1788, was perhaps the great culmination of the Newtonian mathematical tradition. In this work mechanics was unified with an elegance in expression and a rigor in presentation that was unprecedented to that time. So ordered and appropriate is Lagrange's exposition that Hamilton described it as a "scientific poem." Thoroughly in the Newtonian tradition by loyalty and intent, Lagrange broke with this tradition and the Euclidean perspective by presenting his comprehensive and rigorous

---

[6] At the time of the origination of phenomenology and language analysis by Husserl and Wittgenstein respectively, both men were concerned with larger epistemological problems, and it is not immediately apparent that mathematics played a crucial role in their philosophical development. It is also true that their final positions concerning mathematics have not found so significant a place in the technical study of the foundations of mathematics as did their earlier positions. Thus, my contention that mathematics had a marked influence on the later positions of Husserl and Wittgenstein needs detailed verification, which I have attempted in my *Aspects of the Influence of Mathematics on Contemporary Theology* (Ph.D. dissertation, Dept. of Religion, Claremont Graduate School), chaps. 2, 4.

[7] E. T. Bell, *Men of Mathematics* (New York: Simon & Schuster, Inc., 1937), p. 170.

mathematical system of mechanics *without the use of geometric symbolism.* He was fond of saying that the *Mécanique analytique* does not contain a single geometrical diagram. In Newton's *Principia,* by contrast, *every* mathematical relationship is presented by geometric figure. Lagrange substituted for Newton's geometrical presentation one that consisted of equations of variables and numbers.

Lagrange succeeded in presenting a mathematical mechanics without the use of geometric figure or a geometrical understanding of infinitesimals. His success did not challenge the legitimacy of geometrical intuition in analysis. This was to come later in the work of Weierstrass. He did provide a successful alternative mode of presentation of the calculus. At the turn of the century he was engaged in a work to develop the calculus without any concept of infinitesimal and without Newton's concept of limit. His *Lessons on the Calculus of Functions* (1801) gave an impulse to Cauchy and others to finish the work and free the calculus from the difficult, and sometimes contradictory, intuitive geometrical elements.

Augustine Louis Cauchy (1789–1857) introduced a rigor in mathematics that separated the new analysis of the nineteenth century from the old analysis of the eighteenth century. In order to ground the calculus in foundations that were logically acceptable, Cauchy emphasized a focus of attention on the properties of the real numbers rather than on geometric figures. As a result he eliminated (in principle) "motion" from the calculus. Newton had introduced moving points into the set of Cartesian coordinates and defined the derivative (his fluxion) as the rate of change of a moving point (his fluent). Limits in the Newtonian tradition were understood in terms of the "approach" of a point to a particular value. Cauchy made it possible to dismiss all such intuitions of movement. Consider his famous test for the convergence of a series:

> The series $u_1 + u_2 + \ldots$ converges if and only if for all positive integral values of p there exists a positive integer n such that the absolute value of
> $$u_{n\,1} + u_{n\,2} + \ldots + u_{n\,p}$$
> is less than any preassigned positive real number.

This test for convergence, though also known by Bolzano, ante-dated Weierstrass's definition of a general limit of a function, which begins, "If for any $\epsilon > 0$, there exists a $\delta > 0, \ldots$", an approach so universally accepted that it needs no introduction to any student of calculus. In both these definitions, the convergence of a series or the limit of a function is defined rigorously in terms of conditions involving the properties of the real numbers. There is no motion of a geometric point. If there is any activity, process, or motion, it is transferred to the mathematician. The test for convergence as it is formulated derives from the mathematician's hypothetical *choice* of an arbitrarily small real number ϵ and an arbitrarily large integer p and the test whether there exists an integer n so that the portion of the series symbolized above is less than the number ϵ. Cauchy's convergence conditions are not based on these finite choices by the mathematician but on the choices involving "for all," that is, "for all positive integral values of p," etcetera, and hence do not devolve from any specific activity of the mathematician but depend on the logical nature of the definition. Nevertheless, this more rigorous definition of convergence, and the similar techniques for definitions of limit, focus attention more on the mathematician's constitution of the existence of the limit than did the older Newtonian concepts.

Cauchy's definition of convergence and Weierstrass's later definition of limit represent a change in the understanding of analysis that tends to upset the traditional Euclidean balance between constructivity and objectivity. The change of intuition from moving objective points to the more rigorous definition that allows the consideration of the mathematician's choice, indicates a greater emphasis on the constructive aspects of the mathematician than did Euclidean or Newtonian presuppositions.

The final blow to the assumed adequacy of geometrical intuition came at the hands of Weierstrass.[8] We have seen that

8 Although Bolzano is now credited with producing a continuous curve that at no point possesses a derivative before Weierstrass, it was through Weierstrass that the mathematical community became aware of the new mathematical development.

geometrical symbolism was being replaced by equations of variables and real numbers. Weierstrass produced an example that showed a direct contradiction in intuition involving the traditional Newtonian concepts. Newton introduced "movement" into the Cartesian framework of geometry and conceived a continuous curve to be generated by a moving point. Movement of a point along a curve as measured in terms of Cartesian coordinates presupposes the movement of two points along the coordinates —the x and y axes. The derivative at any point on the curve represents the ratio of the velocity of the point moving along the y-axis to the velocity of the point moving along the x-axis. Weierstrass (1815–1879) demonstrated the existence of a continuous curve that at no point possesses a derivative. If we maintain a geometric intuition that includes movement in the Cartesian coordinates, we have to consider a curve being generated where at no time is there a ratio between the velocities of the y and x movement respectively. We somehow come to the mind-boggling conclusion that a curve is being generated by a moving point that at no time can move. Or, alternatively, we must imagine a point moving that at no time has a definite velocity. These arbitrarily chosen examples of geometric intuition, which break down when considering this type of curve, are not just examples of certain geometric viewpoints that will not work. They point to the fact that no geometrical intuition is adequate to describe what is actually the case mathematically when the curve is presented in terms of limits involving sets of real numbers handled in terms of a rigorous logic.

Weierstrass's example of a continuous curve that at no point possesses a derivative was a result of the analysis of his day made possible by the increased powers of formalization that were emerging in the nineteenth century. The new formal devices allowed the presentation of a curve that could not be pictured geometrically. The astonishing thing about the curve is that, though incapable of geometrical representation, it was found to be descriptive of scientific phenomena—namely, of Brownian movement. Thus, not only was the assumed adequacy of geometric figure to present mathematics challenged by the example, but also challenged was the assumption that physical phenomena are more naturally susceptible of geometrical characterization than to characterization by other abstract and formal means.

Weierstrass, practicing a mathematical rigor surpassing even that of Cauchy, continued the work of formalizing analysis. He was able to give formal definitions of the concepts of limit, continuity, and convergence, in terms of his theory of irrational numbers, that cleared up difficulties associated with the calculus since its discovery. In the work of Lagrange, Cauchy, and Weierstrass we see the advent of a new mathematics of analysis, where one of the most fundamental aspects of Euclidean tradition is given up, that of the assumed adequacy of geometrical figure and intuition.

Furthemore, the assumed compatibility of Euclidean geometry and space itself was ruptured by the discovery of Lobachevsky (1793–1856) of non-Euclidean mathematical spaces. His discovery essentially relativized Euclidean geometry as but one among a number of axiomatized algebraic mathematical systems. One had to understand Euclidean geometry in terms of its essentially (nonspatial) mathematical properties, for it could not be decided then which, if any, of the mathematical systems actually described "space." In the middle of the century Cayley was actively exploring spaces of dimension higher than three.

With the breakdown of Euclidean geometric intuition, the natural candidate for replacement of geometric figure was the mathematical content that had been in competition with geometric symbolism throughout the Greek and modern age, namely ordinary number. The natural numbers did not take the place of geometric symbolism and intuition merely by default of the geometric symbolism. The primary reason for skepticism concerning geometric intuition was its inadequacy to represent known (formal) mathematical relationships without paradox. A foundation of mathematics built on number could not be accepted unless natural number was able to illuminate mathematical theory with an accuracy that had not been obtainable with geometric figure. The emphasis on natural number in the dominant English philosophy from Locke to Hume, and the great popularization of this position on the Continent by Kant, perhaps had some influence on the mathematician's search for a grounding of mathematical theory *in* number. But it was the actual accomplishment of the Berlin school, Kummer, Kronecker, Weierstrass, Dedekind, etcetera, of both resolving previously paradoxical concepts in analysis by use of theories and definitions built exclusively on number and also developing entirely new areas in mathematics built on number, that effected the transition in general intuition among mathematicians from geometric figure to natural number.

The fundamental shift in intuition from geometric figure to that of the natural numbers further upset the traditional Euclidean understanding of the relationship of the mathematician's constructive ability to that of the objectivity of mathematical relations. In the Euclidean perspective mathematical relationships were considered to be objective and "out there." A natural number, however, may be thought of as created by the act of counting. Dedekind once said "numbers are the free creations of the human mind."[9] Mathematics may appear to be merely a subjective creation of the human intellect.

At the turn of the nineteenth century the greatest mathematical genius since Newton, Johann Friederich Carl Gauss, was twenty-three years old. He had already discovered and written in his diary (never published in his lifetime) the germinal development of almost all the new mathematics of the nineteenth century that was later to be rediscovered or more fully developed by his successors. There was a rigor in all of Gauss's mathematics that, in fact, made his formulation of new mathematics possible. It caused him to question the uniqueness of Euclidean geometry at the age of sixteen and led him to consider other possibilities at that time. The nature of his "formalism" gave him a transcendence over traditional mathematics and allowed him to investigate in new directions. He was the first true rigorist of the century, and

[9] Richard Dedekind, *Essays on the Theory of Numbers*, trans. Wooster W. Beman (New York: Dover Publications, Inc., 1963), p. 31.

his rigor spread to the whole of nineteenth-century mathematics, though primarily through the voluminous works of Cauchy, since Gauss published only infrequently.

On the German scene, until the very last of the century in the work of Hilbert, rigor and formalism were not separated from an assumed mathematical content. The purpose of rigor and formalism was to allow adequate representation *of* the content and not to separate mathematical formalism from traditional or newly discovered content. There was little sympathy for mathematics conceived as merely "the manipulation of symbols."

In England, however, mathematicians decisively separated a formal axiomatic method from any necessary relationship to number or geometrical magnitude. In 1830 Peacock published his *Treatise on Algebra,* in which he declared that the variables of an algebraic system need not necessarily represent numbers. Throughout the Greek mathematical tradition, variables represented line segments or, alternatively, magnitudes. In the algebraic tradition the variables, x, y, z, etc., had been used to represent numbers. The variables in mathematical systems had been conceived prior to the nineteenth century as aids to generalization but always as representing line segments or numbers. Peacock clearly broke with this tradition and focused his attention on the variables themselves, which he described as arbitrary marks that are combined according to certain operations. This particular degree of abstraction was not obtained on the Continent but remained a part of the peculiar tradition of English mathematics until the symbolic logic of Boole crossed the Channel through the logical works of Schröder, Peano, and others. It was then that formalism found its most radical exponent in David Hilbert.

The significance of the growing formalism in the nineteenth century may be seen in the perspective that it gives one about the relationship of formal mathematical systems to their interpretations. The mathematical system may be seen to transcend its interpretation due to the fact that one system may have many different interpretations. One can formulate a system that appears to have no known relationship to anything in the world, or one that has many different relationships. Through a study of group structure, for example, one may learn and understand the nature of such structure independent of any observation of this structure in the content of mathematics or in the physical world. From this vantage point one can then observe that a group structure has interpretation in many different situations—in sets of operations performed on numbers, in numbers themselves (the natural numbers form a group), in physical symmetry, and the like.

The advent of a radical formalism in the nineteenth century has posed a new problem for mathematicians and philosophers and intensified an old one. The new problem is whether there is any privileged content in mathematics, that is, whether mathematics as a whole can be interpreted in terms of some fundamental content, like geometrical figure, natural number, and so on. I have observed that the inadequacy of geometric figure in analysis precipitated a shift to number as the primary content of the discipline. But number itself was later found to be inadequate as a content for the whole of mathematics, and there occurred a shift to logic (*Principia Mathematica*, etc.) as the primary content. As I shall show in chapter 5, the increasing formalism of the mathematics of *Principia Mathematica* disallowed intuitive logic as the fundamental content of mathematics. The question of *which* mathematical content, geometrical figure, number, etcetera, is most appropriate for the ground of mathematics has throughout the history of mathematics been a significant one. Whether there is *any* *content* at all that is sufficient to ground the whole of mathematics is a new concern of the nineteenth and twentieth centuries. There is the open possibility that there may be no such content.

The old problem is the question whether the mathematician discovers or creates mathematics. The polarity of the problem can be seen in the dynamic tension between the formal aspects of mathematics and an assumed mathematical content. The viewpoint that no mathematical content can adequately characterize mathematics is the one held by modern Formalists who insist that the description of mathematics by reference to its content is not properly a part of mathematics but of philosophy or some other discipline. Mathematical content is viewed by them as too culturally conditioned, too much influenced by philosophical presuppositions to be able to lift up the exact nature of mathematics. Mathematics consists for the Formalists in pure, pristine, formalistic devices, which are in clear contrast to traditional mathematical content. In opposition to this viewpoint, however, are the Intuitionists, who claim that it may not be possible to do any formal mathematics at all without some, perhaps implicit, background of mathematical content. The formalist David Hilbert, for example, required an intuitive logical content as his metalanguage by means of which he constructed his purely formalistic systems. In the intuitionist view, since one has to have *some* intuitive background of content to do any formal mathematics, he had best critically examine this background lest he be producing formal nonsense. Accordingly, the Intuitionists affirm that certain sections of modern formal mathematics may indeed be manifest nonsense, in particular that which accepts uncritically the existence of infinite sets, and that which presumes to use the axiom of choice.

The tension between formalism in mathematics and a position that emphasizes mathematical content of some sort is closely allied with the "fundamental problem" of whether mathematics is created or discovered. Euclidean mathematics achieved a satisfactory (if not brilliant) solution of the problem by relegating the constructive abilities of the mathematician to a secondary status of confirming the existence of the objective mathematical relationships. Through the philosophy of Locke, and in conjunction with certain of the continental philosophers, Descartes, Leibniz, and Pascal, the constructive abilities of the mathematician were enhanced to the diminution of the objective status of mathematical objects. The human subject was seen to transcend mathematics in a unique way. Yet, with the continued advance of mathematical science, man was seen to be only a part of a larger whole that could be described mathematically. Formalism may be understood to be the representation of the pure constructive abilities of the mathematician unhindered by any objective content. The mathematician's transcendence of mathematical form is heightened, because it is he who creates mathematical form by the manipulation of symbols. Yet, as the second aspect of the tension between formalism and mathematical content indicates, the mathematician in creating mathematical form may be doing so in terms of a background of mathematical content.

The intensification of both poles of the fundamental problem in our day, with an emphasis on both the transcendence of the mathematician of mathematical form and an emphasis on the objective and normative status of mathematical objects, has stimulated new formulations of the relationship of mathematics to mathematical form.

The new mathematics has completely disrupted the Euclidean assumptions. No longer are there assured mathematical objects that one seeks to pattern by schematic mathematical devices. No longer is there an assured unity of mathematics by virtue of one system. No longer is the mathematician viewed as exclusive discoverer of mathematical content. No longer is there an assured overarching systematic relatedness to the universe described by mathematical means. There may be order, but it is a partial order characterized by one system among many others. The only remaining clear characteristic of the Euclidean perspective is the emphasis on axiomatic method. But this too has changed. The axiomatic method today as objective system is a rigorous, formalized structure having no necessary relationship to intuitive *content*. In short, the Euclidean perspective, in terms of which much of early Christian theology was formulated, has been found inadequate. New perspectives have arisen in its place and are presently influencing contemporary theology.

Phenomenology and Existentialism as Derived from Husserl [10]

Before becoming a philosopher, Edmund Husserl was a professional mathematician, having studied under Kronecker and

---

[10] See Granville C. Henry, Jr., "Aspects of the Influence of Mathematics on Contemporary Philosophy," *Philosophia Mathematica* 3, no. 2 (Dec. 1966).

written his doctoral dissertation in analysis under Weierstrass. As a participant in the Berlin school, he adopted readily the dominant understanding of the nature of mathematical existence that was emerging there. The content of mathematics was assumed to be primarily that of the natural numbers. In accord with the general feeling of his fellow mathematicians, Husserl understood that it was the task of the *mathematician* to show how all mathematics could be built up out of the natural numbers. It was the task of the *philosopher*, however, to examine the essential nature of such numbers.

After taking up philosophy, Husserl immediately began the task that he considered appropriate, an analysis of the nature of number. It was obvious to him that the natural numbers were obtained through the acts of counting. Yet in the cardinal-ordinal controversy, which illustrates the tension between the subjective constitution and the objective existence of numbers, Husserl sided with Weierstrass on the primacy of the cardinal numbers. They were to Husserl in some sense "there" as part of the nature of an objective set of things.

In his formal study of number, *Philosophie der Arithmetik, Psychologische und Logische Untersuchungen,*[11] Husserl speaks in the first chapter about numbers, multiplicities, and so on, as objectively existing. In the second chapter, however, with apparently little awareness of the transition, Husserl discusses, not the actually presented totalities, numbers, etcetera, but the origination of the *concept* of totalities and numbers. The origination of the concepts is, according to Husserl, most adequately analyzed by psychology, and the remainder of the book consists of this kind of analysis.

Gottlob Frege caught this change in emphasis and criticized Husserl severely for making everything in mathematics subjective. Husserl's mistake, which he subsequently acknowledged, is quite understandable. The natural numbers had traditionally been put alongside geometric figure, with each being interpreted in terms

---

[11] Edmund Husserl, *Philosophie der Arithmetik; Psychologische und Logische Untersuchungen* (Halle: C. E. M. Pfeffer, 1891).

of the other. With the attempt to found all mathematics, including geometric relationships, on the natural numbers, and, thus, without the objectifying influence of geometric figure, the subjective aspects of counting were bound to assume dominance.

The subjective-objective problem became critical for Husserl when he became aware of a high formalism in the guise of the new logic. As he tells us in the Preface to *Logische Untersuchungen*,[12] he became aware that the formalism of mathematics not only transcends an interpretation in number but transcends *any* interpretation. The formalism of logic, for example, could have interpretations in sets, in propositions, and in some aspects of numbers, yet could not be legitimately identified exclusively with any one. The giving up of the natural numbers as the primary content of mathematics and the concern with logic focused Husserl's attention on the more objective aspects of mathematical relationships. Yet he understood the formalism that characterized logic to be radically created *by* consciousness. The questions posed by these considerations caused Husserl to undergo a complete reorientation of his philosophical position. He wanted to take into account the legitimate aspects of subjectivity and objectivity in mathematics without slighting either. The result of his endeavor was phenomenology.

When one becomes aware of the transcendence by mathematical form as exemplified by new formalistic devices of all traditional mathematical content, he can go systematically in one of two directions. He can sever the formal mathematics from any necessary relationship to any content whatsoever and espouse a position of formalism. Or he can modify a fundamentally constensive[13] position so that the mathematical or philosophical

---

[12] Edmund Husserl, *Logische Untersuchungen* (Halle: Niemeyer, vol. 1, 1900, vol. 2, 1901).

[13] The word *constensive* was coined by Haskell B. Curry as a translation for the German *inhaltlich*. Curry claims that there are two main types of opinion in regard to the nature of contemporary mathematics, the constensive and the formal. In the constensive viewpoint mathematics is assumed to have a definite subject matter or content. The object with which the mathematical statements deal are understood

objects are adequate both as interpretations of formal mathematical systems and as the ground out of which formal systems themselves come. Husserl chose the latter. He sought for a philosophical content that would be at once obviously objective to man and that would form the natural unity of mathematics, both in terms of its ontological identity as content and in terms of its logical relatedness.

Such a content was not easy to find. Husserl was keenly aware of the inadequacies of past content and was very sensitive to the difficulties of getting at what he thought was the true content. If mathematical relationships are objective to man, they ought to be seen simply as *there*. But their *thereness* is not openly the case either to the trained mathematician or to the philosopher. There is something in the natural attitude of man, as Husserl saw it, that prevents the true content of mathematics from appearing in its primordiality. The difficulty does not lie with the obscurity of mathematical objects but with our understanding of the nature of objectivity. Thus Husserl saw as his task the clarification of general philosophical methods by which objectivity in general might be obtained.[14]

With his attention focused firmly on known mathematical relationships, Husserl sought to get at the true nature of objectivity as it belongs to these relationships and thus to the nature of objectivity in general. The result of his search was an ostensible breakthrough to the whole panorama of mathematical content, which he saw to be a variety of logical *eidetic* objects. This was a content where the individual mathematical objects were seen as they exist in themselves, as they are related to each other, and as

to exist in some sense and the statements are considered true as they conform with the facts of this existence. According to the formal point of view, mathematics is characterized "more by its method than its subject matter." Haskell B. Curry, *Foundations of Mathematical Logic* (New York: McGraw-Hill, 1963), p. 8.

[14] Formal mathematics in its largest extension was finally considered by Husserl to be the study of object in general. For an enlightening study in this and other matters of Husserl's logic see E. Winance, "Intention and Nature of Husserl's Logic," *Philosophia Mathematica* 2 (December 1965): 69–85.

they are related to other kinds of objects. When one is in the appropriate posture that allows access to the objects, the "principle of all principles" is in effect: "whatever presents itself in 'intuition' in primordial form . . . is simply to be accepted as it gives itself out to be."[15] According to Husserl, things are in their ultimate truth simply as they truly appear. Philosophy is primarily a matter of looking. We should take note here that Husserl's understanding of objectivity in general, like that of Plato and many other Western philosophers, was patterned after an understanding of mathematical objectivity.

But how does one get into the correct position in order to "see" mathematical objects? In order to observe objects in their givenness, one must, as Husserl insists, practice philosophical *epochē* (abstention). *Epochē* is the radical disengagement of the philosopher from a natural attitude and standpoint that attributes "being" or "existence" to perceived objects. In the natural standpoint, maintains Husserl, one is burdened down with an impossible array of presuppositions that hinder apprehension of objects as they are.

In the process of *epochē*, all existence predicates are isolated from objects in the world, the material being of the psychological ego is bracketed, subjective experience as "internal" ideas is set aside, the physical sciences are "parenthesized," and so on. When one does arrive at the final result of *epochē*, he has apparently severed his conscious activities from any attribution of existence at all. In this process one gets at objectivities in their clarity and manifoldness. The fact that we have bracketed "existence" from the book that we may now see, for example, does not take anything away from our perception of it. On the contrary, according to Husserl, only then can we see it in its clarity. But what about the existential status of the one practicing *epochē*? Does everything succumb to *epochē*? The momentous fact that becomes apparent through *epochē*, as Husserl tell us, is that the pure I

[15] Edmund Husserl, *Ideas ; General Introduction to Pure Phenomenology,* trans. W. R. Boyce Gibson (New York : Collier Books, 1962), p. 83.

remains untouched. The Ego life necessarily remains and is not a part of the world.[16] It is pure consciousness, the Transcendental Ego. Husserl, in an ironic turn, got the pure objectivity of mathematical relationships by a process that led to a most radical subjectivity.

In his mature position, Husserl could recapture much of the Euclidean perspective: a universal mathematical content; a *mathesis universalis* that was a universal characterization of all objects and to which even the psychological ego must conform; and the legitimate objectivity of individual mathematical relationships. Yet he could also show forth the radical createdness of these relationships. They were understood to be *intended* by transcendental subjectivity. The idea of intentionality was received by Husserl through Brentano from medieval sources, where it was an attempt originally to explain those aspects of objectivity which attend psychical experiences intended by a subject. With a dissolving of the existence of the psychological ego through *epochē*, intentionality can no longer refer to objectivities "inside" a psychological subject, but relates consciousness to the "objects" themselves. Husserl saw intentionality as the means by which he could interpret those aspects of radical creativity which he had observed in the new mathematics.

We can see Husserl's philosophy developing from an intensification of both poles of what we have called the fundamental problem—the seen subjective constitution of mathematical objects as well as their purely objective status—an intensification that appears to have a definite correlation with developments in mathematics.

Husserl's program for getting at true objectivities had immediate results in nonphilosophical and nonmathematical areas and brought forth new disciplines—the phenomenology of law, psychology, religion, history, sociology, etcetera. Perhaps the most incisive influence of phenomenology on contemporary philosophy

[16] Edmund Husserl, *Cartesian Meditations: An Introduction to Phenomenology*, trans. Dorian Cairns (The Hague: Martinus Nijhoff, 1960), p. 25.

and theology, however, has come through the existential philosophy of Sartre and Heidegger. Both men considered themselves at one time as students of Husserl and acknowledged his profound influence on their thought. Each philosopher, however, disagreed with Husserl about the existence and primordiality of the Transcendental Ego. Each thought that the Transcendental Ego obscured, "made opaque," objectivities and that its existence must be denied in order to continue Husserl's program of "getting to the objects themselves." Without the Transcendental Ego of Husserl, the objects as seen by phenomenology are the prime reality and appear nakedly as "existing"—the study of which is existentialism.

An immediate question arises when one associates mathematics too closely with the philosophy of existentialism. What about the nineteenth-century "existentialist" philosophers, Kierkegaard and Nietzsche, who produced their position without reference to, and often with considerable hostility to, mathematics. I acknowledge that the "fathers of existentialism" were not influenced significantly by mathematics, but I liken the situation between them and contemporary existentialists to that between Socrates and Plato. Plato apparently gave the nonmathematical content of Socrates a structure that was patterned in many ways after his understanding of the nature of mathematical existence. Heidegger and Sartre have given the content of Kierkegaard and Nietzsche, which consists of aspects of subjectivity previously obscured by certain metaphysical presuppositions, a structure in terms of the intentional analysis of Husserl. Tools that were originally devised to examine the nature of mathematical existence have found their way into an analysis of nonmathematical content.

It is not just that the solution of problems in mathematics provides tools to *examine* content in philosophy. The content is often affected by the tools and is channeled by presuppositions associated with the tools. The existentialism of Sartre and Heidegger, for example, differs in "feel" and method from that of Aquinas. Existence to Aquinas was characterized by objectively existing forms, the truths of God, which transcend it and are "above it." Existence to Sartre and Heidegger is shown forth by phenomenology, which understands appropriate objectivities as intended by consciousness. Since all objects are intended ones, everything as an object has a tinge of subjectivity because of the intimate relationship of subjectivity to transcendent consciousness. Though centering on existence in the world, the contemporary existentialists view this existence from "above," whereas Aquinas, and the whole classical and medieval age, viewed such existence from "below." This change in philosophical perspective corresponds to a change in ideas of mathematical existence where, for Aquinas, mathematical forms, in accord with the classical Euclidean perspective, were objective and "above" man, existing independently of him and not created by him, whereas in a more contemporary perspective such forms are objective yet radically dependent on the creative faculties of consciousness.

Wittgenstein and Language Analysis[17]

Ludwig Wittgenstein, though not a professional mathematician like Husserl, concerned himself with the foundations of mathematics and how they are related to philosophy. His competence in mathematics was very great and he spoke with ease in some of the most difficult areas of the subject. His philosophy has had considerable influence on the contemporary understanding of the nature of mathematics. Conversely, mathematics has had a great impact on the philosophy of Wittgenstein.

In his *Tractatus Logico-Philosophicus,* which had a tangential but critical influence on the logical positivist movement, Wittgenstein sought to rectify the instability of *Principia Mathematica* through an appropriate philosophical program. Though reacting violently against any Platonic understanding of the nature of mathematical objects, Wittgenstein did remain in main-line

[17] See Granville C. Henry, Jr., "Aspects of the Influence of Mathematics on Contemporary Philosophy," *Philosophia Mathematica* 3, no. 2 (Dec. 1966).

continuity with Western mathematical and philosophical thought. He sought for a unified philosophy based on an elegant mathematical characterization. From the mathematical system of logic and especially through an understanding of tautology, Wittgenstein thought that the nature of all other mathematics could be understood. Furthermore, with an appropriate understanding of "facts" and their relationship to mathematical and logical form, Wittgenstein believed that almost all significant philosophical problems could be solved.

But Wittgenstein, in the *Tractatus,* in spite of its brilliance, had not taken into account the radicality of the "fundamental problem" that I have set forth. His position was primarily Euclidean. In the *Tractatus* there is *one* logical space as is shown forth by the facts, and this logical space has a function quite similar to that of physical space. Just as physical space includes every extended thing, so logical space includes all the facts. As Wittgenstein states, "logical space includes the world."[18] Indeed, as he further proclaims, "The facts in logical space are the world."[19]

The mathematical system in the *Tractatus,* which is apparently one homogenous whole, however, cannot be objectified in itself. Such objectification would have been for Wittgenstein too close to a Platonic understanding of mathematical objects. The facts that in the *Tractatus* are ontologically primary "show forth" the logical space, which then becomes the "limit of the world." And here limit is something that one approaches through ontologically real entities, the facts, but that in itself does not exist in any ontic sense at all. Furthermore, the nonexistence of mathematical objects can be seen in Wittgenstein's characterization of mathematics as tautological. A tautology in logic is always true. This, to Wittgenstein, indicates that it can, therefore, be in no

[18] Ludwig Wittgenstein, *Tractatus Logico-Philosophicus,* trans. D. F. Pears and B. F. McGuinness (London: Routledge & Kegan Paul, 1961), 1.1, p. 7.
[19] *Ibid.,* 1.13.

way representative of reality. In one of his stronger statements, Wittgenstein maintains that tautology is the "disintegration of the combination of signs" and has no "meaning."[20]

Wittgenstein's decision to take up philosophical work again after considerable inactivity subsequent to the publication of the *Tractatus* appears definitely to have been motivated by his concern with the foundations of mathematics. Like that of Husserl, his mature philosophy comes as a result of attention to certain "crises" in mathematics. Contacts with the logician Frank Ramsey and the philosopher Moritz Schlick, and hearing a lecture by the great intuitionist mathematician Brouwer, set him again to the task of philosophy.[21]

The great change from the *Tractatus* to *Philosophical Investigations* and *Remarks on the Foundations of Mathematics*, in regard to mathematical understanding, consists primarily in three things: a realization that mathematics is not primarily logic, a realization that mathematics is not one homogenous whole identifiable by an essence or content, and a developing awareness of aspects of objectivity that attend individual mathematical relationships. As in the case of Husserl, a revised understanding of the nature of mathematics entailed for Wittgenstein a change in his understanding of the relationship of human creativity to mathematical relationships.

With the giving up of logical technique as the primary characteristic of mathematics, Wittgenstein did not seek some new content or method to take its place, but went quite radically to the position that there is no content, essence, or technique that exclusively identifies mathematics. Mathematics, for Wittgenstein in his later works, consists of an enormous variety of different contents, usages, techniques, and marginal structures, which as a *motley* or *family* cannot be identified by a predicate or set. The multiplicity of mathematics is so great, as Wittgenstein saw it, that any attempt to organize it philosophically is bound to obscure

[20] *Ibid.*, 4.4666, p. 71.
[21] See Norman Malcolm and G. H. Von Wright, *Ludwig Wittgenstein: A Memoir* (London: Oxford University Press, 1958), pp. 12–13.

the precision and exactness of *some* mathematics. Yet, by common usage or conventional methods, one can normally decide whether a particular structure or usage is a part of mathematics or not.

How can we understand what this vast panorama of mathematical relationships is, and in particular, how can we understand some of the perplexing problems associated with mathematics: the transcendence by system of interpretation; the transcendence by mathematician of system; the logical rigidity of mathematical form as it, at times, controls the activities of the mathematician? The answer, according to Wittgenstein, is to be found in an appropriate understanding of the nature of language, and, in particular, with man's involvement in language. Language games, as presented by Wittgenstein, are a form of social activity where different players have different parts. Some games are communal, other games are played alone. Some have fixed and rigid rules (most "mathematical games" are of this sort), others do not. These language games as we describe them and, more important, as we play them, turn out to be the final epistemological explanation. Understanding of mathematics (and most other things) turns out in the final analysis to be the ability to play a certain game.

With mathematics understood, in part, as the "rule" of a particular kind of game, we can begin to understand Wittgenstein's affirmation of the objectivity of mathematical relationships. We first have to be aware that there are many functions of rules in a vast variety of games. But some rules can be codified in tables and, indeed, may form an object or instrument in a game itself. Such instruments then have an obvious empirical objectivity. But even these physical objects may have a transcendent use in the game, say, somewhat like that of the standard meter in Paris. It is the one thing that we can say is neither one meter long or is not one meter long.[22] It has no "length" in terms of the meaning of length in most games of measuring that depend on it. This is like the understanding of the number one in antiquity, which had no magnitude because it was the standard of magnitude.

[22] Ludwig Wittgenstein, *Philosophical Investigations,* trans. G. E. M. Anscombe (New York: The Macmillian Co., 1953), p. 25e.

Furthermore, there is an aspect of objectivity in mathematical relationships as given by Wittgenstein's later philosophy that is quite similar to that of Husserl's ideal objects. Wittgenstein repeatedly insists that the rule of a language game may not be susceptible of any explicit formulation. The knowing of a game, however, may allow one to understand, and, as it were, to "see" the rule as precise and exactly determined. Even for those games where the rule may be explicitly formulated, one may "see" the rule apart from such formulation by playing the game. Wittgenstein is much concerned that we recognize the accuracy of such "seeing" and of the objectivity of that which is "seen."[23] The objectivity of mathematical relationships as understood by means of appropriate language games is far stronger, and different from, mathematics understood in terms of the ethereal tautology or the non-objectifiable logic of the *Tractatus*.

We have said that part of the "fundamental problem" is to explain how subjectively created entities can be rigidly binding over human concerns. Wittgenstein answers this aspect of the problem in a simple and attractive way. Mathematical relationships as rules of certain language games are rigidly binding if one is playing the game. If they are not binding, then one is not playing the game, but perhaps some other. In either case the games were originally created by some cultural activity, and one has the freedom to participate or not to.

Although mathematics is ultimately created by man, he can look in the solidly existing structure of games and find things, and in particular, mathematical things. The act of formulating and finding, however, will be a new game. The *discovery* of new mathematics is to a large degree invention, in that the mathematical objects are discovered by and through a new game. Gödel, for example, could make very surprising discoveries in the mathematical structure of *Principia Mathematica* by means of new techniques and definitions.

As Wittgenstein moved to appreciate the individuality, uniqueness, and objectivity of each mathematical relationship, he was

[23] See *Philosophical Investigations,* section xi,

led, like Husserl, to affirm the radically created nature of such relationships. Unlike Husserl, however, he sought to avoid metaphysical and ontological categories and interpreted this aspect of mathematics in terms of the almost unlimited ability of man to make up games. The *intention* of Husserl that showed forth the necessity of a deep involvement or participation by the mathematician in order to "see" or "understand" mathematics is presented by Wittgenstein as that precise or necessary involvement *which the respective mathematical game requires*. Such an involvement is necessarily total in terms of the requirements of the game. Wittgenstein insists on equally as deep a personal involvement in the doing of mathematics as does Husserl.

The Theological Relevance of Phenomenology and Language Analysis[24]

Why are techniques originally developed for an analysis of the nature of mathematical relationships valuable for theological study? A theological belief, like a mathematical relationship, is deeply rooted in the subjective and creative processes of men. But this belief is not mere emotion; it is not adequately analyzed by psychological means. It often has a precise structural relationship, which has normative control over the believer, his culture, and, at times, his cosmos. Phenomenology and language analysis, which were devised in large part to answer how and in what way mathematical relationships could be both subjective and objective, are applicable to the very same concern in theology. Since we have come through a period of psychologism in religion, the results of phenomenology thus far have been primarily to present in their great variety the manifold objects of religion. Language analysis has so far been quite reductionistic, due, I believe, to its illegitimate lingering attachment to empiricism.

The great value of phenomenology and linguistic analytical

[24] See Granville C. Henry, Jr., "Mathematics, Phenomenology, and Language Analysis in Contemporary Theology," *Journal of the American Academy of Religion* 35, no. 4 (Dec. 1967).

tools for the study of religion is that prejudices and presuppositions that have traditionally hindered the best descriptive work of scholars may be, to a large extent, cleared away. One can analyze the objects that religious experience intends or creates without making value judgments about their truth or their existence in a special way. Indeed, phenomenological or linguistic analytical techniques allow one often to determine what kind of existence is intended. In the examination of Saint Paul and his religious experience and development, for example, we are not limited merely to the discussion of objective metaphysical objects—God conceived in the light of the Hebrew-Christian tradition—or of a description of the historical phenomena (which necessarily has its own presuppositions about existence), or of a psychological description that considers Paul's internal development primarily. Instead, we can go to those objects Paul intended in all of their variety and as they relate to all aspects of human concern.[25] The analysis deriving from Husserl and, in part, from Wittgenstein has allowed a return, in a way never before possible, not merely to the "beliefs" of the ancient church, but to an understanding of the objects to which these beliefs refer. We should not underestimate the importance of phenomenology and language analysis for contemporary theology.

Phenomenology or language analysis, however, can have only a descriptive function in analyzing mathematical relationships and religious intentional objects. In mathematics, for example, the tools can lift up a vast variety of potential mathematical relationships in their diversity, whether in their transcendent objectivity or as "ingressed" (Whitehead's word) in physical phenomena, but with these tools we cannot decide whether a certain set of mathematical relationships (say, those characterizing the law of conservation of energy) apply to *all* things. That, after all, would be a metaphysical generalization. Nor can we use the tools to say that a certain set of relationships applies exactly to a limited set

[25] See Rudolf Bultmann's analysis of Paul in his *Theology of the New Testament*, vol. 1, trans. K. Grobel (New York: Charles Scribner's Sons, 1951), part 2.

of phenomena. That is the function of empirical verification.

Paul Tillich, while affirming that "theology must apply the phenomenological approach to all its basic concepts," was very careful to make a similar distinction for theology to that just indicated. An error occurs, according to Tillich, when a typical revelatory event as seen by phenomenology is used to affirm the universal meaning of revelation. This procedure becomes illegitimate as soon as contradictory cases of revelation are encountered by phenomenological intuition.[26] Phenomenology cannot decide what criterion is to govern the choice between such cases. A critical element must be introduced into pure phenomenology, Tillich claims, and, indeed, is introduced by phenomenologists, whether they recognize it or not.

The danger in the use of phenomenology or language analysis for theology is to act under the assumption that only that which is "seen" phenomenologically or with the tools of language analysis is true. Such an assumption is, of course, not phenomenologically determined. Often, powerful metaphysical or theological presuppositions are transmitted through the assumed posture of phenomenology or language analysis. As a case in point let us look at some aspects of Bultmann's theology.

Bultmann's Phenomenology

Many of the positions of Rudolf Bultmann that are difficult for the English world to understand and that have caused great turmoil and consternation in theological circles may be clarified by interpreting them in terms of his thoroughgoing phenomenological stance. Myth to Bultmann, for example, is that which "gives to the transcendent reality an immanent, this worldly objectivity."[27] The divine appears as the worldly and the human in myth. Bultmann does not intend by this statement of the meaning of myth

---

[26] Paul Tillich, *Systematic Theology,* 3 vols. (Chicago: The University of Chicago Press, 1951, 1957, 1963), 1: 106–8.
[27] Rudolf Bultmann, *Jesus Christ and Mythology* (New York: Charles Scribner's Sons, 1958), p. 19.

to imply that that which myth "talks about" is in any way less real than wordly objects. It is *phenomenologically different*. The transcendent, the Holy, God's act, and the like, are not to be objectified as worldly objects or worldly happenings, according to Bultmann, for then they lose precisely the character that is uniquely theirs. But they can be objectified in their true intentional meaning and as they appear and present themselves. The point is that the Transcendent is not the type of object that myth makes it appear to be, but it has a legitimate objectivity that can be apprehended only phenomenologically. Myth in its deeper meaning points to that which is genuinely objective and phenomenologically existent and which can appear through the myth if the observer is able to take an appropriate stance. The task of theology, according to Bultmann, is to demythologize the myth in order to get to the "correct" and legitimate understanding of the objectivities of the faith that appear through myth.

In our scientific age, where objects are normally thought of as the objects of science, to consider mythology literally is detrimental to the intention of the myth, so believes Bultmann, for that which is objectified mythologically is, more often than not, interpreted similarly to that which is objectified scientifically. To ask, for example, if there really is a hell, thinking as we do, that if there is then it must have objective features of the same type of objectivity as does our physical world (Is its fire like our fire?, etc.), is to entirely miss the point of the myth. It is a fundamental phenomenological mistake "in seeing" that is involved. The intentional objects that are meant by the use of language about hell in the New Testament are multiform and are exceedingly important for an understanding of our own human existence and its relationship to God. So it is with most other of the basic concerns of the New Testament. Phenomenology is able to see and discover vital meanings, and ones (supposedly) close to those of the early church, which have been hidden in our day by our inability to see past the objective language in which the myths are couched.

To deny the this-worldly objectivity of God, of miracles, and the like, is, as Bultmann maintains, not to deny the legitimate objectivity that these things have, and consequently place theology primarily in the subjective or psychological realm. It is the phenomenological stance of Husserl, and more particularly that of Heidegger, that allows Bultmann to present the full objective understanding of the things of faith while maintaining a radical grounding of them in human existence. This objectivity may be had without recourse to a purely subjective or psychological description.

Bultmann claims that "only such statements about God are legitimate as express the existential relation between God and man."[28] The only legitimate theological statements about God, from Bultmann's perspective, are those that are "grounded in human existence." But such grounding does not mean that God's action is deprived of objective reality, "that it is reduced to a purely subjective, psychological experience; that God exists only as an inner event in the soul."[29] According to Bultmann, "from the statement that to speak of God is to speak of myself, it by no means follows that God is not outside the believer."[30] The action of God can be understood both as an objective event (in an appropriate phenomenological stance) and as radically grounded in human existence and its historicity.

We may ask, "Does Bultmann's use of phenomenology determine, in some sense, specific theological content?" The answer is only a qualified, "Yes." There are many theological streams that have conditioned Bultmann's position, and most of these had their advent before phenomenology. Because of his Lutheran tradition, Bultmann emphasizes the primacy of faith as opposed to any security that rests on objective knowledge. That man is not saved by his "correct ideas" is, for Bultmann, equally as important a maxim for true Christianity as is the traditional Lutheran claim that man is not saved by his good works.

Bultmann concentrates his analysis on the nature of man's

[28] *Ibid.*, p. 69.
[29] *Ibid.*, p. 70.
[30] *Ibid.*

encounter with God and not on the nature of God considered in any metaphysical sense. His is an explanation of the self-understanding that comes into being with faith. The philosophical sources on which Bultmann relies serve him essentially as a tool for the presentation of content that is determined primarily by religious orientation and theological insight.

That philosophy is not to *determine* the content of the faith is clearly stated by Bultmann in his description of the appropriate relationship of philosophy to theology. Man approaches the New Testament, according to Bultmann, with some necessary preunderstanding that is often influenced heavily by some philosophical source. That these philosophical sources have determined in large part how the Bible has been interpreted in the past can not be denied, nor can it be denied that certain philosophical positions are influential on interpretation of the Bible today. What must be grasped, however, is that the Bible becomes, in its truly Christian function, a word addressed personally to me that not only describes my real existence, but, in fact, according to Bultmann, *gives to me* authentic existence. In this function, through the act of God as proclaimed in the *kerygma,* the giving or determining of my new existence may shatter the preunderstanding and preconceptions that I may have brought to the Bible originally. No philosophy, affirms Bultmann, is able to circumscribe completely, with adequate description and adequate understanding, that which comes to me and in a sense becomes me through my faith encounter with God.

But some philosophical positions are more adequate than others. Since theology is primarily, for Bultmann, the scientific exposition of self-understanding that comes through faith, a philosophy that has as its focus the nature of human existence is more adequate than one that does not. Since any philosophical preunderstanding is bound to be modified or changed (or at least is not secure from change) through the becoming of new human existence in encounter with God, a philosophy that is open to ontic changes in human existence and human understanding of it while still maintaining adequate ontological descriptions of human existence in general, is preferable to one that in its rigidness is shattered completely by the encounter with God. For these reasons, Bultmann believes that existential philosophy is more adequate than others. This does not mean that existential philosophy can determine what man ought to be, or can say anything specifically about particular human conditions of existence that may become the subject matter of Christian theology. We do not baptize existential philosophy, but only use it as a descriptive device to present the nature of Christian human existence that we discover through encounter with God.

It must be said, however, that the philosophy that Bultmann received from Husserl and Heidegger, in its compatibility with and usefulness for his theological enterprise, has tended, along with other significant forces, to determine aspects of his theology. Particularly does this show itself in Bultmann's understanding of God's relationship to the world. The world for Bultmann, as the totality of spatiotemporal phenomena, is a closed system. All this-worldly phenomena can and should be explained only by worldly phenomena. The course of nature, as Bultmann states, is not interrupted or "perforated by supernatural powers."[31] God, according to Bultmann, can never be introduced as a part of an explanation of happenings in this world. He is hidden to all except the eyes of faith. But in the eyes of faith, the whole of the world is seen as absolutely dependent on the Transcendent God, and even specific events (like the healing of a child) are seen as acts of God. This does not mean that the healing of a child is not to be explained in terms of natural phenomena—it is and should be so explained. But there is a "nevertheless" understanding of God's act as decisive in the event without having to attribute to God causal efficacy of a physical, psychological, or psychical sort.

Part of Bultmann's understanding of God's relationship to the world comes, of course, from his Lutheran background. But it is confirmed and in part determined by his phenomenological stance. Having grounded knowledge of all objects in terms of their appearing to be and being a part of human existence, Bultmann

[31] *Ibid.*, p. 15.

cannot accept metaphysical constructs that in some way describe God's causal action in the world. The "hiddenness of God," as it is important to human existence, is phenomenologically visible to Bultmann. But where does one *see* (phenomenologically) God's acting in the world (or on it) as most traditional theological metaphysics and almost all myths have portrayed? "Nowhere," Bultmann would answer.

Bultmann's position in this regard is reflected most pointedly through his understanding of the resurrection of Christ. No one in modern times has said with so much accuracy and comprehensiveness what the resurrection of Christ means for an understanding of human existence as has Bultmann. And here I mean to commend not only Bultmann but the whole phenomenological enterprise for what it can do and has done for theology. His clarification of what Paul and the early church meant and intended through their corporate existence as the "resurrected community" appears to be a return to orthodoxy in that what Paul intends is taken in its simplicity and accuracy as he, Paul, intended it, and is not subjected to radical modifications in terms of contemporary theological perspectives. Bultmann has performed an unprecedented service for the Church and for Christian theology by allowing a return to what Paul meant and by showing through phenomenological analysis the theological objects to which he referred. But the great importance of the resurrection for Christian human existence in Bultmann's writings does not allow him to say anything, from a phenomenological stance, about the historical fact of the empty tomb. The primary thing that can be said is that from the perspective of the New Testament and of most Christian literature, the importance of the resurrection "for me" far exceeds any affirmation of the historical event of the empty tomb. The fact of the empty tomb and questions about it lie outside the purview of phenomenological vision.

I am aware that Bultmann's position that resurrection does not mean the resuscitation of a corpse and that his consequent skepticism about the empty tomb came primarily from his historical studies of the New Testament. But his position in this regard is complemented by an overemphasis on the phenomenological method. He is too much captured by the perspective that what one cannot *see* phenomenologically simply can not *be*. Because one can not *see* (phenomenologically) God act causally in the worldly nexus, one therefore assumes that he *does not so act*. The empty tomb not only *was not*, from Bultmann's historical studies, but also *could not have been* from his phenomenological presuppositions. Bultmann, in my estimation, is guilty of extending a tool that was developed initially for mathematical and logical objects, and has subsequently found a remarkable use in theology, but beyond its legitimate bounds. He is using it as a criterion for coming to *negative theological opinions* concerning matters that are beyond phenomenoligical vision.

Restrictive Language Analysis

The same type of mistake made by Bultmann is, in my estimation, made by Paul M. van Buren in his book *The Secular Meaning of the Gospel*. Although this work, now over a decade old, has been evaluated, criticized, and superseded by more recent use of language analysis, including that of the author himself,[32] it has become almost a "classic" for a consistent and thorough use of language analysis in the study of the Christian Gospel. Van Buren's mistake in this work is not in the overuse of phenomenology, as was Bultmann's, but in the illegitimate use of language analysis. Like Bultmann, he employs too freely a method that was originally devised for solution of problems in mathematics, without consideration of the metaphysical issues that are a part of the method.

One of the things that we are learning in this decade, as mentioned earlier, is that the function of language analysis in theology is very similar to the function of phenomenology in theology. Both disciplines are used to clarify and present inten-

[32] Paul M. van Buren, *The Secular Meaning of the Gospel Based on an Analysis of its Language* (New York: The Macmillan Co., 1963). See also *Theological Explorations* (New York: The Macmillan Co., 1968).

tional theological meanings as they have been structured in language. An illegitimate use of either tool, phenomenology or language analysis, occurs when normative or metaphysical questions are decided on the basis of such descriptive tools. Whether an empirical perspective is the "correct" one for theology or "true" for theology is not an issue that can be decided by language analysis. We can decide what an empirical perspective means by language analysis but we cannot decide whether it is THE perspective that must necessarily be accepted for theology.

Van Buren uses language analysis to confirm and describe his own empirical presuppositions. He states that he has

> made use of the method of certain linguistic analysts because their method reflects the empirical attitudes which appear to us characteristic of a secular thought.[33]

What he states here is, for the most part, true. Language analysis did grow out of a movement that had its early roots in empiricism, and was called in this beginning stage *logical empiricism*. But it was precisely the breakthrough made by Wittgenstein, and others contemporary with him, that has allowed language analysis to be truly applicable to theology. And this breakthrough was conditioned more by mathematics than by empirical considerations, and, indeed, if anything, has moved language analysis away from empirical presuppositions.

Van Buren acknowledges that the secular thought that he seeks to describe is highly reductive. To the question whether traditional theology has a good deal more than a historical, intentional, or ethical dimension, Van Buren asks another question, "In a secular age, what would that 'more' be." He then answers "It is our inability to find any empirical linguistic anchorage for that 'more' that has led to our interpretation."[34]

Van Buren considers language analysis to be in a natural liaison with empiricism. Whatever can not be justified by empirical language has no legitimate intelligible meaning to him. I have

[33] *Ibid.*, p. 195.
[34] *Ibid.*, p. 198.

criticized Bultmann for his insensitivity to the fact that phenomenology as a mathematical tool has limitations in theology. I criticize van Buren more severely. Not only does he make language analysis the arbiter of whether a particular theological content is legitimate (the empty tomb, etcetera),[35] but his use of language analysis is so restrictive and reductive as to deny the existence of the discipline that was more responsible than any other for giving it birth—mathematics. If mathematics were tied to the kind of empirical presuppositions that van Buren espouses, it could never really begin. Mathematics is *not* primarily empirically oriented. It was the need for tools to describe the *nonempirical* nature of mathematics that precipitated the phenomenology of Husserl and the later language analysis of Wittgenstein. To reduce by means of language analysis that which is valid in theology to that which can be expressed in empirical language is patently illegitimate. Were he more sensitive to the power of language analysis to describe nonempirical objectivities, van Buren's theological content would be much richer and his program far less reductive. As this work stands, however, its author construes language analysis to be a *justification* of empirical presuppositions. This is an obvious overextension of its function.

Phenomenology, Language Analysis, and a Doctrine of God

In examining van Buren's use of language analysis in *The Secular Meaning of the Gospel*, I have chosen one of the more radical and restrictive theological positions of the day. Traditional theological content, and especially traditional ways of believing it, do not fare well in his book. I have claimed, and from an analysis of the relationship of phenomenology and language analysis to mathematics firmly believe, that these tools have had, and can further have, a very positive effect on contemporary theology. I have mentioned the very positive contributions of Bultmann, and van Buren's work itself can be understood as a very positive, helpful, and legitimate analysis of the relationship of *empiricism*

[35] *Ibid.*, pp. 127–28.

to the Christian Gospel. One particular traditional doctrine, however, seems very vulnerable to these new tools—that of God's objectivity and causal action. We have seen how both Bultmann and van Buren attack this doctrine. There seems to be an alternation in the study of God by the tools of phenomenology and language analysis, first a positive, but groping analysis of God, followed by a devastating and leveling attack on the foundations previously built. Phenomenology and language analysis seem quite adequate for an analysis of aspects of religious existence in *relationship* to God (however conceived), but seem inhospitable toward "seeing" God in any traditional metaphysical or mythical sense.

The philosopher who did most to positively introduce language analysis into theological discussion was John Wisdom. In the 1920s the question was asked by the logical positivist movement whether theism was a position that could be determined by an experimental verification. Since the answer is obviously No!, the theistic position was thereby considered meaningless and forthwith discredited. Wisdom in 1944, by use of his parable of the gardener, pointed out that though the issue of theism could not be determined by empirical verification, it was still a meaningful one.[36] The two men who returned to the long-neglected garden agreed on all that they found in the garden. There was no difference in their understanding of what they would find in the garden if they looked further, nor what they would find if they looked at other gardens. Yet, one man affirmed that he believed in an invisible gardener and the other affirmed that he did not. "At this stage, in the context," says Wisdom

the gardener hypothesis has ceased to be experimental, the difference between one who accepts and one who rejects it is not now a matter of the one expecting something the other does not expect.[37]

[36] John Wisdom, "Gods," *Logic and Language*, ed. A. G. N. Flew. 1st ser. (Oxford: Basil Blackwell, 1951), pp. 187–206.
[37] *Ibid.*, p. 192.

The situation that was found in relation to the garden, where two men had the same facts before them, saw the same things, and agreed that they were the same, yet had two entirely different yet meaningful understandings of the facts, is repeated in many very significant and important areas of human concern. Wisdom points out that in philosophy, metaphysics, and psychoanalysis, there is a point where no new information is added yet where significant new and vital understanding is achieved.[38] At this point it is not merely a question of understanding of words, or of different interpretations of the same facts, but of significant new insights into reality. As Wittgenstein shows in his discussion of picture puzzles, it is not a case of original data to which we append an interpretation, but of seeing data in terms of an interpretation. We see the mathematical sequence in its exactness only by knowing how to "go on." There is danger, says Wisdom, in dismissing the paradoxes of metaphysicians and psychoanalysts as a different use of words from their literal conventional meanings, for in doing so we may miss entirely the new insight that is intended by not participating in "the shock of taking a paradox literally."[39] Wisdom attempts to show how *new* meanings, new aspects of reality are discovered and formulated by metaphysicians and psychoanalysts, often in terms of paradox, which is a mix-up, but an appropriate one, of existent language games. With this he is emphasizing the aspect of phenomenological seeing in reality that we have observed developing in the later Wittgenstein. It is the recognition of the full range of intentional meanings in language analysis, including the religious, that has precipitated through Wisdom's works a widening interest in language analysis among theologians and a new interest in theology among some analysts. Language analysis is relevant for an analysis of the religious problem of God, and has been used frequently in this function, but, as in the case of the gardeners, more accurately shows the intentions of man than the nature of God.

[38] John Wisdom, *Philosophy and Psycho-Analysis* (Oxford: Basil Blackwell, 1957), pp. 248–82.
[39] *Ibid.,* p. 273.

One of the first clear usages of a Wittgensteinian position to formulate *positively* a theological position is in John Hick's *Faith and Knowledge*.[40] In this work, Hick gives the traditional meanings of knowledge, belief, and faith and indicates where he agrees and disagrees, and finally arrives at a description of his understanding of faith as an act of "total interpretation." Religious faith is understood by him to share a common epistemological structure with cognition in other fields, where to know any object is to know our environment as significant in a certain way. To "know God by faith . . . means that we interpret, not only this or that item of our experience, but our experience as a whole, in theistic terms."[41] According to Hick, the world is to be understood as an ambiguous set of symbols through which we may or may not "see" God. He states that the discovery of God "lying behind" the world is not like the discovery of a man concealed behind a screen, or that of the "discovery" of inferred electrons, but rather like the discovery of the pattern in a puzzle picture. At this crucial point of his argument he refers to the *Philosoph:cal Investigations* and utilizes Wittgenstein's epistemological analysis of what it means "to see."[42]

Wittgenstein uses puzzle pictures in 2:xi, of *Philosophical Investigations* to analyze the place of interpretation in seeing. He is concerned to discredit the illegitimate idea that we think we "see" data to which is appended an interpretation. In place of this viewpoint, Wittgenstein affirms (with many examples) that interpretation is inextricably bound to seeing. We actually see things *as* we interpret them. The kind of seeing that Wittgenstein is analyzing is the seeing that goes on in and through symbols, such as words, pictures, mathematics, and sense data.

Hick claims that God is seen in the world, which is one vast multiplicity of symbols, in terms of our interpretation. Because we see God by means of interpretation, however, does not mean

[40] John Hick, *Faith and Knowledge* (New York: Cornell University Press, 1957).
[41] *Ibid.*, p. 165.
[42] *Ibid.*, p. 185.

that we see him to any degree less than the multitude of other things that are seen by and through interpretation. The seeing of God, according to Hick, does not differ in kind from most other seeing, but only in degree. Whereas other things are seen through some localized set of symbols, God is capable of being seen through the totality of all symbols presenting themselves.

Hick feels that Wittgenstein's analysis of "seeing" is not quite adequate for what happens when we see God, because the totality that the religious interpretation discloses entails the participation of the interpreter in a "situation which makes *continual* practical demands upon him."[43] I have emphasized the word *continual,* for it is here, I think, that the true difference between Hick and Wittgenstein lies. Hick is saying that Wittgenstein's analysis is inadequate for the understanding in faith that we *always* see the demands of God on us. Wittgenstein, of course, would agree, for his multiplicity of language games did not allow him to affirm an *always* in any metaphysical sense. Not even mathematical objects could always be seen, but depended on the particular games of seeing, that is, they themselves were seen only punctiliously. I fear that Hick may too quickly have departed from Wittgenstein's discussion of seeing. One may understand that he is always under the hand of God, but does he not see this only sporadically? Does not the seeing of God, if He can be seen at all, have the same type of punctiliousness that other types of seeing have?

I have used Hick's work as an example because I consider it to be a positive affirmation of an objective God based on the language analysis of Wittgenstein. It is not the eternally existing metaphysical God that is affirmed, although this is not itself denied, but the God who is "seen" through faith. As in the other language games of Wittgenstein, one does not merely see, but he sees something, that is, something objective, but not necessarily empirical. Hick balks at a typical Wittgensteinian analysis because he wants more substantiality to belong to the God who is seen. Whether he can have this, or even the punctilious seeing that is more in line with Wittgenstein's original language games, is a

[43] *Ibid.,* p. 186.

matter that remains, at least in our present discussion, to be analyzed. Hick's position is essentially an anomolous one in the general trend of usage of phenomenology and language analysis. On the whole, as measured by the majority of theologians who use the tools, neither phenomenology nor language analysis allows the seeing of an objective God.

To support my observation that phenomenology and language analysis, at least as they are in some respects patterned after modes of knowing in mathematics, inhibit any knowledge of an objective God, let us look at traditions that have in the past affirmed an objective, substantial God to see whether the recent use of phenomenology has effected any appreciable change in outlook concerning this aspect of God's existence. An examination of contemporary Thomism, especially the arguments for the existence of God, provides such an opportunity, although this analysis will be unfairly brief and in no way comprehensive.

In the *Summa Contra Gentiles* of Aquinas, Book I, Chaper 13 (3) there is the following familiar argument:

> Everything that is moved is moved by another. That some things are in motion—for example, the sun—is evident from sense. Therefore, it is moved by something else that moves it. This mover is itself either moved or not moved. If it is not, we have reached our conclusion—namely, that we must posit some unmoved mover. This we call God. If it is moved, it is moved by another mover. We must, consequently, either proceed to infinity, or we must arrive at some unmoved mover. Now it is impossible to proceed to infinity. Hence, we most posit some unmoved mover.[44]

This argument, if compared carefully, can be seen to be very similar to the existence proofs in the *Elements* of Euclid. If we define God as an unmoved mover, and then prove the propositions (as do, in fact, both Aristotle and Aquinas) (1) everything that is moved is moved by another, and (2) in movers and things

[44] Aquinas, *On the Truth of the Catholic Faith; Summa Contra Gentiles*, trans. Anton C. Pegis. 3 vols. (Garden City: Image Books, 1957), 1: 86.

moved one cannot proceed to infinity, the form of the argument is almost identical with that of the existence proofs. In terms of a comparison of the *form* of the argument with that in the *Elements,* the argument of Aquinas is an existence proof of the definition of God.

In the Euclidean perspective, the relationship between the constructive ability of the mathematician and the objective status of the mathematical objects is carefully worked out. There is no question that mathematical objects exist apart from and prior to man's discovery of them. There is no hint given that a mathematician may *bring into existence* a figure by constructing it. The mathematical objects are ontologically real in themselves and do not depend on the mathematician for their existence. The function of a definition is to point out, or lead one to, these mathematical entities as they are available to human insight.

Nowhere is more care taken than in the *Elements* however, to insure that the definitions are not merely verbal but do actually refer to "existent" mathematical figures. The Greek mathematicians were very sensitive to the fact that the defining of something in no way assured its reality. The mere formal procedure of defining does not produce existence. A rigorous procedure is utilized in the *Elements* in order to insure that the definitions are about real things, for example, that a square really exists. Such a procedure may be called an existence proof.

That the *Elements* is concerned to prove the existence of the entities that it describes is not readily apparent. The definitions are given first, in an intuitive and straightforward manner, and one naturally assumes the existence of the things described. The actual constructions or existence proofs that justify the existence of which the definitions speak are found in propositions far removed from the initial definitions. The proof of the existence of a square, for example, is in proposition 46 of the first book. The proof consists of an actual construction, using principles that have been proved prior to proposition 46.

The constructive aspects of Euclidean mathematics, here called existence proofs, are clearly subordinated to the objective aspects of Euclidean mathematics. A square is assumed to exist apart from human demonstration of it. The existence proof *confirms* the fact of the existence of the figure. Such proofs checked human fallibility that otherwise might attribute existence to (ideal) things that could not exist. The argument of Aquinas (and Aristotle) as it compares in form to that of the *Elements* confirms the existence of an already-assumed God whose definition is an unmoved mover. God's existence, like the mathematical objects of Euclid, is apprehended intuitively; proofs only confirm this prior intuition.

With the fundamental shift from the Euclidean perspective that occurred in the nineteenth century to a viewpoint that emphasized the radical createdness of mathematical relationships associated with their intentional objectivity (a development that precipitated, as I have claimed, the phenomenology of Husserl), we would expect those who are concerned with the arguments for the existence of God to shift their perspective accordingly.[45]

Catholic theologians Maritain and Gilson, and Anglical theologians Mascall and Farrer, have sought to separate Thomas from his Aristotelianism and to emphasize the Christian characteristics of his thought that distinguish him from Aristotle. The central idea in modern Thomism (as it was in classical Thomism) is that any finite substance entails God's existence. In any finite substance, its essence is seen to be separated from its existence. This fact, as seen in Thomistic philosophy, demands the existence of a substance whose essence is his existence, namely God.

---

[45] One of the important channels of influence of Husserlian phenomenology into Thomistic thought was the study session in September 1932 of the *Société Thomiste,* which considered Thomism and German contemporary phenomenology. Present at this session were Jacques Maritain, Etienne Gilson, Alexandre Koyre, Edith Stein, and many others. Husserl's metaphysical conclusions, and in particular his Idealism, were underplayed at this session in favor of those aspects of his philosophy which could aid Thomism. It was thought that his method could be used to "show forth" the contents of the faith without radically modifying the metaphysical assumptions of the faith. Accordingly we find much use of the phenomenological method in the works of Maritain and Gilson with little reference to phenomenology itself. Erich Przywara has made use of phenomenology to a greater extent than either Maritain or Gilson.

The two fundamental changes in the Thomism of the twentieth century are: (1) the substance that entails God's existence is seen to be primarily human existence and not the general thinghood existence, rocks, trees, etcetera, of Aquinas, and (2) what is to be apprehended through the arguments is primarily a metaphysical *relationship*—not God himself—between human existence and God's existence. The metaphysical relationship, which is claimed to be absolutely unique, is seen to be both objective to and grounded in human existence. One sees it primarily in human existence because it is there that the necessary finiteness is apprehended.

By means of the apprehended relationship, one can, of course go on and say traditional things about God. But these Thomistic attributes are affirmed on the authority of the traditional metaphysical perspective and not on the authority of what is phenomenologically seen in the argument. The two are not incompatible, but rest on different authorities. The phenomenological viewpoint, following the newer perspectives in mathematical argument, allows one to go only so far. The added metaphysical characteristics can not be justified on an exclusively phenomenological authority, or, for that matter, any mathematical or logical one, but depend on some other.

I am concerned only to point out here that the major changes that have occurred in the understanding of traditional Thomistic arguments are in accord with the shifts in perspective that have accompanied the phenomenological viewpoint of the new mathematics. It is not surprising that a tradition that has always been close to the understanding of the nature of mathematical argument should modify itself to be in accord with contemporary developments.

Paul Tillich has been very careful to separate a phenomenological method from a metaphysical one. Although using phenomenology extensively—he does assert that the beginning of each of the five parts of *Systematic Theology* is a phenomenological analysis in which is given "a description of the meaning of the determining ideas, before asserting and discussing their truth and actuality"[46]—he does not attempt to describe the nature of God by phenomenological means. He can describe phenomenologically, however, aspects of human existence, many of which reflect what I have called the fundamental problem associated with the new mathematics, namely, the adequate description of how mathematics can be both radically created yet essentially objective. The fundamental problem finds manifestation, for example, in his discussion of the polarity between ecstatic reason and technical reason,[47] in the polarity between subjective and objective reason,[48] in the tension between controlling and receiving knowledge,[49] and so on. In each of these examinations of the nature of reason by Tillich, a basic existential dilemma appears. The human subject in his use of reason is both transcendent of it and necessarily conformable to it. Ecstatic reason, for example, must be subjected to the norms and criticism of technical reason, yet it, itself, is the source of technical reason. There is tension between controlling knowledge and receiving knowledge; one is "safe . . . but not ultimately significant"; the other "can be ultimately significant, but it cannot give certainty."[50]

The basic tension between controlling and receiving knowledge, between technical and ecstatic reason, between subjective and objective reason, and the like, indicates a basic polarity in all of human existence. Our fundamental problem, which I have shown as arising out of mathematics, is but one aspect, for Tillich, of a basic polarity, instability and tension in all of human existence. Tillich here reflects, of course, the classical Christian Thomistic tradition, which perceives essence and existence as bifurcated in all finite existence. He has extended this position however much further than Thomas or the Thomists, going beyond the mere distinction of essence and existence in objective substances and considering a wide range of tensions and dichotomies in human

---

[46] Tillich, *Systematic Theology*, 1: 106.
[47] *Ibid.*, p. 53.
[48] *Ibid.*, p. 75.
[49] *Ibid.*, p. 105.
[50] *Ibid.*

existence. Each of the aspects of polarity in human existence can
be analyzed by phenomenological means.

Although God is the only source of unity for the basic polarity
of human existence for both Tillich and the Thomists, He also
participates, according to Tillich, in certain aspects of this polarity.
In our fundamental problem we have been concerned with the
mathematician's ability to create and transcend mathematics while
at the same time being conformable to its norms. Tillich calls the
ability of human existence to transcend itself and other existence
the "ecstatic nature" of existence. This "ecstatic" existence is also
always understood to be conformed to norms as a part of existence. Tillich uses the word *ecstatic* for his doctrine of God and
calls on his understanding of "ecstatic" existence to illuminate
this doctrine.

There are three ways of understanding God, according to
Tillich, the first being the traditional supernatural way, where God
is considered to be a being (the highest one) among other beings.
The second position, called naturalism, is where God is brought
close to being identical with nature. The third position, which
Tillich affirms, is the "ecstatic" one, where "ecstatic" means
"self-transcendent.": "God as the ground of being infinitely
transcends that of which he is the ground."[51] God as the ground
of being is the source of being. In Him, through Him, by Him,
all being is constituted. He also infinitely transcends it; He
transcends those objects that are constituted by and through Him.
Though transcending being, He is always "there" as the ground
of being.

I cannot take the care to develop with accuracy Tillich's
concept of God. It is to our purpose here only to show its
similarity to concepts of human existence as seen phenomenologically and to point out the close relationship of it to the
fundamental problem that I claim is associated with contemporary
mathematics and that precipitated Husserlian phenomenology.
There is no question that Tillich's view of God is basically a

[51] *Ibid.*, 2: 7.

religious one. But there is also no question that he was made aware of new developments in mathematics and philosophies built on these developments.

Tillich does not use phenomenology as the authority for stating that his doctrine of God is true. Phenomenology in his work is used to describe the nature of human existence in its relationship to God, but is not used as a criterion for truth or falsity. What Tillich has done is to apply the traditional theological argument that what is of genuine existence in man must be found in God, who is the ground of such existence. God so understood, as reflective of a basic human existence, can not be objectified as a metaphysical One. We find in Tillich, as well as in other theologians who depend heavily on phenomenology or language analysis, a hesitancy and inability to affirm that God is a metaphysical subject who is also a metaphysical object over against man.

We have seen the very positive use of phenomenology and language analysis in the work of Bultmann, Hick, some Thomists, and Tillich, associated with at times a groping use of these tools to characterize God but also with a hesitancy to claim that they can legitimately affirm a traditionally objective God. These positive results have been challenged radically by a group of theologians who also depend upon phenomenology and language analysis. Though receiving most of their stimulus from Nietzsche, Hegel, and Blake, the "death of God" theologians as theologians acknowledge their dependence on Bultmann, Tillich, Wach, Eliade, and others who have used phenomenology as a primary tool. Through his almost exclusive use of phenomenology, Bultmann does not consider legitimate the metaphysical or mythical God. Tillich makes an explicit separation between the metaphysical and the phenomenological dimensions. If one cannot accept the metaphysical dimension, and in our day many can not, he is left with the phenomenological dimension. One can "see" phenomenologically the intention of God in the past, but he cannot, by means of phenomenology, "see" God as intended by (a certain sector of) culture today. Thus, as confirmed by phenomenological or linguistic analytical vision, God is dead.

I essentially agree with the phenomenologists and linguistic analysts who claim that an objective God cannot be affirmed through these tools. The mathematical tools of phenomenology and language analysis have not confirmed that God is the metaphysical One, and, indeed, seem incapable of doing so. We may yet, however, understand God to be objective in a traditional sense by metaphysical means in which the system so formulated may include the full range of phenomenological analysis. We can do so, however, as I see it, only if we have some adequate understanding of the nature of causality, and in particular, some way of understanding God's causal action. The developments of mathematics and the understanding of causality are closely related. Both seem intimately involved with phenomenology and language analysis, as I shall attempt to show in the next chapter.

4
Mathematics and Causality

In chapter 2, I pointed out that during the Greek move into axial existence, philosophers held mathematical structure to be a model of appropriate, precise knowledge that could be obtained by an autonomous reason. In the move of the basis of existence from the mythological realm to that structure emphasizing mathematical precision and objectification, the subconscious, subrational, and vague forces of nature became alien forces to be subjugated to the new powers of reason. As the relentless and cumulative process of mathematical rationalization continued, and as Western man began to dwell more completely in this new kind of existence, the forces of nature began either to be characterized by quantification or to disappear further from rational awareness.

The brilliant conquests of science attest to the power of mathematization to represent aspects of nature and its forces. In the case of the understanding of causality, however, some initial success in rationalization was obtained by Plato and Aristotle, and reemphasized by Kant, but on the whole, causality as a presented phenomenon has tended to recede further into the background of consciousness. Any rational characterization of it has become problematical.

At this point I am not concerned to say what causality is or to give any philosophical description that might bring its true nature into some kind of clarity. I am concerned, however, that the reader recognize that in most ordinary circumstances he is patently aware of causal forces, has actually an understanding of causality, and is able to communicate in ordinary language about it. When young Jimmy says that it was his brother who caused him to break the vase, his claim is intelligible to us. How do we know what Jimmy means by his statement? We know primarily because we have been involved in countless experiences of exercising our power on someone else and, conversely, of feeling the power of others. We know that there may have been psychological, situational, and, perhaps, physical coercion directed to Jim from his brother. And although the situation that Jim is describing may be very complicated, a mother or father may have a clear understanding of what actually happened. Yet, if we try to sort out what is exactly the cause-and-effect relationship, we find ourselves in considerable difficulty. In such a process of precise analysis, even that which we thought we understood about the particular causal situation may seem to disappear.

Strict Mathematization Dissolves Causality[1]

I have been surprised by certain kinds of misunderstandings between scientists and theologians regarding causality in each other's fields. I have heard theologians (or people interested in theology) say that of course we must have an understanding of causation in theology but that it cannot be like that of science, where things are rigidly bound by pervasive forces. On the other hand I have seen scientists (or people interested in science) show great perplexity at theologians' supposed interest in spiritual causal forces of some sort and especially in God's causal action in the world. The truth is that both groups have almost given up any use of a concept of efficient causation in scientific systems or

[1] See Granville C. Henry, Jr., "Mathematical Objectification and Common Sense Causality in Science and Religion." *Journal of the Blaisdell Institute* 4, no. 1 (Jan. 1969).

theologies that are highly structured or intensely analytical. Science and theology are very close today on the point of causality in their disciplines—neither has much to say about it.

Not only have theology and science given up an emphasized concept of causality in their theoretical and analytical structures, but both disciplines are in marked contrast with the experience and daily life of the average man, whether he be a participant in technology or religion. The virtual disappearance of efficient causation from contemporary physical science is strange, since it stands over against the massive persuasions of traditional common sense. The elimination of kinds of efficient causation in theology goes against the almost universal statement in myths and the naive descriptions of religious experience that God causes certain selected events to happen.

Under the impact of Bultmannian, Tillichian, and Barthian theology, the common sensibilities of the ordinary (relatively well-informed) American Christian do appear to be changing in regard to his understanding of God's causal efficacy on the world. The immediate and sympathetic response to the "death of God" theology, for example, was due in large part to a loss of the sense of God's causal efficacy, for traditionally in religion and theology God's existence has been understood primarily in terms of His causal action. Furthermore, I think that one of the reasons for the great interest in a secular or worldly Christianity is not only the breakdown in theology of an understanding of God's causal efficacy but a beginning breakdown of an understanding of ordinary worldly phenomena. The scholarly discipline of theology, as contrasted with various modes of religion, has often grown out of the security of a supposedly well-understood causal understanding of the world. When this understanding begins to break down, attention focuses on the world in an attempt to put it back together again emotionally and conceptually, using whatever means, including Christianity if it is helpful. Christian theology, according to those who promote a secular Christianity is, therefore, supposed to have its primary function in understanding the world and not in understanding God.

Thus, the situation appears to reflect a genuine division between the objectified and theoretical realms and the practical and mythological realms, with the practical-mythological in science and theology, as represented by technology and religion, gradually beginning to give way as led by the theoretical. The reader probably ought to object here and say that I have the order wrong, and that the truth is that the theoretical is reflecting the practical in both science and religion. To a degree, of course, this is a correct analysis. I believe, however, that the loss of causality in the theoretical aspects of science and theology comes in a large measure from the structure of theoretical thought itself as conditioned by mathematics, which as a pure discipline may be severed from the practical realm.

As science has become more mathematical, it has become less causal. Two basic explanations account for this. The first is that the generalized, objectivized mathematical systems that have evolved in science and that have been found through massive empirical evidence to characterize certain general aspects of the physical world leave less and less room for what has traditionally been called efficient causation. For example, if we consider in sequence the Aristotelian, Newtonian, and Einsteinian systems, we find a progressive diminution of the role of efficient causation. Aristotle's system required an efficient force to maintain motion. Newton's system allowed for aspects of self-movement for inanimate objects as guaranteed by his principle of inertia:

> Every body continues in its state of rest or of uniform motion in a right line unless it is compelled to change that state by forces impressed upon it.[2]

In Einsteinian general relativity, the acceleration that had been conceived as due to gravitational forces in the Newtonian system is reinterpreted to be a result of space-time curvature that does not act as a force but as a certain kind of condition or restraint that can be described in terms of static relationships.

[2] *Principia*, Law I, Bk. I, trans, Andrew Motte, rev. Florian Cajori (Berkeley, University of California Press, 1962).

The advent of quantum mechanics interpreted statistically has further loosened the strict causal bonds linking events or states as understood by scientists and philosophers. An infinite number of unpredictable states may arise from a given condition in keeping with a rigorous and empirically "proved" mathematical theory concerning the atom. One can have a good approximation of the probability of, say, an electron being in one state or another, but there is no determination of the exact future of an individual electron, no matter how much we know of initial conditions. The indeterminacy principle of Heisenberg restricts our simultaneous knowledge of both momentum and position of an individual small particle. The more accurately we know momentum, the less accurately we know position, and vice versa. The whole idea of *individual* particles becomes vague because their detection as individual is limited by the indeterminacy principle. If we shine a small source of monochromatic light on a screen with two small holes in it and let the light that emerges fall on a photographic plate on the opposite side, we get the familiar patterns on the plate that result from the interference of the secondary waves originating from the two holes. The chemical process occurring at the photographic plate, however, is a quantum one, indicating that the waves impinging on the plate are light quanta. Can we not assume then, believing the individual quanta to be energy packets of some sort, that the quantum goes through either one hole or the other? If we do we get contradictions with the known facts of the experiment.[3] They indicate that any naive concept of particles or quanta is called in question. Yet the mathematical theory describing the situation is unambiguous. This and numerous other comparable situations have led Heisenberg to affirm that the ultimate determination of the nature of the fundamental particles will be a mathematical one, that is, that the fundamental particles will be understood to be actual mathematical structures. As a result of the strict mathematization, Heisenberg has said simply,

[3] See Werner Heisenberg, *Physics and Philosophy; The Revolution in Modern Science* (New York: Harper & Row, 1962), paperback, pp. 51, 52.

"The law of causality is no longer applied in quantum theory."[4]

Heisenberg, however, did not want to do away altogether with an understanding of cause-and-effect relationships in science. Indeed, the assumption of some such relationship is necessary for *appropriate scientific methodology*. According to the Copenhagen interpretation of quantum theory, a description of the experimental equipment and the larger world "which does not belong to the object of experiment" must be done in terms of classical concepts of physics, which entail space, time, and causality.[5] Thus causality, which is banished from the mathematical description of quantum mechanics, does have, as Heisenberg says, "a limited range of applicability."[6]

The Indeterminacy Principle, which may appear to forbid concepts of causality within the mathematical interpretation of quantum mechanics, is a systematic restriction of our knowledge that is necessary in order that the major theories of atomic and nuclear structure stand. According to its present place in physical theory and the general ways of interpreting it, the limitations imposed by the theory cannot be overcome by future empirical or mathematical discoveries. It is possible, of course, that a scientific revolution may change the foundations of atomic theory and relax the restrictive nature of the principle. But it is difficult to know of this until it happens. Heisenberg's principle appears to be a foundation part of the physical theory itself.

The Indeterminacy Principle, however, does not rule out a cause-and-effect relationship among the microparticles themselves. There may be a rigid causality and determinism among the non-observable particles, but we can not claim this or its contrary from the mathematical theories themselves. This would require an analysis apart from mathematics, but of course consistent with it, an analysis of the nature of the *being* of the particles, involving a metaphysical dimension.

Do we need to go to metaphysics? Might it not be possible

[4] *Ibid.*, p. 88.
[5] *Ibid.*, p. 90.
[6] *Ibid.*

to find within the mathematics itself, among those particles that Heisenberg believes will ultimately be understood *to be* mathematical relationships, a mathematical structure that also may be understood *to be* cause and effect? Certainly the present interpretations of quantum mechanics seem to deny this. I think the nature of *mathematics* and mathematical relationships also prohibits it. In the realm of pure abstraction and quantification there is no agency, nor is there any structure that appears to characterize agency.

This brings us to the second explanation why the mathematization of science has made it less causal. Mathematical abstractions and relationships that form the dominant part of science are clearly in themselves a-causal and have no agency whatsoever. I could justify this statement by a historical examination or even better by asking certain questions, such as, "In what way is a Boolean algebra causal?" Perhaps I should ask the reader to choose any mathematical figure or set of relationships that is familiar; a particular triangle, the set of natural numbers, this year's income tax calculations, and question whether these relationships are either the cause of something or necessarily caused by something. The answer, I think, is an obvious No. I shall say more about this aspect of mathematical form, but for now I ask simply that it be accepted.

Of course, some mathematical relationships that in themselves as mathematics are necessarily a-causal may refer to processes in which causality plays a prominent part. The most famous example of a mathematical theory that is applicable to physical processes and the one that has been most frequently and most persuasively used to justify a doctrine of strict causality is Newton's law of gravitation (1) $F = GmM/r^2$ associated with his second law (2) $F = Ma$ which tells, for example, why one is caused to fall toward the ground. It is ostensibly the force of gravity given by the law of gravitation that causes the acceleration demanded by the second law. Let us examine some aspects of Newtonian mechanics to see if, in fact, it does show the structure of causation.

It is not difficult to see how Newtonian mechanics could be

considered as exemplifying a world in which cause and effect is rigidly binding. If we accept personal agency as a basic model of causal action—for example, if we accept that another person is the cause of our hand dropping when he presses down on it—we may have similar sensations when a weight is substituted that presses down with comparable force. We feel the weight "pushing." We see our hand drop. By analogy with the act of the human agent, the weight then may be said to be the cause of our hand dropping. By further extension and insight, we can see that the weight presses on our hand due to the gravitational attractive force of the earth according to (1). The weight is a mediate cause of movement depending on the ultimate cause of gravitation associated with the earth. The understanding of the earth or other astronomical bodies as causes of the force of attraction allows the vague but powerful mythological perspectives that so naturally associate themselves with "earth" and "heaven" to infiltrate the strictly mathematical assumptions. If we introduce considerations of other forces; chemical, electric, magnetic, and so forth, we may describe very accurately the movements of weight and hand according to a mathematical extension of (2). It is then a very liberating experience to be able to interpret the vast welter of causal forces that we can actually feel and do know intimately with the mathematical precision that allows us to correlate them with distance and movement. Once we have an adequate knowledge of initial conditions in any situation and the relevant differential equations before us that may be derived from the mathematical assumptions of Newtonian mechanics, we may predict with almost unerring precision the future state of a closed system under observation. If we can correlate the forces we know by common experience with the mathematical variables of the mathematical system, then it is very easy to see and understand the cause-and-effect relationships as related to one another by a rigid determinism modeled after the rigid and necessary structural relationships of the mathematical system. This feeling of an exactly structured deterministic relationship of cause and effect may be enhanced through a further study of the mathematical relationships themselves. The study and significant mastery of the mathematics of Newtonian mechanics may give one the overwhelming conviction that he is now able to see, experience, and understand forces and cause-and-effect relationships that were only vague and indeterminate before. Certainly this was the dominant experience of scientists and many philosophers in the eighteenth and nineteenth centuries.

But what do the mathematical formulas of Newton show us of the actual causes? Do we mean that "gravity" causes the hand to fall? Gravity is not mentioned at all in the relationships given. Only force, mass, distance, and time are symbolized (acceleration is defined in terms of distance and time). Perhaps, then, it is the mass of the weight and the earth (which are represented in the formulas) that "causes" the attraction and, hence, acceleration of the weight to the earth. That may be so, but the formulas only describe that force which exists between two masses and say nothing about "causes." Indeed, if we center on "force" as the ultimate clue to the explanation of the causes involved, we will probably have to define it in terms of the second law itself, that is, in terms of mass and acceleration. Such circularity points up the painful fact that, as we ask for precision about the nature of causes, we are forced almost immediately to the mathematics where, because the mathematics is objectified and made precise itself, *there is no explanation of the nature of cause.* Strictly speaking, from the mathematics itself and without reference to our intuitive feelings about the relationship of the mathematics to the world, the best that we can say is that Newtonian mechanics shows forth the effects of causes that may or may not be close at hand. That is, it allows an understanding of the relationship of particles of mass, time, and space in a closed system where the understanding is primarily simple description only.

Newton was much less "Newtonian" in his idea of causality than were many of his followers. Though believing quite firmly in cause and effect, he clearly showed and explicitly stated that the order of inquiry in physical science should be first to determine the laws mathematically and only then to inquire into the nature of basic causes. In his search for causes of a primary sort, however, he had notorious difficulty. Particularly perplexing to him was the source and cause of gravity, for which, in the final analysis, he could give no adequate explanation.[7]

It was a recognition that the precision gained through an adequate mathematical characterization did in fact separate physical theory from causal considerations that made possible (through the traditions of Locke and Berkeley) the dissolving of the ontological relationship of cause and effect in the philosophy of David Hume. Hume was one of the first philosophers to recognize and state emphatically that causality had little to do with the mathematical relationship of implication. For him causality was to be found, if found at all, in experience, and with this position I am in complete agreement. But the experience of which Hume spoke was a very special kind, a kind that was interpreted through the philosophical tradition beginning in the modern world with Descartes and confirmed in the English tradition by Newton, Locke, and Berkeley. The continental rationalists and English empiricists, of course, had many basic differences. They were firmly agreed, though, on the criterion of validity of ideas and experiences. Descartes set as his model of valid ideas the clarity and distinctness of accepted and well-known mathematical relationships. Hume accepted as his model the vividness and luminescence of certain kinds of sense experience. For both, the degree of acceptance of ideas and sense experience was dependent upon the degree of objectification obtained by them. Hume recognized that the experimental philosophy of Newton was not built exclusively on abstract ideas but also on experiment and experience, and accordingly he made a radical distinction between thoughts or ideas and sense impressions. The experience that Hume considered crucial for science, however, was an experience that had the same qualities of objectification as Descartes's ideas—a self-evident

[7] "But hitherto I have not been able to discover the cause of those properties of gravity from phenomena, and I frame no hypotheses; for whatever is not deduced from the phenomena is to be called an hypothesis, and hypotheses . . . have no place in experimental philosophy." *Principia,* Bk. III, General Scholium.

clarity and distinctness. Hume states that "all sensations . . . are strong and vivid," and that "all ideas, especially abstract ones, are naturally faint and obscure."[8] His contention is manifestly false. As one focuses on, say, a green leaf, the sensation of greenness is, as Hume claims, strong and clear. But in the act of focusing one's attention on the leaf, he relegates a vast area of sense experience to a penumbra of vagueness. Some things may be perfectly visible but quite unclear, for example, the leaf on another tree quite nearby. The degree of objectification or intensity of focus determines the self-clarity of the sense experience but at the same time narrows the angle where other things blend into vagueness. In the language of the phenomenologists, all intentional objects have a horizon determined by the object intended. Entities within the horizon giving themselves to sense experience, however, have various degrees of determinateness and ultimately shade off in a continuum of obscurity and vagueness. With regard to ideas being necessarily vague as compared to sense experience, Hume is wrong here also. Depending again on the posture of intention, an idea may be equally as vivid as a sensation—but in a different way. One can attend, for example, to the shape of a leaf as a symbol of a particular mathematical idea or relationship in such a manner and with such intensity that its color and indeed its actual shape are secondary. The objectified sensations of Hume and the geometrical ideas of Descartes are much closer ontologically to each other than either is to the vast, almost overwhelming, vague, and distant ideas and sensations that are at or near the edge of consciousness. These nonprecise experiences are of immense importance for an understanding of human motivation, action, and religion, and are the realm in which an adequate appreciation and understanding of causality is to be found.

If one accepts that cause and effect are to be found only in experience, and if one accepts only the kind of sense experience that Hume allows, then he cannot find, as Hume correctly main-

---

[8] David Hume, *An Enquiry Concerning Human Understanding,* Section 2, in *The English Philosophers from Bacon to Mill,* ed. E. A. Burtt (New York: Modern Library, 1939), p. 595.

tains, any power or necessary connection between events giving the experience. But if one allows a wider range of experience, I do not think Hume's negative conclusion is valid. Hume's "customary connection" with which he describes our apprehension of causality is, of course, a wider experience itself.

It should be clear that I am not saying that the search for causes has vanished from all science. It is very important to find the cause of cancer, for example, for in doing so we believe that a cure may be effected. But even when the true cause is found, if the past history of science is any reliable guide to the future, the precision required to understand the causative agents' relationship to bodily processes in general will make a concept of causality problematical. It is as if we are using two levels of language, one to speak of causality in terms of agency or responsibility, and the other to get the required scientific objectification and precision for chemical, physical, and biological understanding. The burden of my discussion so far is that the latter languages, especially as they are couched in the objective terminology of mathematics. resist any incorporation into the other and vice versa.

In contemporary religion and theology, the gradual disappearance of concepts of God's causal efficacy on the world is an example of the continued process of objectification and reductionism characteristic of Western thought. This process in theology is similar to and often modeled after the *necessary* modes of objectification and isolation in science. Exact concepts in science are the result of considering only a very limited aspect of presented phenomena in terms of idealized circumstances that are often impossible to obtain in actuality. After such isolation, the sought-for relationships are captured and represented most faithfully by the sterile literal variables of mathematics which, as appropriately formulated, need not have any intuitive content. By arduous training the scientist learns to disengage his naive feelings and concepts and to focus the realities of experiment into abstract, objective mathematical relationships—which tend to dissolve concepts of causality.

When theology and philosophy have looked to science as a

model of accuracy, they have usually attempted a commensurate objectification and isolation and thereby have effected a sharp reduction in content, including concepts of causation. In an eloquent and contemporary plea for reductionism in theology, van Buren notes that:

> in almost every field of human learning the metaphysical and cosmological aspect has disappeared and the subject matter has been "limited" to the human, the historical, the empirical,

and concludes that "theology cannot escape this tendency if it is to be a serious mode of contemporary thought."[9] The examples he gives, of "limitation," however—the change of astrology to astronomy, alchemy to chemistry, and the elimination of purpose from medieval painting—are all examples of disciplines acquiring more isolation *through a more thorough mathematization*.[10]

Though objectification in theology today patterned after the kind of objectification in mathematics is much more indirect than in science or even in philosophy, it is evident, specifically in theologians who are dependent on philosophical movements that themselves have close contact with mathematics. I have outlined in some detail in the last chapter how theologians utilizing phenomenology and language analysis have, on the whole, eliminated both a concept of an objectified God and His causal involvement in the world. My concern is that theologians not get caught up in the frenzied task of further objectification resulting in a reductionistic theology without realizing the similarities of their programs with powerful movements in the field of science and mathematics. These developments in science and mathematics are an outgrowth of the original move into axial existence of the Greeks, where the exactness of mathematics was considered normative, and they are

---

[9] Paul M. van Buren, *The Secular Meaning of the Gospel Based on an Analysis of Its Language* (New York: The Macmillian Co., 1963), p. 198.

[10] For an analysis of the relationship of mathematics to late medieval painting, see Morris Kline, *Mathematics in Western Culture* (New York: Oxford University Press, 1964), chapters 10 and 11.

continuing to separate Western man from his subconscious, from his roots in a mythological religion, and indeed from the "real world." Science as a professional and somewhat narrowly defined discipline can continue to exist and flourish under these circumstances—although it would be more enjoyable if an adequate concept of causality could be developed for it. But religion, and especially the Christian religion, cannot continue to exist or be relevant under an exclusive interpretation of this kind of development and movement. Christianity must continue to tie in with its mythological sources. It must have an experience of God and his causal action.

Causality Becomes Mathematical

The move into axial existence by the Greeks helped effectually to separate certain aspects of their existence from their mythological past. As Greek philosophers moved into the kind of objectification exemplified by mathematics, many of the ways of feeling and understanding causality began to be lost to consciousness. The force of mathematization began to dissolve older feelings and understandings of causality in the manner indicated above. As mathematics ostensibly was able to isolate aspects of causality and give them precision, the understanding of causality in human experience *became more mathematical*. It became more mathematical, however, as it was identified or associated with those portions of legitimate mathematics that were partially but not wholly formalized. This process has been endemic to Western philosophy. It began with the Greek thinkers and has continued throughout our philosophical tradition as carried on by major representative thinkers.

In order to grasp what happened to the understanding of causality during the axial revolution, we need to look briefly at preaxial Hebrew and Greek linguistic formulations of causal ideas.

Hebrew, in common with other Semitic languages, has causative meanings built into the structure of the language itself. By appropriate changes on a basis stem, verbs are able to express a simple affirmative meaning (Qal), for example, "to love"; an intensive (Pi'el), "to love passionately"; or a causative (Hiph'il), "to make to love," "to cause to love." The causative in the Old Testament is almost exclusively to be understood in terms of the action taken by one person on another. For example: "And Jesse made (caused) seven of his sons to pass before Samuel" (1 Sam. 16 : 10). It is used frequently of God, who is seen to cause men to do, feel, and be certain things. "And I (Yahweh) will cause you to know what to do" (1 Sam. 16: 3). There is causal action taken by God on natural phenomena, and causal action taken by animals on men, but almost never is there an understanding of natural agents or the forces of nature as causally effective on men. When such agents are employed in the Old Testament, there is almost always a direct reference to some personal agency, primarily God, who is the source of action lying behind the immediate means of natural events. An interesting variant on the ordinary understanding of the *hiph'il* is the so-called permissive use. In this interpretation, agency is understood to be taken not primarily on the person to whom the verb refers but on those circumstances and persons surrounding him, either in terms of action or restriction. Certain clarity and appropriateness of meaning are obtained when some *hiph'ils* are translated as permissives; for example, Pharoah's heart is permitted to be hardened, instead of directly caused to be hardened by God.[11]

Implicit within the Hebrew idea and understanding of causality on the one hand was an understanding of agency, the feeling of power or compulsion by another (normally person or personal force); and on the other hand was the sense that the source of this agency could be identified. It was the drive toward identification of those kinds of agency the Hebrews considered most important that led to their objectification of the mythological God, Yahweh, as the one who had the ultimate privilege of exercising determining agency on all things. They moved from a typical position of honoring local gods who exercised local power to an

[11] I am indebted to Professor William H. Brownlee for pointing out this use of the *hiph'il* to me.

identification that their local God had in fact supreme and ultimately exclusive power.

The key word for understanding causality in Greek culture is *aitia,* the word used by Aristotle, and found in the New Testament, for cause. In its earlier form *aitia* meant guilt, blame, responsibility. The one who was guilty was presumed to have *done something* that affected others in a (usually) deleterious manner. An agency for change was presumed, and was held to be responsible for the known bad effects. Results known to have occurred required a cause, and when such cause was found, it was seen to be identically the guilty or responsible person. In the Athenian law courts, to find a person guilty was also to find the cause of the crime or action. The search for and discovery of a cause was like finding out "who dunnit" in contemporary mystery novels.[12] One appreciates the simplicity of the act and the difficulty of identifying the one acting. There may be multiple causation, of course, when a number of guilty ones are found, but reflecting law court usage, one understands a given person to be guilty or not, a cause or not a cause.

In both Hebrew and Greek meanings at the earliest level, causality was understood as primarily agency between persons. This is clear from the meaning of *aitia* in Greek and from an actual study of the *hiph'il* usage in the Old Testament. I want to propose that the ancient intersubjective model of causality is really the one that has both intelligible meaning and sufficient adequacy for an understanding of causality today. We may have difficulty in returning to an intersubjective model as that kind of commonsense experience that tells us most about causality. The model seems patently too anthropomorphic for science—and possibly also for religion. Of what advantage is it to speak of causation among atomic particles by means of some human model? Was it not the overthrowing of the peculiarly human aspects of final or purposive causation in the Renaissance that allowed efficient causation to become more mathematical, thereby

[12] I heard of this example from Professor Harry Jaffa, who I think was quoting Professor Leo Strauss at the time.

precipitating the birth of modern science at the hands of Galileo? Since Newton are we not accustomed to think of causation as occurring primarily at a mechanical level?

The answer is a qualified Yes. The assumption throughout, however, is that we do in fact know what causation is at the nonhuman or mechanical level. The point I want to make is that our conviction that we know what causality is at the mechanical level is due to our "placing" or transferring human, commonsense, understandings of causality into some aspects of semi-formalized but primarily intuitive mathematics. When this mathematics is made more formal or more thoroughly objectified, the concepts of causality placed there, as mentioned above, tend to be dissolved.

Though causality was originally understood in Greek primarily in terms of intersubjective relationships, it did have implicit within its linguistic structure and use many aspects that could refer to nonpersonal situations. The objectification that occurred during the early axial period in Greece shifted an emphasis toward the *identification* of causes and away from insuring strict personal agency. This resulted in causal relationships being extended to nonpersonal relata. A cause in much of the later Greek literature became the identification of a prior state or action. Thus, in this literature, *aitia* may be best translated as *occasion, case,* or *reason*. For example, in the New Testament: "she declared unto him before all the people the reason [for what cause] she had touched him" (Luke 8:47). Here *aitia* is used to refer to a situation, in this case a flow of blood, that resulted in a subsequent condition or action. The move into axial existence by the Greeks tended to fragmentize and enlarge the domain of causal situations and reduce respectively the number of associations of pure agency associated with causal explanations.

The move into axial existence by the Hebrews, however, intensified the aspects of agency associated with causality through their identification of the ultimate source of agency in Yahweh. In both movements, Greek and Hebrew, there was a tension between accepting a multiplicity of causal agents working independently and affirming some one explanation that explained their interrelationships or some one agent who was ultimately responsible for all secondary causal interactions. In affirming that Yahweh had ultimate responsibility and agency, the Hebrews became faced with the problem of theodicy. Hence for them there had to be some way in which men could be understood to take limited causal action without attributing all responsibility and blame to Yahweh. The Greeks sought desperately for some one interpretation of the multiplicity of causal interactions that they observed, finding partial answers in the *arche* of Thales, Anaximander, and Anaximenes, in the *logos* of Heraclitus, in the atomism of Democritus and Empedocles, in the numbers and numerical relationships of the Pythagoreans, and finally in the *ideas* of Plato and the causal structures of Aristotle.

In the first book of the *Metaphysics,* Aristotle gives a review of his four causes—the formal, material, efficient, and final—and presents a history of the development of the idea of cause with exposition and criticism of previous viewpoints. The earliest philosophers, according to Aristotle, recognized only the material cause. They were looking for an underlying matter or substrate, a physical or material basic constituent of the universe. For Thales, it was water; for Anaximander it was the *apeiron* (indefinite, infinite), and for Anaximenes it was air or *pneuma* (spirit, breath). From our perspective the *arche* of the Milesians seems not only noncausal but thoroughly nonmathematical. From Aristotle's viewpoint, due to the isolation and objectification of mathematics that was occurring in his day, he could also view the *arche* as primarily material. I think, however, that Aristotle's advanced knowledge of mathematics obscured for him, and for us, an earlier legitimate contact of causal ideas with mathematics.

I do not want to get into an old controversy about how much mathematics Thales in fact did. He could not have proved the five theorems Proclus claims that he did.[13] Nor was his just a

13 (1) a circle is bisected by its diameter, (2) angles at the base of isoceles triangles are equal, (3) the vertically opposite angles of intersecting straight lines are equal, (4) triangles which have a side and adjacent angles equal are themselves equal, and (5) an angle inscribed in a semicircle is a right angle.

simple extension of Egyptian mathematical rules to new practical situations.[14] He did some *new* mathematics in a more general fashion than was done previously. He accomplished some remarkable mensuration feats in terms of some glimpses of the more abstract principles. I can say this with some authority, I think, because Anaximander, a student of Thales, produced a quite sophisticated *mathematical* cosmology. In no tradition that I know of is Anaximander said to have made primarily mathematical discoveries. The source of his knowledge of mathematics appears to have been none other than Thales. And Anaximander's use of mathematics is definitely more than an empirical rule generalized to new situations. Furthermore, Anaximenes, a student of Anaximander, proposed for the first time in history that one could understand things (and he apparently meant *all* things) in terms of quantitative changes of the basic *arche*, which for him was *pneuma*. The beginning of the mathematical aspect of the Milesian tradition apparently goes back legitimately to Thales, and was not initiated by Pythagorean sources.

The striking thing about Milesian thought is its extent and generality. We know that deductive mathematics, even the sensible pictorial type of Milesian and Pythagorean thought, brings with it powerful and particular concepts of the *all*. The Milesian *arche* can be understood as causal primarily because it was the only concept of structured being available. As such, it had to bear the whole weight of interpretation of all causal understandings, including the answer to the *reason why* as well as the source of efficient agency. What does it mean to talk of correlating causality with mathematical structure in Milesian thought when what evidence we have indicates that it held little distinction between mathematical relationships and material *arche*? The correlation may be made precisely because of the confusion of the two on their part. From the advent of mathematical thought at the hands of Thales

---

[14] J. Burnet concludes after careful historical analysis that Thales only applied an empirical rule that he learned in Egypt to practical problems that the Egyptians had never faced. J. Burnet, *Early Greek Philosophy*, 4th ed. (London, 1930), p. 45.

to the time of Plato there was a groping toward understanding of mathematics as transcendent form, though in all cases prior to Plato mathematics was understood to be *part of* the constituent world. The material and formal were not precisely distinguished.

As a consequence of his more adequate knowledge of mathematics, Plato was not able to continue to find true causal efficacy as residing in the old intuitional ground of mathematics, either in the *arche* of the Milesians or in the sensibly physical reality of the Pythagoreans, but in a natural way saw it to reside in the *new* intuitional ground of mathematics, the ideal realm of abstract essences. I need to point out that though mathematics was more formalized and objectified in Plato's time than in the early Pythagorean and Milesian eras, it was not so formalized as it was to become at the hands of Aristotle and the mathematicians contemporary with him. It appears that if a mathematical theory or body of knowledge is to be that structure most adequate for a particular contemporary understanding of causality, it must be recently more adequately formalized but not so formalized that the objectification associated with this formalization dissolves the attending causal intuitions. There is a delicate balance here, a developmental period when mathematical theory is most susceptible to causal interpretation.

When a mathematical theory changes so that the old intuitional ground is no longer capable of bearing the whole weight of causal interpretation, the old understanding of causality is not necessarily discarded *in toto*. It is often kept as an adjunct to the more adequate and newer discoveries of causal structure. Thus, Aristotle claimed that Plato had used two causes, the material and formal, each of which Aristotle recognized as legitimate. Aristotle, however, accepts the material and formal as valid only in terms of his emphasis on, and at times claimed discovery of, efficient causation.

I agree with Aristotle that the intuitions and feelings associated with the understanding of efficient causation are close to the root level of true insight into causality. Without an adequate understanding of efficient causation, the other causes—material, formal, and final—have little or no meaning. The primary difficulty today in this matter is a loss of an appropriate concept of efficient causation in science, philosophy, and theology. Much of the philosophical and theological emphasis to save final causes or reintroduce teleological goals is misplaced. I do not think we can have any idea of how a *telos* may influence events without some knowledge of how past events are related causally to present and future ones. In Aristotle's philosophy I see a basic, common-sense, societal, interpersonal understanding of causality trying to come forth in his doctrine of efficient causes. We have seen this process in the *arche* and essences of previous philosophers. In Aristotle's understanding of efficient cause, however, I think we are closer to the truth and can accept some aspects of his practical insight as legitimate. At least we can accept *efficient cause* as the name of that true causality which we seek to find and explore.

Although Aristotle was very close to what may have been a legitimate and true insight into the exact nature of causality in his affirmation of efficient causation, he too ultimately found a mathematical structure to interpret this intuition. That mathematics which was relatively new, recently formalized, but still primarily intuitive for Aristotle was the discipline of logic. Logic itself was not recognized as appropriate content of mathematics by Aristotle (or any Greek thinker) but was considered a tool for the presentation, explication, and verification of mathematics. By means of logic one could decide the truth of a mathematical statement in the geometry of Euclid.

It was Aristotle's own more adequate formalization of logic—which in its further formalization today we must consider as true content of mathematics—that allowed him to criticize the doctrine of essences as held by Plato. It was this new mathematics, the beginning formalization and objectification of logic itself, that forced Aristotle to see that the old objectifications in Platonic essences were inadequate and at points philosophically wrong. Aristotle's further objectification of mathematics again shifted the ground of causal understanding.

In what mathematical structure did Aristotle ultimately find causal connection? Primarily it was found in the structure of logical connection, that is, implication itself. This is, of course, not clearly stated by Aristotle himself, because his understanding of logic was not sufficiently developed to see the extent of connection between causality and deduction.

In *Posterior Analytics,* Aristotle argues that all reasoned acquisition of knowledge proceeds from that which is already known, and he lists the kinds of things prior knowledge of which may lead to new knowledge, through argument or demonstration as facts, or meanings, or both.[15] In each of these cases, however, he illustrates facts and meanings by mathematical examples where it is clearly intended and forthrightly stated that what is prior ontologically is prior logically, that is, what possess the pre-existent solidity, the necessary truth to be ontologically causal, are the premises and axioms of logical discourse.[16]

His crucial argument is in Section 2, where he states that

> We consider that we have unqualified knowledge of anything . . . when we believe that we know (i) that the cause from which the fact results is the cause of that fact, and (ii) that the fact cannot be otherwise.[17]

Though allowing for the possibility of other ways of knowing, Aristotle affirms that we do definitely know factual data by demonstration. That which we know by demonstration is dependent upon premises and axioms that are "true, primary, immediate, better known than, prior to, and causative of the conclusion."[18]

Are the axioms or theses of argument the source, that is, the causative ground, of known facts? We might say that perhaps they are in discussion, argument, or mathematical proof, but not necessarily so in the actual world. The distinction between verbal description *of* the world and happenings in the world was, of

[15] *Post Anal.,* 71a1-13, trans. Hugh Tredennick, *Loeb Classical Library* (Cambridge, Mass.: Harvard University Press, 1960).
[16] *Ibid.,* 72a6-19.
[17] *Ibid.,* 71b10.
[18] *Ibid.,* 71b20.

course, recognized by Aristotle. But in his work, as often in our speech, there is a tacit assumption that language does reflect what happens in the world and often quite accurately so. If we understand the genuine axioms or bases of thought to represent generalized forms, which in Platonic thought constitute precisely that which is actual and in Aristotelian thought may be actual, we may understand this true actuality as causally determining that which is dependent upon them. Just as some premises entail a conclusion, some cause or causes generate an effect.

In the *Physics*[19] Aristotle discusses the relationship between necessity in mathematics and necessity in nature and claims that they are quite similar though apparently inverted in direction. His argument by example is essentially this: the properties of a straight line necessarily entail that the angles of a triangle equal two right angles, but not necessarily conversely. However, the contrapositive is true that "if the angles are not equal to two right angles, then the triangle can not be straight sided."[20] In nature, especially for things that achieve a goal or end, a final cause, if the end has been secured (if the thing actually has come to be), then the antecedent conditions must be or have been. Accordingly, the failure of the existence of antecedent conditions necessarily entails the nonexistence of the end or actual entity. Aristotle is affirming that causal connection is dependent upon antecedent conditions, on analysis that can be understood without reference to a *mathematical* connection. By using mathematical examples, however, Aristotle effects an implicit connection between causal and logical matters.

Put in its more strict logical form, and with the recognition on our part that the contrapositive is logically equivalent to the direct implication, Aristotle is calling attention to the similarity between the properties of straight lines entailing the properties of triangles and the end result entailing its antecedent conditions. Aristotle does not make an identification between logical necessity

---

[19] *Phys.* Bk. II, chap. 9, trans. Wicksteed and Cornford, *Loeb Classical Library.*
[20] *Ibid.,* 200a19.

and the guidance given by final causes; he notes carefully that one is logical and thereby involves no action and that the other is not. But because logic had not been sufficiently objectified, that is, made formal and static, by Aristotelian categories, but was interpreted as guiding human thought, it could in Aristotelian thought show forth causal connections.

For example, Aristotle actually gives an illustration of transition from *potential* to *actual*, terms usually reserved for physical causal process, by means of the demonstration of a geometrical figure. We know that the sum of the interior angles of a triangle are equal to two right angles, because, according to Aristotle, we are capable of *drawing a line* parallel to an original side of the triangle.[21] Since we know that the angles about a point on a straight line are equal to two right angles, it becomes immediately apparent that the triangle also has interior angles equal to two right angles. The potential constructions, that is, the actual (eternal) mathematical relationships in the triangle, are "discovered by being brought to actuality"[22] by an act of thinking. We acquire knowledge, as Aristotle here maintains, by constructive action. The constructive action, which is clearly causal in this case, is closely identified with the form of deduction employed, that is, if logic in this case does represent the form of thought, it is the pattern for causal action.

Because Aristotle recognized the "eternal structure" of implication, that is, as he recognized it to be similar in nature to mathematical objects, geometrical figures, numbers, and so on, he had no hesitancy in separating all causes (except the minimally formal) from logic. Because he understood logic to be that rational discipline that guides the mathematician in his action of deduction, or more pointedly, as he saw the rational categories of logic to be binding on the activities of the physical world, he could then see causal activities to be intimately related to essentially logical ones.

[21] *Meta.*, 1051a25, trans. H. G. Apostle, *Aristotle's Metaphysics* (Bloomington, Ind: Indiana University Press, 1966), p. 158.
[22] *Ibid.*, 1051a30.

Untangling the knotty issues of this problem, for Aristotle or for us today, is no simple matter. A traditional way of handling it has been to assume that *formal* logic is concerned primarily with the *form* of thought. The tricky philosophical problems of the relationship of logic to the physical world are handled in terms of the general understanding of the relationship of thought to these realities. Causality in the physical world is understood to be related to logical structure in a manner compatible with the understood logical rational characterization *of* the physical world.

If mathematical objects are seen to be simply a part of thought, logic may then as the *form* of thought be seen as a characterization of the methods of creating mathematics in thought. If mathematical objects, though, are understood to transcend thought, to be existent in themselves in some way, the function of logic as the form of thought is to *discover* these external mathematical relationships. In either case the relationship of causal concerns to logic is subject to considerable confusion. The structures of causality may be closely identified with the internal structures of logic. Then causality in the external world is essentially unknown. Or causality may be identified as some real connective in the external world, which may be known, but essentially known by thought. If mathematical objects are seen to be discovered by thought, the logic that is used to discover mathematical objects is easily confused with the thought that grasps causal relations. The connections of logic may again be mistaken for the connections *of* cause in thought.

In Kant's time the burgeoning awareness of the constructed nature of the natural numbers and the awareness of the possibility of having a purely constructive geometry were changing the accepted understanding of the nature of mathematics. It was not that philosophers or mathematicians were eager to abandon the Euclidean perspective: the obvious homogeneity, objectivity, precision, and certainty of mathematics associated with its clear ability to describe the objectively existent physical world. The mathematician-philosophers Descartes, Leibniz, and Newton each affirmed a strong Euclidean position, but only after having laid considerable emphasis on the subjective processes that appear to produce or create mathematics. It was the nonmathematician Locke who more consistently founded a philosophical position that stressed the psychological constitution of the natural numbers and from them the creation of all mathematics and thus set the stage for the repudiation of many aspects of the Euclidean perspective. To Locke, and subsequently to Kant, the natural numbers were the result of the mind's putting together sensations of unity to get the numbers, two, three, and so on.

The fundamental problem of mathematical studies for Kant was how to take with utmost seriousness the constructed nature of mathematics and yet maintain, against Hume, its power to give a normative, objective, and certain description of the phenomenal world. His famous answer was that mathematics is *synthetic-a priori,* that is, constructed by consciousness out of the "pre-existent" and given intuitions of space and time. Cause and effect as one of the categories of understanding was given by Kant an almost identical ontological standing with geometrical and mathematical relationships. It is, according to Kant, a synthetic creation of consciousness not necessarily given by the external world but which as an internal "form for possible experience" is rigidly binding over all phenomenal experience.

Patterned after the ostensible homogeneity, necessity, and unifiedness of mathematics, cause and effect was seen by Kant to be an unbroken pattern connecting all phenomena and thus destroying all freedom from the realm of nature as empirically understood. Freedom, according to Kant, is to be found only in the power of reason in the noumena, and in particular that noumenon of which we are somehow aware as our own subjective person. The working out of these distinctions produced the disjuncture of nature and history that has had, for example, such a tremendous influence on continental theology. Religion and faith as given by theological description are to be found primarily in the realm of history, for in the realm of nature as given by science, cause and effect hold almost complete sway.

In order to show how a more thorough mathematization

dissolves concepts of causality, I described in the last section how a Newtonian mechanics, ultimately built on a Newtonian calculus, mathematized causality. The chief expositor of a Newtonian causality, Laplace, explained in his *Theory of Probability* how an Intelligence who "would know at a given instant of time all forces acting in nature and the position of all things of which the world consists," could behold the *complete* past and future![23] How? By calculations with Newton's second law put in the form of differential equations—three of them,

$$m_k \frac{d^2 x_k}{dt^2} = X_k, \qquad m_k \frac{d^2 y_k}{dt^2} = Y_k, \qquad m_k \frac{d^2 z_k}{dt^2} = Z_k,$$

for each mass point m_1, m_2, . . . , m_N, where X_k, Y_k, Z_k are functions of the coordinates x_1, y_1, z_1, . . . , x_N, y_N, z_N. The knowledge of the location and mass of each mass point, and the force upon it, by the theory of differential equations could allow the prediction of any future state (position and forces) of the mass points. Since there is no mathematical distinction between past and future here, such determination would apply also to any past state.

The mathematical description in this case by means of differential equations was understood to be a *law of causality*—a description of causal relations. The actual causal intuitions associated with the mathematics are roughly of two sorts. We can either understand the causal connections among the particles to be the forces exercised on a particle by all the rest of them, essentially by a kind of psychological transfer of feelings as described in the last section, or we can view the "causal connection" to exist between the whole system of particles at any one time t_k and some other future time. In either case, however, the basic con-

---

[23] Quoted from Philip Frank, *Philosophy of Science ; The Link Between Science and Philosophy* (Englewood Cliffs: Prentice-Hall, Inc., 1957), p. 263.

nection in the mathematical description is a mathematical connection. By virtue of a mathematical characterization, we ensure this.

We have seen in this discussion that there are two general ways of mathematizing causality, to associate causality with the mathematics describing essentially physical processes, an attempt that found its greatest success in Newtonian mechanics, and to associate causality with structures of logic that ostensibly portray processes of consciousness, an attempt that has dominated continental thought. Though these two modes of interpreting causality seem in themselves to harbor the greatest philosophical differences, differences that can be elaborated into the disjunction between objective and subjective, and even into the philosophical doctrines of realism and idealism, they share a common relationship to mathematics and thereby a common fate as mathematics has become more thoroughly objectified.

A mediating position between understanding causality as an ontological connective of physical processes or as the structures of consciousness seems available in terms of probabilistic and statistical theories of causality. Patrick Suppes's small monograph *A Probabilistic Theory of Causality* is clearly one of the best recent summaries as well as a significant creative formulation of theories of causality based upon probability theory.[24] In addition to his probabilistic theory of causality, Suppes also presents other mathematical theories of causality, specifically *algebraic* ones, that are interpreted in terms of his probabilistic theory. His definition of event B being a *prima facie* cause of event A: (1) event B is prior in time to event A, (2) the probability of event B is greater than zero, and (3) the probability of event A conditioned upon event B is greater than the probability of event A alone,[25] allows us to understand events B and A to be, depending, of course, on their interpretation in a particular theory, actual events in the real world connected by an ontological

[24] Patrick Suppes, *A Probabilistic Theory of Causality* (Amsterdam: North-Holland, 1970).

[25] *Ibid.*, p. 12.

causal bind, represented and defined, however, in terms of the indeterminacies of knowledge captured in terms of probability theory.

These indeterminacies attend individual outcomes that define the events under examination as subsets of a set of total possible outcomes. The probability of (the event of) a fair coin being heads is, of course, one-half. This does not mean that, in any small even number of tosses, one will get exactly one-half heads and one-half tails. On an individual toss one is in ignorance (from the theory) whether heads or tails will result. It does mean that, as the number of tosses become large in number, the ratio between heads and tails does approach one-half. If probabilities are assigned to events from empirical measures, they have to be so assigned in the context of a general theory so that the events themselves turn out to be subsets of the space of possible outcomes. That event B is a *prima facie* cause of event A does not mean that there is a necessary "constant connection" between the happening of B and the happening of A, but that when B occurs there is a higher probability of A occurring than if B had not occurred at all. B may occur without A ever following. Or A may occur without the precedence of B. But the event A is dependent in a precisely quantitative way on the event B. If A does *always* follow B, then in addition to B being a *prima facie* cause of A, it is also a *sufficient* cause of A, that is, the probability of event A conditioned upon the event B is numerically one.

A probabilistic theory of causality is a rich theory. Not only can one define *prima facie* and sufficient causes, but also spurious causes, direct causes, indirect causes, supplementary causes, and negative causes. These causes are precise in their characterization and intuitive in their relationship. They give meaningful description to what are apparent causal connections, especially in scientific theory.

As Suppes points out, very recent literature in the sciences does use causal terminology in its presentation of results more frequently than past literature. This occurs in the "hard" sciences, quantum mechanics, for example, as well as in the social sciences.

Why is this so? I think that it is a recognition that there are new concepts of causality as well as new terminology to present these concepts in the precise algebraic, probabilistic, and statistical theories of causality now available. This does not mean that scientific authors present precise causal connections in terms of probabilistic or statistical theories. It does mean that they know, or believe, that it is possible to do so, and feel freer, therefore, to use more common intuitive causal terminology.

Russell once claimed:

> All philosophers, of every school, imagine that causation is one of the fundamental axioms or postulates of science, yet, oddly enough, in advanced sciences such as gravitational astronomy, the word 'cause' never occurs. . . . The law of causality, I believe, like much that passes muster among philosophers, is a relic of a bygone age.[26]

Russell was right for his time, and right for our time for most of present-day science. I have tried to give reasons for the demise of causal language in the previous section, "Strict Mathematization Dissolves Causality." But science has changed since Russell's day and new mathematical concepts of causality have been formulated in our day. Causality is again becoming mathematical. Will these new mathematical concepts of causality, however, suffer the same relativization as those of the past? Will Russell's statement be applicable to contemporary science? I certainly think so, and for the same reasons given in the previous section.

One way to appreciate this approaching relativization is to notice that in each of the new approaches to causality, whether algebraic, probabilistic, or statistical, precision of concept about causality is dependent upon interpreting causality in terms of an exactly specified mathematical theory. In probabilistic causality, for example, in order to be precise mathematically about causes, one must have, according to the grounding work of Kolmogorov (1933) that gave probability its axiomatic foundations, and hence

[26] Bertrand Russell, "On the Notion of Cause," *Proceedings of the Aristotelian Society* 13 (1913): 1–26.

its precision, a nonempty set X of possible outcomes, a family F of subsets of X representing events, and a real valued function P on F that satisfies the Kolmogorov axioms. In this case P(E) for E in F, that is, for E a subset of X, represents the probability of event E. In order to talk about the specific probability of an event, and thus, in order to be able to define what we mean by event B "causing" A, we must have in mind a background, though exactly specified, sample space X of possible outcomes. That is, in order to talk about specific causes by means of probability theory, we must do so in terms of previously delineated sample spaces. I say spaces, rather than space, because there are necessarily a multiplicity of them, dependent upon the subject matter under examination in which one seeks to define causal relationships. There is no one sample space adequate for all events, just as there is no one axiomatic system for all algebras, and specifically all those algebras that define causal relations. As Suppes puts it: "The analysis of causes and their identification must always be relative to a conceptual framework.'[27] The precise mathematical frameworks, however, are infinite in number. This does not mean, however, that true concepts of causality are multifold. There may be a common characteristic of the many systems, the definition of *prima facie* cause, for example, that captures the legitimate intuitive meaning of cause. And this is the question. For if such definition does not represent what we may think is the ubiquity of causal relationship, then we do hesitate to use the word *cause*. For we know that *prima facie* cause, for example, is defined in terms of exact probability concepts. And instead of calling event B a *cause* of A, we say simply, and, of course, more accurately in terms of the theory, that the probability of event A conditioned upon the event B is greater that the probability of A alone.[28]

In an attempt to clarify the nature of causality, or to discover that there really is none, two paths appear to be open to us. The first is to continue the traditional (but often unrecognized) procedure of making an understanding of causality precise by model-

[27] Suppes, p. 90.
[28] I am assuming here that the first two parts of the definition hold.

ing it after some aspects of mathematics. If the range of causal meanings is multiform, and the range of mathematical connections is infinitely more so, perhaps there is a legitimate possible matching of some mathematical structures with actual causal ones. It may be that probabilistic theories of causality, for example, adequately refined, are what we truly need as an adequate characterization of causality.

The second path is to try to distinguish between the vague, imprecise feelings of causation and the precise formulations that we create in rational and mathematical objectification. That is, it may be true that we can never give causality an appropriate structure, due to some perhaps peculiar epistemological difficulties. We may have to devise some modes of investigation other than the precise rational ones for the examination of this very important part of our ordinary experience. We may be able to use mathematics, in its precision and structured intensity, to contrast that which in its vagueness differs from what can be "clearly and indubitably known."

Mathematics Shows Forth Causality by Contrast

How might we go about illustrating and clarifying a non-mathematical causality? Could it be done by the recent tools of phenomenology and language analysis? We might think so, since these tools do allow a kind of integration of feelings and objective structures. There are aspects of causality that are illuminated by, say, certain language games of Wittgenstein or the phenomenological analysis of bodily functions by Merleau-Ponty. Yet, it appears to me that the root nature of causality is systematically obscured by both phenomenology and language analysis.

Although arising primarily out of mathematical content, phenomenology and language analysis are able, as we well know, to illuminate content other than mathematical. Their ability to present a vast variety of different kinds of content makes them as useful as they are in philosophy, theology, sociology, psychology, and so on. But some content does resist phenomenological analysis.

Causality appears to be near the boundary of what can and cannot be seen phenomenologically. Causality tends to disappear as content approaching the mathematical in clarity is presented. This point was clearly brought out by Husserl, who insisted that one must at all costs get rid of the naive understandings of existence and causality through *epoché* in order to begin to "see" phenomenologically. According to the Husserlian tradition, the excising of feelings of causality is a necessary condition for the success of phenomenology. Somehow, it seems that the feelings of causation interfere with the presentation of other content and vice versa. It should be no surprise, as already indicated in the previous chapter, that theologians who rely heavily on phenomenological tools tend to obscure or eliminate concepts of causal efficacy.

Part of the title of this section, "Mathematics Shows Forth Causality," may appear to be a misnomer, since the burden of the discussion so far has shown that the new tools arising out of mathematics tend to eliminate, not illuminate, causality. In the case of Whitehead, however, the only other major mathematician-philosopher who has influenced theology, I think that we may say that in his philosophy mathematics has illuminated causality—by contrast. It was Whitehead's clear awareness through his mathematical studies of an understanding of mathematical existence, an awareness that I shall document in more detail in the next chapter, that allowed him to contrast those experiences of true causation, which he called the mode of causal efficacy, with those experiences similar in vividness and structure to mathematical relationships, which he called the mode of presentational immediacy. Whitehead believed that most traditional philosophy, especially that coming from Hume and Kant, had emphasized too much the vividly presented aspect of experience and had neglected the vague but ever-present experiences of causation.

I am not going to attempt any detailed explanation of Whitehead's understanding of causal efficacy. This could adequately be done only after a general introduction to his metaphysical philosophy, and there are many good such introductions available today, as well as excellent theological positions built upon his causal philosophy.[29] I prefer to give an example of how one experiences causal forces, and show how these experiences are related to the kinds of objectification experienced in a mathematization of the cosmos, and delay a more exact examination of Whitehead's philosophy until we can make a specific examination of its relationship to mathematics. At that time the more general problems of natural theology, the limitations of metaphysics and the function of skepticism, can be made more apparent in terms of their at times close alliance with contemporary mathematics.

I think Whitehead's clearest example illustrating causal action, and he gives very few examples outside of a general metaphysical treatment, is of a man who blinks from the turning on of a light in a darkened room.[30] Asked why he blinks, he claims that the light made him blink. He actually feels and experiences this to be so. It is not just the experience of light flash and lid shutting that appears but the causal connection between them. Whitehead claims that his feeling of causal efficacy is what enables him to get the right time sequence between the light flash and lid shutting. Upon reflection, especially of a philosophical kind, the man may have genuine doubts about any "general" explanation of his causal experiences—as Wittgenstein points out in so many of his language games about causality. But while he is experiencing it, especially if he is not focusing on the causal experience itself, it is quite plain, to all of us, that causal action is involved and causal experience is manifest.

This causal experience is not of the same kind of presentational intensity as the light flash and the lid shutting. Ordered in a scale of experiential intensity (the normal order, of course, conditioned by the focus of intention), we would find that the light flash comes first, the lid shutting second, and the causal feelings last. We may

[29] See for example the general introduction by Victor Lowe, "Whitehead's Metaphysical System," in *Process Philosophy and Christian Thought*, ed. Brown, James and Reeves (Indianapolis: Bobbs-Merrill Co., 1971).

[30] Alfred North Whitehead, *Process and Reality; An Essay in Cosmology* (New York: Harper & Row, 1960), paperback, pp. 265–66.

not consciously notice the lid shutting at all, much less the common causal experiences, because of their vague bodily character. We have been conditioned by eons of evolution to take for granted the common bodily experiences, and notice the exceptional—the punctuation by pain or the visually discriminatory experiences that portend danger, sexual, or aesthetic interest, and the general conditions that insure our survival. But the vague bodily experiences are there forming the immense background for the intensely presentational ones. The feeling of muscle contraction around the eye, the feeling in the eye of its support by the body, the mild pain *in* the eye upon light flash, the sense that the eye *sees,* all of these in association with multitudes more of vague but interrelated experiences of very minimal intensity, insure a notice of a single intended climactic one. What we fail to notice, often, is that the intense, well-defined presentation is dependent, even experientially, on the plethora of intimately related, almost unnoticed, bodily conditions that do not call attention to themselves during the experience.

Mathematically and philosophically, in association with the scientific disciplines, we may try to figure out how the light flash *causes* the lid blink. The generation and transmission of light by electromagnetic waves, the transfer of energy of these waves to the retina of the eye along with discriminatory characteristics that tell color, the transmission of this energy by neural connectives to brain receptors, which then in some (presently mysterious) process condition bodily actions that both close lids and present the experience of light flash—all can be described mathematically to the degree that science has progressed in its actual characterization of the processes involved. As I have indicated, this scientific-mathematical characterization does not allow the causal aspect to show forth. Only if one introduces a general metaphysical connective between basic metaphysically characterized structures of being, can a generally causal connective be made manifest, and then it partakes of the general liabilities of any metaphysical speculation.

If we grant with Whitehead that there are some real experiences of causal efficacy that we can feel through our own bodies, though perhaps they are vague and obscure in their actual presentation, we still must seek to structure them in some manner in order for them to be intelligible in a basic culture that prizes other more intense modes of knowing. Especially is such clarification necessary if some adequate understanding of causality is to be made relevant to science—and in terms of my analysis, since religion follows science, to religion also. Whitehead's general metaphysical description of causality has certain primary characteristics: causal agency, in contrast to a description by means of antecedent conditions,[31] is a real connective between actual entities, asymmetric in time, that determines (limits, constitutes) what now is in terms of what then was. It is this agency that we can experience—though vaguely. When Whitehead claims that agents are prior in time to that which they condition, he is pointing out not that the structure of causal efficacy is subject to temporal categories, but that the nature and structure of time itself is dependent on and constituted by the structures of causal connection. The presently understood limitation on the maximum speed of influence to that of the speed of light (roughly 3×10^{10} cm./sec.) is simply the way causal efficacy propagates in this age. It need not have always been that way nor will it necessarily be so in the future. Causal agency as such never determines completely, but only influences the outcome of events. Determination by causal forces is a matter of degree, some things being more completely determined than others. Any event, however, must be susceptible to being referred back to its antecedent causes, and in this way the ponderous ability of the past to determine significantly the present must be recognized. Memory and perception, in a Whiteheadian perspective, have the same temporal structure as causal agency. Memory remembers past causes. What is given in perception is past causes.[32] The problem here, however, for a Whiteheadian understanding of

[31] In the *Introduction,* section "A Note on Causality," there is a brief discussion of the nature of antecedent conditions.
[32] I am indebted to Charles Hartshorne for pointing out this aspect of Whitehead's philosophy.

causation, is that the process that allows rational intensification of the contents of both memory and perception, seems to relegate to the penumbra of vagueness the actual causal connections.

This is a problem in Whitehead's philosophy that I have attempted to show throughout this section—that mathematization tends to dissolve causality. Whitehead clearly acknowledges the problem and maintains that as one experiences in the mode of presentational immediacy, experiences in the mode of causal efficacy are obscured. I have difficulty, for example, as I examine my own experience, say, of the blinking of the eyes upon turning on the light, of deciding in what mode the so-called causal experiences are actually felt. As I understand Whitehead, "by the time" I actually feel them with any clarity, they are in the mode of presentational immediacy. How can one actually get at true feelings in the mode of causal efficacy?

This problem is reflected in Whitehead's metaphysics itself, and is apparently a serious one. In order to show the problem more adequately, I shall use a portion of Leclerc's description of Whitehead's metaphysics, not because I disagree with him, but because his precision of exposition allows a concise statement of the major difficulty. Leclerc is speaking of causation and objectification of actual entities.

> In his [Whitehead's] doctrine an "efficient cause" is a past actuality, as objectified. An efficient cause cannot "act"; it is an "efficient cause" by virtue of its "pastness." The past does not "act" in the present, for as past, its activity is over; it merely "functions" in the present by being "a ground of obligation" conditioning the activity of present *actual* entities.[33]

Since accepting this as a very accurate characterization of Whitehead's position on efficient causation, I can state the problem, I think, simply. I understand, according to Whitehead, that the feelings of causal efficacy constitute the *experiential* authority for understanding that there is a past at all. If these feelings, however,

[33] Ivor Leclerc, *Whitehead's Metaphysics: An Introductory Exposition* (New York: The Macmillan Co., 1958), p. 110.

are actually due to the activity of the present actual entity, as is maintained, and if according to the ontological principle, this activity in the present actual entity is the sole true existence, how can one possibly escape the solipsism of the present moment and affirm a past, or other actual entities besides oneself?

In contrast to the dilemma of solipsism, which may be interpreted to be an affirmation of complete and arbitrary freedom (since there is nothing other than oneself to interfere with the being and activities of consciousness), we may come to an opposing dilemma in a Whiteheadian perspective that denies freedom altogether by interpreting the becoming of an actual occasion in a sequential manner where causation between phases of the sequence is presumed to act in a manner similar to the causal relations between actual entities themselves. On this basis Edward Pols has recently criticized very severely the Whiteheadian concepts of process philosophy for contemporary theology.[34] If these concepts are not adequate *within* Whiteheadian philosophy, they certainly lose their effectiveness for theology.

The underlying difficulty may not be specifically in Whitehead's metaphysics, but in the nature of metaphysics itself. Using Whiteheadian terminology, the very exposition of any metaphysical position must be in terms of the structural relationships of eternal objects. Even the characterizations of the nature of actual entities in Whitehead's metaphysics must be ultimately done by the connections of eternal objects. I am not saying what Whitehead says so well concerning the ontological relationship of eternal objects to actual entities, but that this very description, especially as we make it precise, utilizes eternal objects. Thus the very structures of eternal objects, modeled expressly by Whitehead after his understanding of

[34] Edward Pols, *Whitehead's Metaphysics: A Critical Examination of Process and Reality* (Carbondale: Southern Illinois University Press, 1967). See the response by Lewis Ford, "Can Whitehead Provide for Real Subjective Agency? A Reply to Edward Pols' Critique," *The Modern Schoolman* (January 1970), and John B. Cobb, Jr. "Freedom in Whitehead's Philosophy: A Response to Edward Pols," *The Southern Journal of Philosophy* 7 no. 4 (Winter 1969–70).

mathematical objects, as eternal and nontemporal, and as connected without any implicit categories of freedom, structure the metaphysical system as system in such a way that it, when viewed as comprehensive description of phenomenal things, tends to obscure the past, categories of freedom, other entities, and especially causality. It is this tightly knit, rational character of metaphysics that makes it possible to affirm the difficulties of solipsism on the one hand or the negation of freedom in a developing actual entity on the other hand.

The solution to the problem is not to pursue ever relentlessly a more thorough objectification and rationalization of the metaphysical position in order to make it adequate, although, of course, appropriate modification of any metaphysical position is essential to maintain contemporary relevance, but to recognize, as did Whitehead, the essential difference in kind between causal experiences and rational ones within which metaphysics is formulated. We have observed the functions of objectification in the Pythagorean society and the religious thinkers of the Upanishads. Any negation requires an objectification. Negation and rejection often enhance *experience*, that is, allow the experiencing of things otherwise obscured by rational categories. The Pythagoreans experienced a rational world through their objectified categories. The writers of the Upanishads experienced a new world of being through their objectification and rejection of rational categories. Whitehead's categories, as precisely objectified, can therefore be rejected or contrasted by his own authority, with causal experiences. However his metaphysical structures contain the rational pattern by which *actual* causal connections may exist.

The rational structure of causality in Whitehead's philosophy, that is, the connective of prehension, can be mathematized (in part) and correlated with the mathematical structures of relativity. This has not been done, to my knowledge, and I have not done it. Whitehead could have done it in terms of the mathematization of time, space, and entities (perishable like his later actual entities) within time and space that he proposed in "On Mathematical

Concepts of the Material World" but he did not because he had not yet come to his position of "nonmathematical" causality.[35] The general procedure for understanding the structures of causality between entities is from Whitehead's metaphysical structure itself that each actual entity receives causal influence from all other actual entities in its immediate past, but no causal influence from its contemporaries. *Past, future,* and *contemporary* are defined mathematically by relativity theory in terms of the fixed maximum speed of light.

Furthermore, it is also true, I believe, that his philosophical position concerning the becoming of actual entities was developed near the end of his studies in mathematics and was motivated in a significant way by his concern to explain both the creative (constructive) nature of mathematical relationships and their objective status. His ontological principle guaranteed that what would have been intuitive mathematical processes within consciousness in most other philosophies were ontologically real, actual states of different but successive actual entities in his philosophy. Through this device, Whitehead was able to have a close relationship between the nonprecise experiential aspects of causality and that which has close similarities to the traditional mode of making causality precise by patterning it after the mathematical activities necessary to get at a fixed and valid mathematical structure.

This mathematizing of causality by Whitehead is effective in showing forth true causal experiences only if one is able to reject—perhaps the correct word is contrast—the mathematical structure with the ontologically different causal experiences themselves. This is what actually happens, I think, in the awareness of those who follow in some manner a Whiteheadian metaphysics. It shows forth in a kind of "conversion" of those studying White-

---

[35] Whitehead, "On Mathematical Concepts of the Material World," in F. S. C. Northrop and Mason W. Gross, eds., *Alfred North Whitehead: An Anthology* (New York: The Macmillan Co., 1961), pp. 7–82.

head, who initially is hopelessly pontifically rational, but who then in some apparently mysterious manner allows the experience of causal forces apparently hidden. The structures of causality in Whiteheadian philosophy allow the *possibility* of actual causal relationships where, perhaps, we had not previously expected to find them, and in our rational contemplation of them, we find, by appropriate procedures of contrast, that they are, in part, actually there. We experience what we now conceive to be rationally possible. Or conversely, we characterize rationally what we have known causally to be present.

Whitehead's causal philosophy is a needed corrective for an a-causal science and theology. I find the causal experiences to be primary and their philosophical characterization secondary. It may be that the experience of causality in science and religion is dependent, at least in our age, on adequate metaphysics, but the metaphysics is ultimately a secondary structure based on, if it is in any way valid, the actual world. For religion, some causal understanding of the world, its subjects, and its God, is crucial. The religion of Christianity, apart from some minor professional *theological* manifestations, has always considered God to be causally active.

The *experience* of God's causal action on man has also been a prominent part of Christian life. In conversion, baptism, eucharist, prayer, and everyday activities, God's action, according to almost all devotional literature, and especially the Holy Scriptures, is present, and manifests itself in the believer's actual experience. Read any primary accounts of Christian religious movements, such as, the Wesleyan revival or the present Jesus People movement, and ask: "Do these people believe themselves to experience God?" The answer is, of course, Yes. But this experience is not just of a God who sustains all men in their possibilities of existence, but of one who acts particularly and does specific things, such as giving the power to overcome the temptation of drugs or, for that matter, raising a particular man from the dead! The conviction among ordinary Christian believers throughout the whole Christian era that God acts specifically and causally may be wrong, but it is hard to deny that this conviction has been dominant. If theology is to represent the normative experience of believers, it must allow for actual causal description of God's action. Present process theology does allow this.

In my contrast of causal experiences with the precisely rational or mathematically exact, I have warned, at least implicitly, against accepting unconditionally any metaphysical position. The metaphysical position, because it contrasts with the actual causal, may not and probably does not, reflect the actual structures of causal relation. Furthermore, because of the similarity of metaphysical structure to mathematical structure, we may use known qualities of mathematical structure to criticize a hasty and unduly enthusiastic acceptance of any metaphysical structure. Since Whitehead's philosophy has recently been so extensively used for theology and forms the prime example of a metaphysical position in use today, I ought to give, as I have for Husserl and Wittgenstein, a brief history of his dependence on mathematics for his philosophical position. Then we can see how the discipline of mathematics may affect the general questions of metaphysical adequacy, the problems of skepticism, and, as a continuation of the discussion of this chapter, the understanding of causality.

5
Mathematics and Contemporary Process Theology

In its religious adequacy, precision of thought, and delineation of significant issues, contemporary process theology has progressed far beyond its inception in the philosophy of Whitehead. The basic Whiteheadian distinctions, however, are still very much present. The descriptions of actual entities, eternal objects, and their relationships involving time and space, continue to be the heart of process theology even though the subject matter discussed may center on traditional theological topics such as a doctrine of God, Christology, the nature of good and evil, and the like. Whitehead's reaction to the new mathematics had a significant influence on his mature philosophical position. The very distinctions of eternal objects and actual entities were the result of many years of consideration of the foundations of mathematics. Contemporary mathematics may yet shed further light on the metaphysical aspects of process theology, but in order to engage in contemporary criticism, we need a general grasp of the initial relationship of mathematics to Whitehead's early thought.

240

Whitehead's Mathematical Development[1]

Whitehead began his serious philosophical writings after years spent as a professional mathematician, during which time he was intensely concerned almost exclusively with mathematics or its foundations. His professional philosophical contributions came late in life and only after he was convinced that problems in the foundations of mathematics could not be solved mathematically. It can fairly be said that Whitehead approached his philosophical interests historically through his own involvement in mathematics. For us, a look at his mathematical development can help point out some aspects of his intended meaning concerning *eternal objects,* which from many perspectives within the general philosophical tradition are problematical, and *actual entities* on whose clear concept all major theological doctrines of process theology depend.

Whitehead's general concern in mathematics may be classified as a search for the true nature of mathematical existence. For the professional mathematician Whitehead, this meant no more than an appropriate understanding of number, magnitude, geometrical figure, algebraic structure, and so on, that would allow both old and new mathematics to fit into some unified whole with all aspects of pure mathematics interpretable in some common mathematical medium. New mathematical developments, for many of which Whitehead himself was responsible, caused him periodically to revise his understanding of this common medium and ultimately forced him to a *philosophical* position that he thought adequate for the new mathematics. I shall trace his development in this regard.

In his first major work, *A Treatise on Universal Algebra with Applications* (UA),[2] published in 1898, Whitehead was very sensitive to the fact that the new algebras, which constitute the

[1] See Granville C. Henry, Jr., "Whitehead's Philosophical Response to the New Mathematics," *The Southern Journal of Philosophy* 7, no. 4 (Winter 1969–70).

[2] Alfred North Whitehead, *A Treatise on Universal Algebra with Applications* (New York: Hafner, 1960).

primary subject matter of the book, represented a definite break with past mathematics and were, consequently, looked on with suspicion by many mathematicians. Accordingly, he issued a plea in the preface for their inclusion as legitimate mathematics.[3] In order to show that these algebras, which he believed capable of unification in a Universal Algebra, have claim to be an integral part of mathematics proper, Whitehead defined the nature of mathematics as "the development of all types of formal, necessary, deductive reasoning."[4] This definition shows his feeling for and continuity with the English formalist school, which attempted to free mathematical formulation from necessary intuitive content. The further clarification of this definition by the explication of the words *formal, necessary,* and *deductive* is an excellent description of the working philosophy of this formalist school, and I recommend it to the reader.[5] By defining mathematics in terms of a "high" formalism, Whitehead could insist that the new algebras discussed in UA are a definite part of the subject matter of mathematics in that they conform to the definition.

Whereas Whitehead recognized and accepted, and, indeed, vigorously affirmed the formal nature of mathematics as the "dealing with marks" according to "conventional laws,"[6] and also accepted the existence of a multiplicity of different mathematical systems that may have no necessary relationship to number or quantity, yet are capable of being produced by such formalistic procedures, his primary goal in UA, as far as he was concerned with the foundations of mathematics, was to find a ground of unity for the multiple systems in some common *interpretation.* If one mathematical content could be found such that aspects of it would serve as interpretation of the various formal systems, unity could be had on two fronts, the formal and the intuitional.

The search for an intuitive content for mathematics by Whitehead may seem surprising, since one often hears that mathematical

---

[3] *Ibid.,* p. vi.
[4] *Ibid.*
[5] *Ibid.*
[6] *Ibid.,* p. 11.

formalists seek at all costs to avoid such content. This is not so. The difference between the English formalists at the time Whitehead was writing UA and the Berlin school of mathematicians with whom Husserl worked was primarily a matter of emphasis. Both groups operated symbolically in terms of some content. Whitehead's conviction that there is always some ontological content corresponding to mathematical reality allowed him the freedom to create apparently "fanciful" formalistic speculation with safety, whereas the members of the Berlin school, Kronecker, Dedekind, Weierstrass, and others, held grave doubts that one could find a mathematical content that would *always* correspond to formalistic manipulations. For them there was the ever-present possibility that a mathematical system that was rigorous in all respects still could itself be no more than "formalistic nonsense." Accordingly, they sought for and thought they had found the universal content of all mathematics, namely, natural number.

For both groups, however, the tension between the apparent legitimacy of new formal mathematical systems and an old content that progressively was made inadequate *by* the new systems became critical. In response to this problem both Whitehead and Husserl launched a mathematical and then a philosophical quest to find a true content or kind of mathematical existence that would provide a unified interpretation for the new algebras and logics. The end result for Whitehead was his doctrine of *eternal objects;* for Husserl, his of *intentional objects.* As a professionally trained mathematician, Husserl was influenced philosophically by the same major crises in the foundations of mathematics that influenced Whitehead. In particular it was Husserl's awareness that natural numbers could not form the content of all mathematics that precipitated his search for the true objects of mathematics and resulted in his phenomenological method for apprehending them—as was outlined in chapter 3. As we shall see, it was the breakdown of the thesis of *Principia Mathematica* (PM), namely that logic could form the content of mathematics, that led Whitehead to further investigate the nature of mathematical objects.

In UA Whitehead sought to uphold an old Western idea that

the unity of mathematical systems can be obtained by a generalized idea of space. A generalized concept of space is an abstraction from many portions of mathematics, and hence has an applicability to those portions of mathematics which in themselves have no apparent relationship to the "spaciness" of space. Though capable of forming the interpretation of many different algebraic systems —this is what Whitehead sought to show in UA—historically the mathematical idea of a space arose as an abstraction from geometry.

It would be foolish and inaccurate on our part to see Whitehead's project in UA as the reduction of different algebras to any physical properties of space. Whitehead specifically declares that his higher spaces are mathematical spaces and separate in concept and structure from physical space. Yet we must not forget the difficulty even the most powerful of mathematicians and philosophers of the late nineteenth and early twentieth centuries had in isolating new mathematics abstracted from geometry from intuitions associated with geometry. Whitehead was attempting in UA to make intellectually palatable the new and strange algebras that had been recently created, and the natural and traditional way to accomplish this was to show their interpretation through an extension of the familiar medium of geometry. The medium, however, was not adequate as a content-ground for mathematics, and Whitehead moved slowly toward a new foundation for mathematics, the *logic* of PM.

In Whitehead's next publication after UA, "On Mathematical Concepts of the Material World" (MC),[7] which was first read before the Royal Society in 1905, he sought to provide a multiplicity of different mathematical systems (or general spatial concepts) that are each adequate to characterize the physical world. In this paper we see the mathematician-physicist Whitehead producing systems in pure mathematics designed to represent the most general characteristics of time, space, and entities in time

---

[7] F. S. C. Northrop and Mason W. Gross, eds., *Alfred North Whitehead: An Anthology* (New York: The Macmillan Co., 1961), pp. 7–82.

and space. Many aspects of these mathematical systems found their way into his philosophical positions. It might be helpful to pursue the influence that these systems had on Whitehead's later philosophy, but our present interests are focused on Whitehead's search for the true nature of mathematical existence. This was not the thrust of the paper under consideration, but certain developments within the paper do give us clues concerning Whitehead's modification of his views concerning mathematics.

The terms *general space* and *manifold* that played such an important part in UA are absent from the paper MC. They are to be found, however, in this publication with a new name, *polyadic relations*, where they serve a different function, specifically the description of the physical world. The change in terminology from *general spaces* to *polyadic relations* is a change from terminology about higher geometry to that of logic. In MC Whitehead introduced almost all of the full-blown logical symbolism of PM. The shift was from the generality of mathematical spaces to the generality of logic. This was a shift in orientation from the mathematical objects that are tinged with geometrical intuitions to those that partake of logical intuitions.

UA was not devoid of interest in logic. On the contrary, Boole's symbolic logic was presented in detail and the other algebras were studied "for the sake of the light thereby thrown on the general theory of symbolic reasoning."[8] But there is a decided difference of emphasis in the use of logic between the two works. In UA logic as a formalized tool was not used extensively. It was reflected, as a Boolean algebra, into a general space in order to find unity with other systems. In MC, however, instead of symbolic logic being reflected into a general space and thereby partaking of spatial intuition as in UA, it was used as the *means by which* a multiplicy of essential relations (or if we prefer, general spaces) are presented. General spaces (essential relations) in MC were understood in terms of logic and the intuitions relevant to it and not vice versa, that is, logic understood in terms of general spaces, as was done in UA. There is nothing unusual in the use of

[8] *A Treatise on Universal Algebra with Applications*, p. v.

logic by Whitehead in MC to present what is essentially mathematical content. This has been the traditional procedure since Greek mathematics. The use of logic, however, not merely as the tool of mathematics but as fundamental content of mathematics was a new position taken by Whitehead in PM.

In 1900 Whitehead and Russell went to France and heard Guiseppe Peano tell of his recent work in logic. Peano had enormously increased the extent of symbolic logic by introducing symbols to represent notions "there exists," "is contained in," "the set of all x's such that," and so on, that had found no adequate representation in the logic of Boole. By this symbolism he was able to present in the *Formulaire mathématique* a development of arithmetic that requires only the general principles of logic (adequately symbolized), the undefined terms *number, zero,* and *the successor of*; five postulates about these undefined terms; and definitions of certain fundamental arithmetical operations. The place of logic in Peano's system, however, appears to be essentially a classical one. Logic is a tool for the presentation of mathematical content. The concepts *number, zero,* etcetera, are undefined and presumed to constitute the elements of arithmetic and not the content of logic.

The transition that we have observed in Whitehead's thought from trying to ground mathematics in a generalized mathematical space to the clothing of spaces (or essential relations) in logical terminology, has run full course in PM. Logic was affirmed to be the source of mathematical subject matter. The task of PM, "the mathematical treatment of principles of mathematics," was accompanied by "a backward extension into provinces hitherto abandoned to philosophy,"[9] that is, into logic, which had traditionally been a part of philosophy. What was sought by this "backward extension" was a set of primitive ideas of logic, a set of definitions phrased exclusively in terms of these primitive logical ideas, and a set of primitive propositions (axioms) of logic by which the logical system created from these axioms is sufficient

[9] Alfred North Whitehead and Bertrand Russell, *Principia Mathematica To # 56* (Cambridge: Cambridge University Press, 1962), p. v.

to deduce the ordinary propositions of arithmetic, algebra, geometry, analysis, and so on, from the original primitive ideas.

The primitive logical ideas: "elementary proposition," "propositional function," "negation," "disjunction," and so on, are assumed to have a direct intuitive presentation. They point to logical or mathematical objects that "reveal" themselves to the trained observer. The primitive ideas cannot, of course, be defined, but "are explained by means of descriptions intended to point out to the reader what is meant."[10] Whitehead and Russell, however, showed no trust in self-evidence alone. Too many serious errors had been introduced into mathematics by accepting apparently self-evident premises for them to affirm any infallible quality to such "feelings" of certainty. In spite of many careful statements about the possible unreliability of "self-evidence" in PM, largely motivated by the necessity of introducing the awkward Axiom of Reducibility into its framework, the axioms of PM on the whole do, in fact, partake of a degree of self-evidence that allow them to be accepted by many, even today, as the true intuitive ground of both logic and mathematics. Most well-trained mathematical logicians, however, can no longer accept the logistic thesis as presented by PM.

The breakdown of the thesis of PM occurred primarily, I think, for three reasons: an instability within PM that became critical, the more thorough and more adequate formalization of the mathematics of PM, and the surprising results of Gödel. The instability was the famous Theory of Types formulated by Russell to handle Burali Forti's contradiction and others implicit within PM. Whitehead's original enthusiasm for Russell's solution, reflected in his statement "All the contradictions can be avoided,"[11] turned to mild revulsion when he realized that "our only way of understanding the rule is nonsense."[12]

The continued formalization of the mathematical system of

[10] *Ibid.*, p. 91.
[11] "Mathematics," *Encyclopaedia Britannica*, 11th ed., 17:881
[12] "Mathematics and the Good," *Essays in Science and Philosophy* (New York: Philosophical Library, Inc., 1948), p. 111.

PM has effectively separated the mathematical system as such from the assumed logical content that was presumed to be its ground. The mathematical system of PM, for example, can be presented mathematically by the set theoretic models of P. R. Halmos, where "predicates" are functions, "propositions" are constant functions, quantifiers are mappings, and so on.[13] The natural relationship between propositions and the primitive elements of PM becomes a very unnatural one in these algebras. Yet these newer algebras allow a more powerful grasp of the mathematics of the original system than did PM. The philosophical position that sees mathematics to be a natural generalization from logical reality is no longer necessary and may indeed hinder the acquisition of the true mathematical structure of PM itself.

Gödel's Incompleteness Theorem showed the impossibility of deducing all the theorems of arithmetic from PM or, for that matter, from any system with a finite (or a decidable infinite) number of axioms. Thus, the program of PM to deduce mathematics (all of it) from a simple set of logical axioms is now believed impossible.

It is difficult to ascertain exactly when Whitehead became aware of the full crisis of developments pertinent to the thesis of PM. One does notice that even during the period in which he affirmed without any major reservations that mathematics is simply an extension of logic, he also espoused a more formalistic position.[14] As in the past, however, Whitehead could not maintain exclusively a pure formalism. For him the formalism of mathematics and the reality to which it referred had to be explained in terms of the most general categories applicable to all things, that is, metaphysics. "Even in arithmetic you cannot get rid of a subconscious reference to the unbounded universe."[15] Slowly we see Whitehead's formalism giving way to a generalized content of mathematics that appears at one point as "relations,"

[13] Paul R. Halmos, *Algebraic Logic* (New York: Chelsea, 1962).
[14] "Axioms of Geometry," *Encyclopaedia Britannica*, 11th ed., 11 : 730.
[15] "Mathematics and the Good," p. 111.

at another point as "patterns," and finally crystallizes in terms of his precise understanding of "eternal objects."

Eternal Objects[16]

If we understand Whitehead's doctrine of eternal objects as found in *Science and the Modern World* (SMW) and *Process and Reality* (PR) to be primarily a description of the ontological nature of mathematical relationships and only secondarily a description of other abstract entities like colors or even emotional feelings, much ambiguity and actual error concerning them can be cleared up. I grant that this is not the way Whitehead normally approaches the subject. Many beginning students of Whitehead have their first approach to the meaning of eternal objects through colors. There is no surprise then that a general uneasiness may emerge concerning their supposed radical abstractness or their unique individuality.

I do not think that our common knowledge of the abstract nature of colors or of emotional feelings has undergone any great change since the time of Plato. There is a natural abstraction "red" that we can make from red things. Most of us, however, have considerable hesitancy about declaring "redness" to be in any significant way independent of red things. So also are our feelings concerning particular shades and variations of "redness." How can we declare to exist a certain exact red color if there are not things that have that color red? The general criticisms of the Platonic tradition concerning abstract relationships still hold. Yet we hear Whitehead frequently speaking of both the radically abstract nature of eternal objects and their individual particularity. And eternal objects are held by him to be somehow independent of and prior to *ordinary* empirical things.

Although our knowledge of color abstractions since Plato has not changed appreciably, our understanding of the nature of

[16] See Granville C. Henry, Jr., "Whitehead's Philosophical Response to the New Mathematics," *The Southern Journal of Philosophy* 7, no. 4 (Winter 1969–70).

mathematical abstractions *has changed,* and changed in the direction of reintensifying both their abstract nature and their individuality. These changes came primarily in the nineteenth and early twentieth centuries through the more adequate formalization and objectification of mathematics itself.[17] Although recognizing that an understanding of the transcendence of mathematical form over empirical reality has been a part of Western tradition since Plato, Whitehead clearly accepted that there is a degree of abstraction available to the contemporary mathematician and philosopher that was not available to *any* pre-nineteenth century mathematician. For example, geometry need have no necessary relation to space. As he learned from the breakdown of PM, mathematical logic need not be involved with propositions or any aspect of ordinary language. And number may have nothing to do with counting. "It is only recently that the succession of processes which is involved in any act of counting has been seen to be irrelevant to the idea of number."[18] Mathematical relationships, for Whitehead, as "complete and absolute abstraction,"[19] need not be part of *any* empirical situation.

Mathematics acquires its transcendence by being purely symbolical and axiomatic. By being symbolical it allows us to consider relationships that transcend their own exemplification in the physical world. By being axiomatic it allows us to consider relationships that are not observable in the world—and may never be. This is possible because we can manipulate the axioms of a system and thereby determine new relationships and hence new mathematics without having presentations of these relationships in intuition or in the physical world at all. Colors and emotional feelings share neither of these characteristics.

What Whitehead had in mind as an eternal object is not just the symbolism, however, but a metaphysically real relationship to which the symbolism refers. The referent of the symbolism

[17] See my brief history of mathematics in chap. 3, section "The Breakdown of the Euclidean Perspective in the Nineteenth Century."
[18] "Mathematics," p. 881.
[19] Alfred North Whitehead, *Science and the Modern World* (New York: New American Library of World Literature, Inc., 1960), p. 27.

may be found at times in the physical world, but if this is where we look for it primarily we are not in the "realm of complete and absolute abstraction" and hence are not dealing with pure mathematics. The precise ontological status of a mathematical eternal object is that of a potential relationship for entities in the world. When such a potential relationship is actualized—or to use Whitehead's terminology, *ingresses*—in the world, we are able to see it in and among the things of the world. In order to "see" it, however, we do not have to behold it in the world. One can apprehend a mathematical eternal object directly, according to Whitehead, through the symbolism of mathematics or, for that matter, just as it is in itself.

As abstract, eternal objects have their own individual identity.

> each eternal object is an individual which, in its own peculiar fashion is what it is. This particular individuality . . . cannot be described otherwise than as being itself.[20]

Whitehead's emphasis on the individual objectivity of mathematical relationships is derived from his knowledge of the successive failures of more generalized mathematical theories to explain thoroughly or ground mathematics. As I have mentioned, neither geometrical figure, natural numbers (arithmetic), logic as formulated in PM, nor even set theory can form the general foundation for the totality of legitimate mathematics. During the long course of mathematical history, the general assumption that individual mathematical relationships were dependent on or grounded in larger, more comprehensive theories effectively diluted the focus on the individuality of the relationships themselves. With the breakdown of the thesis of PM, Whitehead saw that the individual mathematical entities could somehow be ontologically prior to their general systematic relatedness, that is, prior to the general field of logic itself, and began to investigate this position in his philosophical works.

What happened to Whitehead's philosophical position concern-

---

[20] *Ibid.*, p. 229.

ing the individuality of mathematical relationships can be understood by those who know Husserlian phenomenology and especially by those who are familiar with Husserl's early works. The similarity of development between the two men is striking. Husserl's phenomenological battle cry "to the objects themselves" was originally raised in concern for mathematical and logical objects and for the same reasons that motivated Whitehead. The philosophical transition for Husserl was far more violent than for Whitehead, because Husserl had been attempting to explain mathematics in terms of a psychologically dominated philosophy based on his understanding from the Berlin school that mathematics itself could be adequately grounded mathematically in natural number and thereby understood in terms of the *acts* of counting. As I attempted to explain earlier, the breakdown of this understanding mathematically, forced Husserl into an almost complete revision of his philosophy, where the emphasis was on the priority of the intentional mathematical objects with a deemphasis of their psychological determination. We all know that Husserl's emphasis on intentional *objects* in no way kept him from incorporating human subjectivity in his philosophy. For Whitehead also, that place or metaphysical ground of mathematics became intensely subjective in his later philosophy, as I shall shortly indicate in the discussion of actual entities.

If there is no systematic mathematical or logical ground that *mathematically* can be the source of all mathematics, where then ontologically do we find mathematics? How can we understand that unity and logical relatedness which mathematics seems actually to possess? Whitehead worked to a metaphysical view that finally saw mathematical relationships as grounded in actual entities, and through this concept he could explain the place and unity of mathematics.

Actual Entities

Whitehead's conception of an actual entity, though not called by this name, emerges early in his philosophical works. In

Principles of Natural Knowledge, The Concept of Nature, and
The Principle of Relativity, which were published during the period
from 1919 to 1922, there is a shift from almost pure mathematical
presentation toward a description of aspects of reality that are
not primiraly mathematical. Apparent in these works is a search
for a reality that underlies mathematics but that cannot be
described by mathematical means.

This reality is called by Whitehead an event or fact. Both
event and fact have to do with the "unbounded universe." Fact is
a relationship of factors. It is a totality and, therefore, not an
entity for cognition. Factors limit or canalize fact. Awareness, for
example, is a limiting factor in fact. The term *limitation* is used
by Whitehead "for the most general concept of finitude."[21]

The interesting point here, as we seek to understand Whitehead's
change in his understanding of mathematics, is that mathematical
entities as abstractions are found as "placed" or "grounded" in
fact. "The number three is nothing else than the aspect of
fact as factors grouped in triplets."[22] Fact, or event as totality, as
found in these earlier works is the nascent concept of an actual
entity, which finally emerges in mature form in *Process and Reality.*
We see in these works the first step toward the grounding of
mathematical objects in an intense human subjectivity. Whitehead's "facts" do not have the intense subjectivity that later
attend his actual entities. He is more concerned at this stage
of his thought to save scientific theory from an illegitimate
mathematization.

Whitehead was convinced that contemporary scientific viewpoints have divorced scientific theory from sense experience. The
color blue, for example, seen in some object is relegated by
current theory to a subjective experience caused by the interaction
of light waves of a particular frequency with the eye, nervous
system, and so on. The electrons, the light waves, which are all
characterized mathematically and *are not seen,* are thought to be
the primary locus of reality, whereas that which is seen, the blue,

21 Northrop and Gross, pp. 306–7.
22 *Ibid.,* p. 308.

is thought to be a subjective experience. And not only that, the blue is taken from the object and given location somewhere in the mind. Whitehead believed that the blue is actually in the object where it is seen.

The error to be corrected, according to Whitehead, is the inappropriate use of mathematical concepts. Mathematical objects in contemporary theory are often given a "concreteness" that is not correctly theirs. We think that points, lines, and other exact mathematical concepts are to be found in the physical world, when, in fact, they are *never* seen there. The mathematical objects are abstracted from sense experience, according to Whitehead, and should never be allowed to be a substitute for it in scientific theory. Whitehead states:

> There can be no true physical science which looks first to mathematics for the provision of a conceptaul model. Such a procedure is to repeat the errors of the logicians of the middle-ages.[23]

If one is not to look to mathematical models for an appropriate scientific theory, where then is he to look? The above statement sounds strange coming from the man whose "Mathematical Concepts of the Material World" consists almost exclusively of mathematical models that attempt to characterize the physical world. Whitehead's answer to this question indicates his change in perspective. One must look first at the world as it appears and describe it accordingly. Scientific theory must have at its foundations what one sees and touches, that is, sense data. But even at this stage, for Whitehead, sense data were not the narrowly understood vividly present experiences upon which most previous empirical philosophy had been built, but larger complexes of "total" experience. This is a phenomenological outlook, which Whitehead accepted. What is real is what one "sees" phenomenologically and not what is projected into the world from a mathematical model.

The primary thing that appears phenomenologically is *fact*.

[23] *Ibid.*, p. 322.

Fact is the totality actually perceived and directly appearing. Mathematical objects find their being and ground *in* this fact.

Objective fact as the totality of that which appears, is transformed into subjective experience itself in Whitehead's characterization of the nature of actual entities in *Process and Reality*. That which is perceived is that which is *felt* subjectively. That which is felt subjectively is actually that which determines and *is* the being of an actual entity. Fact, which was totality objective *to* the perceiving subject in Whitehead's earlier cosmological works, becomes the subjective being *of* an emerging actual entity in *Process and Reality*. An actual entity prehends other existent actual entities of the past and selects from the totality of them what will be the essential nature of its own being. But in experiencing these actual entities, in prehending them for its own purposes, it does so in terms of its own subjective coming to be. That which is "objective" to me, say that tree in the yard, *as* it is seen (felt, smelled, etc.,) by me is a part of my own essential being in the moment.

This transition in Whitehead's thought is similar to the transition made by Husserl toward a radical subjectivity. Indeed, much of Husserl's analysis, and hence a great portion of phenomenological "seeing" is compatible with and finds its place in Whitehead's understanding of the coming to be of an actual entity. The intentional object of Husserl as that which is intended by subjectivity has the same type of subjective grounding as does the object prehended in Whitehead's thought—but only in the later stages of becoming of an actual entity. The object prehended, in Whitehead's thought, though existing initially by itself independently of the entity prehending, is experienced as determinate part of the subjective being of the emerging actual entity itself. That which is perceived vividly in the present moment by an actual entity, that is, the whole range of color presentations, touch sensations, the mathematical relationships of entities, and so on, is declared by Whitehead to be primarily a *projection* of the emerging actual entity.[24] In the mode of presentational immediacy,

[24] *Process and Reality*, pp. 185–97, 255–79, 474–508.

that which is experienced as "there" is put "there," or intended
"there," by the basic subjective processes of the actual entity.
Even the mathematical objects as exemplifying internal and
external relationships in and among the objects observed are
projected from the emergent complex of processes that is determining the actual being of the actual entity itself. In the mode
of presentational immediacy, the mathematical objects are constructed out of basic subjective processes and have their objective-
ness "there" only as a projection of the becoming subject. The
"grounding" of mathematical objects in an underlying subjectivity
(the preexistent and "eternal" Transcendental Ego for Husserl
and the emergent and short-lived actual entity of Whitehead)
conform philosophically to the desire by both Whitehead and
Husserl to recognize adequately the created nature of mathematics
without denying its ultimate objectivity.

The Metaphysics of Whitehead

In discussing the similarities between Husserl and Whitehead,
one should not obscure the basic metaphysical differences between
the two men. Husserl moved from his understanding of mathematical objects as that which is intended by human subjectivity, to a
Transcendental Subjectivity, and then to a Transcendental Idealism.
The authority for his philosophical idealism was, to him, what he
believed that he saw phenomenologically. Whitehead, however,
moved to an examination of the radical subjectivity of human
experience within the context of a metaphysical system that affirms
a clear realism. It is granted by him that an actual entity has
experience of the objective world in terms of its own constituent
being, but this experience is possible, according to Whitehead,
only because the objective world is *there*. Whitehead's realism,
where electrons are considered to be actual entities and not just
the interpretation of statistical mathematics, where the statistical
variance in measurement is due primarily to actual change in
length of the thing and not only to techniques of measurement,
where the blue of an object is in the object and a part of it and

not merely a subjective experience, is often very surprising to the contemporary scientist.

The authority for Whitehead's basic philosophical position is not exclusively that which *appears* phenomenologically. To be sure, Whitehead claimed that any legitimate philosophical thought must be relevant to human experience, or else it comes to naught. As he states in PR: "The elucidation of immediate experience is the sole justification for any thought." [25] But in this elucidation of human experience Whitehead allows speculative generalizations that are the result of "the play of free imagination" and are not necessarily guided by immediate phenomenological insight or authority. There are generalizations involving the *all* that go beyond the bounds of what is seen. For example, how can Whitehead possibly affirm that all actual things are in process, based exclusively upon what is seen phenomenologically? He can not and does not. Such an affirmation is a speculative generalization. Whitehead maintained that in any reputable philosophy there are speculative generalizations and that it is up to the philosopher to make these known so that they may be more adequately analyzed. Because Whitehead recognizes the importance of speculative generalization, and also its great dangers, he subjects his own generalizations to an intensive criticism and sets up criteria for the analysis of such generalizations in any philosophy.

The fundamental differences between Whitehead and Husserl are the result of a different basic insight and a different philosophical method. Husserl's idealism and Whitehead's realism are a difference based on insight. Whitehead's metaphysical emphasis and Husserl's phenomenological emphasis are the result of a different method. Both Husserl and Whitehead allow the insight based upon phenomenological vision a fundamental place in philosophy. Husserl, however, sought to limit philosophy to this type of insight, whereas Whitehead allowed the metaphysical generalization an equally important place.

But what is the nature of a metaphysical generalization in Whitehead's thought? How will our examination of the place of

[25] *Ibid.,* p. 6.

mathematics in Whitehead's philosophy allow us to evaluate its adequacy and function for theology? In answer, I return to the discussion of eternal objects.

If the concept of eternal objects in Whitehead's philosophy was modeled, as I maintain, primarily after his understanding of mathematical existence, and if his concept of actual entities was developed in large part to find a true ground for mathematics, how then are we to understand nonmathematical eternal objects like colors, feelings, and the like, in their relationship to actual events? Are these kinds of eternal objects of the same nature as the mathematical ones? The answer is both Yes and No and is, therefore, hardly satisfactory. Whitehead understood, and process philosophy following him has continued to understand, both under the same general ontological category of eternal object. Both mathematical and nonmathematical eternal objects have the *same* metaphysical function in their relationship to and constitution of actual entities. But there are differences between them beyond the obvious mathematical character of the one and the nonmathematical character of the other. For example, Whitehead speaks of *simple* eternal objects in regard to colors, that is, the basic elemental sensa at the root of the experience of, say, a green leaf.[26] But there are no simple mathematical eternal objects. Points, lines, whole numbers, and so on, which had been considered to be simple by many mathematicians in the nineteenth century are, in fact, very complex structures and are recognized to be so by Whitehead.[27] The attempt to discover "atomic" elements in mathematics, some one set of simple entities from which and out of which all mathematics can be understood and constructed, though pursued in every century of mathematical discovery has consistently failed—if for no other reason than the genius of the mathematical community in discovering new legitimate mathematics

[26] *Science and the Modern World*, p. 240; Compare *Process and Reality*, p. 174.

[27] The complexity of a point may be seen in Part IV, chapter 2 of *Process and Reality*. Any entity, of course, is "simple" if it is an undefined element of the domain of an axiomatic system. This, however, is an epistemological distinction, not an ontological one.

that will not conform. Whitehead knew that there are no simple mathematical eternal objects, at least in terms of contemporary mathematical research, but nevertheless affirmed, though with some considerable ambiguity, the existence of simple sensa. Can colors be simple eternal objects? In a consistent Whiteheadian perspective, I do not think so. They are necessarily complex. A detailed analysis will confirm, I think, that all eternal objects are complex. But here in *my* perspective, as well as in Whitehead's early perspective, I am assuming that the true metaphysical nature of *all* eternal objects possesses those characteristics attendant most visibly to mathematical ones. And this may not be the case at all. Mathematical structures may have a different metaphysical nature from colors, feelings, emotions, etcetera.

The reader may think that I am belaboring the obvious at this point. Of course mathematical eternal objects are different from more sensible ones, and most likely are different in a major ontological way. We know this from common experience, as witnessed by the great divide between the "two cultures" of science and the humanities. Or we know it from a historical examination of previous philosophers. Ought we not also to know the difference between mathematical and other objects of consciousness by a simple philosophical analysis? Such an analysis may not be simple at all. Its difficulty is not peculiar to the specific philosophy of Whitehead, but is manifest in the analysis of any Western philosopher who has used contemporary mathematics to clarify and structure essentially nonmathematical reality. The list of philosophers who have employed a new mathematical technique to produce a new philosophical position, technique, or insight is long and honorable: Plato, Aristotle, Descartes, Leibniz, Spinoza, Pascal, Locke, Kant, Russell, Husserl, Wittgenstein, and many others. In Western thought new mathematical discoveries, or basic mathematical paradoxes, have often opened up new ways of seeing nonmathematical aspects of the world. But in each case, it seems that the very success of a philosophy that has employed mathematical tools or insights to present or clarify nonmathematical content tends to obscure the relationship between the mathematical and nonmathematical itself. This is especially true during the period of the most important influence of the respective philosophy. Subsequent further objectification and development of the mathematics may sharpen the boundaries between what is purely mathematical and what is not. We are capable of adequately making such distinctions in the philosophy of Descartes, for example. But for the philosophy of Whitehead in its present stage, the analysis that I think really ought to be made should proceed cautiously and should proceed in awareness of the major mathematical developments since Whitehead.

There is one aspect of the problem, however, that we can observe at this stage. The problem of the distinction between mathematical and nonmathematical structures is almost an identical one in the philosophies of Husserl and Whitehead. Husserl's logical and mathematical objects intertwine, involve and constitute all other kinds of objects. Husserl's search for an ultimate *mathesis universalis* is one that he thought would characterize "object in general," and hence involves mathematical and logical structures in each thing. The difference between mathematical and nonmathematical in Husserl's thought is not always clear —although he made a superb effort in the direction of clarification. The *similarities* between mathematical and nonmathematical objects are fixed, primarily because both are known—and really *only* known according to the program of Husserl—through the phenomenological method.

In fact we can say, I think, from the perspective and presuppositions of Whiteheadian philosophy, that Husserl's whole program is an exposition and clarification of the realm of Whitehead's eternal objects. What can be seen phenomenologically from a Husserlian perspective is a vast interrelationship and hierarchical structure of eternal objects fanning out in each case from the centrality of intended structure into a horizon. Whitehead's emphasis on "experience" and Husserl's emphasis on "what appears simply" are very similar ground perspectives. What is seen from this common perspective is remarkably similar. Even their description of what Whitehead calls causal feelings has a common, though anomolous, place in relationship to seen static structures.

I have maintained that the objects truly seen through the perspectives of both Whiteheadian and Husserlian philosophy have been conditioned by the ways of seeing mathematical objects. The new ways of seeing mathematical objects were precipitated by mathematical developments that were known to the professional mathematicians Husserl and Whitehead. If my analysis is indeed true and adequate, mathematical objects then take a certain precedence over nonmathematical ones. They determine *how* the nonmathematical ones are seen by modifications of the under-lying perspective of a balance between subjectivity and objectivity. The importance of mathematics, really, for the philosophies of Husserl and Whitehead is comparable to the importance of mathematics, say, for Descartes's philosophy, although the "clear and distinct" criterion for Cartesian philosophy is modified in Husserlian and Whiteheadian philosophy in a manner comparable to the change in understanding mathematical relationships today. The importance of mathematical relationships as models of general epistemological structure in Husserlian and Whiteheadian phil-osophy allows us to affirm their precedence and thereby effect a partition, at least in general categories, between mathematical and nonmathematical objects. As mathematical, I include here the formally logical as objectified mathematically. I both admit and affirm that the exact dividing line between mathematical and nonmathematical is often difficult to ascertain at our present stage. On the whole, however, as ordered in terms of *clarity of appearing*, we have first mathematical presentations and then nonmathematical ones.

There are other presentations, however, in both philosophies: the causal feelings of Whitehead and the naive feelings associated with the psychological ego in Husserlian philosophy. These vague feelings associated with our very particular existence—not the general qualities of thrownness of *Dasein* but the particular feel-ings of, say, my being Granville Henry in this very moment—are neither in the realm of eternal objects nor in the true field of vision of phenomenology. They are not ideal objects. They contrast with mathematical objects in a way that other non-mathematical objects do not.

A crucial difference between Whitehead's philosophy and Husserl's, and indeed between the whole program and results of process philosophy and phenomenology, results from the handling of these causal feelings. Husserl excises them; and Whitehead moves to metaphysical categories in order to include them. For Husserl they are what obscure true phenomological vision. The naive existence in which we live our ordinary lives, with the push and pull, the influencing and being influenced, must be overcome in the true philosophical attitude, since it is in this existence that we are liable to metaphysical presuppositions and attitudes of the most powerful (and perverse) sort. Husserlian phenomenological epochē "inhibits acceptance of the Objective world as existent and any objectively apperceived facts, including those of internal experience." [28]

For Whitehead, however, the anomolous causal feelings that contrast with clear mathematical presentations are extremely important for an adequate philosophical view. They are what determine our naive, particular, psychological existence. They are the historical element of our existence determining immediate being within the freedom of becoming of things. They are structured in our understanding, however, by an appropriate choice of a most general set of eternal objects that then become the metaphysical categories of being in general. The metaphysical generalizations of Whitehead, in answer to my earlier question concerning their nature, are a selection from among the eternal objects (or, we may say, *an* eternal object, when it is understood in its ultimate complexity involving relationships among other eternal objects) that seem to coordinate causal feelings in their relationships to our most immediate experience of being. They must also, therefore, coordinate causal feelings with the clear experiences of eternal objects.

I maintain that Whitehead's metaphysical generalizations are

---

[28] *Cartesian Meditations*, trans. Dorion Cairns, p. 25.

really a subspecies of his eternal objects, in spite of his apparent position to the contrary in the first two chapters of *Process and Reality*. The ultimate categories of "creativity," "many," and "one" are obviously clarified by the structures of eternal objects. I maintain that, as they truly become precise metaphysically, they become eternal objects in their mutual relatedness. Whitehead tells us that the term *one* is not the integral number "one" which, as he says, "is a complex special notion."[29] And of course the number one in its relationship to other numbers is complex and special, indeed, technical in its place among the real numbers. The metaphysical "one" as he intends it includes the notions of the general idea of "a," the definite article "the," and the demonstratives "this" or "that," and stands for the "singularity of an entity."[30] But as made precise, the metaphysical one becomes a close relative of the number one among the eternal objects. It is perhaps a more complex eternal object (although there is no true *measure* of complexity among the eternal objects) than the number one. It identifies the unity (number oneness) of an actual entity as made up of the multiplicity of actual entities in its past, in terms of the vastly complex mathematical structures of becoming. It includes the relationships of stages within the becoming actual entity, the complex relationships involving time and space of the actual entity to its objective past, and also the relationships to the number one, which is itself a complex eternal object. "Many" has to do with the diverse actual entities (each as *one*), and creativity has to do with how the many actual entities become one (but not with how the many eternal objects can be considered to be unified in one object).

Here I am interpreting "creativity" to be a generalization from the experience *that* all pluralities get creatively unified and not as an aswer to *why* they get unified. As such, in the detailed explication of how the many become one and the formed one then becomes a part of the many, creativity is best explained by a complex of eternal objects (effectively unified in one). My con-

---

[29] *Process and Reality*, p. 31.
[30] *Ibid.*

clusion is that the whole *metaphysical* structure of Whitehead —including the many, the one, and creativity, the concepts of actual entities, *and* the concepts involving eternal objects, as *the structure is made precise*, and to the degree that it is made precise—consists exactly of a subset of eternal objects (as Whitehead understands eternal objects) and hence is also one such object.

I cannot doubt, though, that Whitehead intended "one," "many," "creativity," "actual entity," and so on, to have included within their respective meanings *more than* that which is possible through a mere presentation as static structure. (Remember that movement can be characterized by static structure. The derivative may represent velocity but is itself quite static.) The terms *a* or *an*, *this* or *that*, have an existential import, a radical historical dimension, and a feeling of causal determination as one participates in particular existence. "Creativity" may indeed be "the universal of universals"[31] and thus clearly understood as a variety of eternal object, although when so understood its intended preeminence is hard to justify. But it is also "the principle of novelty," where novelty necessarily involves the kind of nonprecise feeling of newness associated at times with actual existence and the novelty we feel that we bring about in response to (or in reaction to) causal forces. In each case, however, it is the structure of Whitehead's metaphysics that allows an understanding of the nonstructural elements of his philosophy.

We have seen an evolution in Whitehead's thought from his considering axiomatic mathematical structures as the most appropriate way to characterize general aspects of the cosmos, that is, time, space, and entities within time and space,[32] to an apparent rejection of mathematical method in philosophy, a rejection that attacked any accepting of first principles on the authority of their mere clarity,[33] to a position that finally affirms (if my analysis is correct) that the general metaphysical categories are themselves

[31] *Ibid.*
[32] See section "Whitehead's Mathematical Development" above.
[33] *Process and Reality,* pp. 11–12

similar in nature and structure to axiomatic mathematical systems. In this final stage, according to Whitehead, we are to form a scheme or matrix that is "stated with the utmost precision and definiteness" and then "argue from it boldly and with rigid logic" and finally confront any conclusion "with circumstances to which it should apply."[34] The intermediate stage of Whitehead's thought represents his discovery and elucidation of experience that can be phenomenologically known, that is, that which is seen to appear and which is *not* handed to the viewer by any preordained axiomatic mathematical structure. The whole authority for accepting any content so seen is its very appearing. There is no guarantee ever that experiences accepted or the content viewed manifest themselves according to any mathematical scheme that has its authority on the clarity of the premises known. My claim is that the way by which these experiences are known phenomenologically is patterned after the way which mathematical structures are themselves known. The shifts in perspective of knowing mathematical relationships effectively opened up newly known nonmathematical content. The contrast between Whitehead's second stage of viewing reality with the first is a contrast primarily in his "seeing" mathematical relationships, where a vision of a rigidly unified mathematics by means of mathematical axioms is no longer acceptable.

We should be careful not to let Whitehead's prohibitions against an illegitimate mathematization prevent us from seeing that in its most mature form his metaphysical principles are very similar to mathematized structures of his "Mathematical Concepts." The differences essentially lie in the way the mathematical structures are seen and in the way these structures are related to the existent world of experience. The extent and range of experience is much enlarged in Whitehead's later thought.

Whithead's criticism against metaphysical argument from clear and distinct principles employing a mathematical method is a valid one, for in no case can one know that a mathematized axiomatic system is applicable to the world from the mere authority of its

[34] *Ibid.,* p. 13.

basic principles alone. The goal of Whiteheadian metaphysical philosophy is an "accurate expression of the final generalities"[35] themselves, based on the authority of human experience. Whitehead's procedure is in effect a scientific one, whereby one creates, discovers and projects mathematical structures, or structures very similar to them, and by means of an involved cultural process that is part of the community of science and the larger academic community, confirms these structures by general experience. The major difference between Whitehead's general metaphysical categories and more limited strictly scientific systems lies in his inclusion of the larger realm of experience perceived through phenomenological vision within his general system. I am claiming that what can be seen phenomenologically has also been conditioned by modes of mathematical seeing and, further, that the general metaphysical principles of Whitehead's thought are a subset of such general mathematical relationships as seen phenomenologically.

A recognition that the nature of Whitehead's metaphysical philosophy, as it is made precise and objectified, is really primarily a subset of his eternal objects, must necessarily also emphasize its *tentative* character. The goal of his ultimate generalizations was, of course, to find some specific generalities that would hold necessarily for all things. But his search for such generalities was never complete and he continued to affirm his sentiment expressed in the beginning of *Process and Reality* that "metaphysical categories are not dogmatic statements of the obvious. They are tentative formulations of the ultimate generalities."[36] If, as I maintain, the metaphysical categories and structures themselves have an ontological similarity to Whitehead's understanding of eternal objects, and these in turn are patterned after known relations in mathematics, we ought then to be able to conclude something from the nature of mathematics itself about this very tentativeness of metaphysical speculation. And, indeed, the newer theories coming out of the foundations of mathematics concerning

[35] *Process and Reality*, p. 12.
[36] *Ibid.*

the ultimate limits of mathematics as a discipline tend to reinforce our hesitancy to accept metaphysical speculation as eternally true or rigidly valid. There must be a necessary skepticism in the way of accepting metaphysical principles or the basic principles on which mathematics operates. I shall examine the nature of this kind of skepticism in association with a historical dimension of Christian skepticism in the next chapter.

Metaphysics and a Theological Objectification of God

An objectivized God can not be found *within* the realm of Whiteheadian eternal objects as phenomenologically seen. A metaphysical structure can be seen that *may* correlate our experiences of God's causal action and that *may* thereby portray some aspect of His activity. But such a structure is not God in His consequent nature, only an attempted description of Him.

Neither can God be found among the objects of phenomenological examination in the Husserlian tradition, nor in an extended Husserlian tradition such as that examined in chapter 2. Nor can God be found within the objectivities of language in a Wittgensteinian tradition. In each of these contemporary traditions of philosophy, that aspect of knowing which was modeled after a way of knowing the new mathematics fails to allow an apprehension or objectification of the traditional Hebrew-Christian God.

This does not mean that a phenomenological analysis prohibits a grasp of a marvelously new realm of, and perspective on, content that is useful religiously. As is obvious to anyone who has studied contemporary religious literature, the advent of phenomenology for the study of religion has greatly enriched its study. We may talk about God's effect on human existence, the nature of the Holy, perspectives toward divine transcendence, the meaning of the future, the priority of eschatology, as well as the traditional doctrines of sin, redemption, and Christology—and talk about these topics in a way that seems more accurate and more adequate religiously.

What is meant when it is said that God cannot be presented

objectively by phenomenological or linguistic analytical means? Does not a phenomenological presentation of transcendence associated with, for example, resurrection experiences point to *one* who is transcendent, or an analysis of the holy indicate *one* who is holy, or an analysis of nonbeing show forth *one* who ultimately IS? The answer is both Yes and No. If phenomenological language is used to confirm mythological or familiar personal language: God as father, God who sends His Son, the God Who creates (according to human models), then the objectification of God is clear in the mythological language. The question is whether there is any intelligible reference to the noun *God*. The *language* indicates its objective reference. But does the language truly signify that of which it speaks? The further one clarifies by phenomenological means what is meant by the mythological language, the further one moves even linguistically from indicating an objective God.

Or if phenomenological language is used to confirm metaphysical language: God as the *One Who Is* (with all the associated philosophical machinery), God as Actual Entity or Personal Society, then, again, God's objective status as described metaphysically is clear. As one uses phenomenological or linguistic analytical language, he may recognize that this language *in itself* does not signify the objective God spoken of metaphysically. But there is no reason why we *must* stick necessarily to one mode of presentation. The two modes, metaphysical and phenomenological-analytical, can be compatible and can together present a theology that is exquisitely precise (whether accurate or not is another question) and apparently adequate to describe a religious existence. In fact, mythological and personal language can be integrated into a complex, but relatively complete, language structure that contains both phenomenological-linguistic analytical and metaphysical language, all of which together form a whole, unified around the religious existence of the community and individual, and representing the intentions of the community, including a precise understanding of God's existence and objectivity. This is what, I think, would be called within the religious community the redemption of language. Yet, it is the metaphysical language within this corpus of language-faith that bears the burden of describing God's existence and objectivity.

The metaphysical language, however, as it is precisely (and mathematically) presented, as it lifts up its object which is ultimately a structure, indicates an objective framework that is among the variety of intentional, phenomenological, or eternal objects. That is, the object of metaphysical language is itself a phenomenological object. As a complex structure, it may show an entity, clearly objectifiable within the structure, that is described in terms of its relationships with other entities. This is how in general, within metaphysics and in particular in process theology, God is objectified. He is identified as an entity within one system having such-and-such relationship with other entities. We know that the metaphysical system is not complete. It merely claims to represent the *most general* of attributes of the cosmos, including God, not *all* of them. We do not know in terms of the metaphysical analysis, even as buttressed by other forms of analysis, whether the emphasis is correct or whether even *any* particular structure or relationship is correct. Thus, in any metaphysics, as precisely formulated, we do not know ultimately, in terms of the formulation, whether the subject or entity defined as God in relationship to others, conforms in fact to the God Who is the source of experience and historical action in the Christian religion or not.

Having said this, however, I want now to emphasize the importance of the metaphysical task. If there are experiences—powerful feelings and orientations concerning the world—that are not part of, or not analyzable into, the realm of eternal objects or phenomenological objectivities, that do not present themselves with their own clear authority as objective structures, then some metaphysical analysis appears necessary in order to correlate and understand "structurewise" their meaning and importance. I think clearly that the Christian religion produces such experiences. If the Resurrection of Christ does engage believers in a historical existence that cannot be predicated exactly and completely as appropriate structure, then I maintain that metaphysics is still altogether necessary, especially in our day of the authority of scientific structures, in order to effect some understanding of this existence.

Can we narrow down the nature of "experience" in some way so as to get a clue to the nature of the connection that can be structured metaphysically? I think, and here I speak personally because of the convictional nature of my statements, that I am acted upon by felt causal forces, some of which identify their agent as God, the God of the Judeo-Christian tradition. I may be determined completely at times by these forces, the power of agency to do so certainly seems to be there, but normally the probability of my conforming to their intended direction is less than one, which makes them similar to other causal forces from *other* ordinary agents. The experience of God's action takes many forms, some of which are mundane and ordinary, others of which have all the phenomenological characteristics of a "wholly other." In short, according to my experience, God acts historically within the created order. My interpretation of experiences of His causal action is clearly molded by my participation within the Christian community.

These causal forces, like my experience of other causal forces, are normally vague, imprecise, and effective, and are to be contrasted with those experiences which are phenomenologically bright, precise, limited, and "mathematical," as I have attempted to outline in chapter 4 and in this chapter also. These forces are what Whitehead attempts to structure metaphysically (and mathematically) as *causal efficacy* and *prehension*. In themselves, however, they are prephilosophical or premetaphysical. One may experience them, be affected by them, irrespective of his philosophical preconditioning. The religious tradition in its earlier sources is careful *not* to present them under the guise of any one philosophy. In the covenantal understanding, God acts, Israel responds. Sometimes Israel acted and God responded! In Christian perspective God acted and acts in the crucifixion of Christ. And many have responded to God's act—in terms of a great variety of philosophical and metaphysical preconditionings.

Having a causal experience of divine action does not, of course, indicate in itself the unity or objectivity of the Judeo-Christian God. Religious literature is filled with examples of mistaken revelation, and especially of mistaken objectifications of the source of communication of influence. Too many have claimed to have been led by God, and then later affirmed (or have had confirmed) that it was in fact other "spirits" who were responsible. The early Hebrews clearly understood that *a* god, Yahweh, was having a causal influence on them and they on him, but it was not until a later tradition, or a later revelation, that they understood that Yahweh was, in fact, in their new monotheistic tradition, Almighty God. I have presented in chapter 4 how processes of objectification led from causal experiences, not to a monotheistic objectified god, but to a nonobjectifiable god, Brahma, of the Upanishads.

Causal experiences, however, do have a vector character. They point to an agent, or agents. When causality is interpreted on a personal model, then agents are seen as persons, as was true in the evolution of the Hebrew understanding of causality. Multiple experiences of causation are seen, by common experience and revelation, to come from a divine person—who has whatever objective unity persons have. Thus God, as seen within the religious tradition, is Father, Creator, Savior, all mythological terms that indicate as best they can His objectivity and unity. It is here that the metaphysical task is crucial. The essential vagueness of the mythological terms does not allow any precision of understanding of God's relationship to the cosmos. A metaphysical analysis can. And such an analysis can point out God's objectivity and unity, within the system, as I have indicated—but, of course, with the limitations on metaphysical systems that we have observed. Some metaphysical systems are more adequate than others because they represent more adequately and faithfully the intentions of the religious community. Whitehead's metaphysics, in my estimation, is the most adequate representation of the causal element in the Christian religion. In addition, at least for me, his characterization precisely of mathematical and metaphysical structures allows me to see and understand more adequately, by contrast, the nature of causal actions, and thus more fully to understand those within the Christian tradition.

There are generalities and structures in the realm of mathematical relationships that can, as we well know, characterize some of the most general aspects of the cosmos. Presentations within the realm of mathematical objects occupy, challenge, and grasp the sensibilities of Western culture, and now in a more thorough way the sensibilities of the rest of the world, by giving control and understanding of a world that without them is chaotic. Though not born in Israel's historical religious existence, these mathematical structures and presentations nevertheless have become a part of the general cultural and academic aspects of Christianity. *From the Jewish and Christian religions we can claim that God knows these relationships and, in knowing them, has the responsibility for the possibilities of how we may know them, and how we know them in relationship to Him.*

In short, it is not *whether* metaphysics is necessary for the Christian theological task, but *how* we understand the function of metaphysics within Christian theology. The radicality of the Christian faith in its potential for genuine and pervasive revolution in the affairs of men, and their underlying intellectual constructs, demands that we absolutize no position. The attractiveness, the aesthetic gain, the religious necessity to combat the chaos of utter relativism, demands that we attempt some metaphysical understanding of the Christian faith. To maintain an appropriate balance between the authority of rational systems and the revolutionizing experiences of belief has always been a concern of Christian theology, manifesting itself in discussions on the polarities of faith and reason, skepticism and belief, and again in our day on the distinctions between the secular and the holy. These considerations bring us to a discussion of the relationship of mathematics to attitudes of skepticism and secularization.

6
Mathematics, Christian Secularity, and Skepticism

The word *secular* in most ordinary language contexts concerns that which pertains to the world, to things *not* religious, *not* sacred or *not* spiritual. An initial use of *secularization* in a sense compatible with its present meaning is found in the treaty of Westphalia, where it was used to distinguish lands that had been transferred from ownership by the church to the princes.[1] The historical process of secularization means, according to Gogarten, "the transformation of institutions, ideas and experiences that were once the work of divine providence into the product of a purely human thought and action."[2] Theodore Runyon has extended this definition so that secularization is "a relativizing process in which that which was previously thought to be absolute, or associated with the absolute, or of high authority and value to

---

[1] Larry Shiner, *The Secularization of History: An Introduction to the Theology of Friedrich Gogarten* (Nashville, Tenn.: Abingdon Press, 1966), p. 25.
[2] *Ibid.*, p. 26.

273

a culture, is reduced to a position of relative authority."[3]

As we consider the definitions of *secular*, as given even by the theologians, it may come as a surprise to recognize that there is a relatively strong and concerted thrust by a number of eminent contemporary theologians and philosophers of religion who also are reflecting and leading a large number of Christian people, to encorporate an understanding of secularization in the heart of Christian self-understanding itself. What appears, at least on the surface, to be alien to the spirit of Christian piety, has been declared under the leadership of Gogarten, Bonhoeffer, and the popularizations of Cox, van Buren, and others to be the particular genius *of* the Judeo-Christian religion. If the new "secular" theology is to be in any way a legitimate Christian theology, it must be either a radical reformulation of orthodox doctrine that is justified by contemporary evidence or revelation (since the activity of God has previously been understood to be present in all things), or a fruition of an obscured development that has roots in the ancient tradition. The latter is clearly the claim and emphasis of the diverse group of theologians who are now championing the appropriateness of a Christian secularization.

The kernel of the new Christian understanding of secularization is contained in the old early Christian kerygmatic message. The good news is that the Resurrection of Christ has defeated the elemental powers and spirits of the world, broken the shackles of a prescriptive law, and freed men to live in relationship to other men and God in an entirely new way. The Gospel confirms and completes the dedivinization of the world that began in early Judaic tradition when Yahweh called the Hebrews away from nature worship into a historical existence. The old spirits that had hallowed the ground, the trees, the mountains, the lakes, the storms, and at times were understood *to be* the stars, were all relativized. The distinctions between sacred and profane were

---

[3] Theodore Runyon, "Secularization and Sacrament: Reflections on the Theology of Friedrich Gogarten," *The Spirit and Power of Christian Secularity,* ed. Albert Schlitzer (Notre Dame, Ind.: University of Notre Dame Press, 1969), p. 124.

theologically obscured in Christian life when meat sacrificed at pagan altars was declared clean for Christian consumption —because the gods of the altars themselves had been neutralized. Christian man was understood to be responsible *to* God *for* the world, and not subject to the divine spirits *in* the world. He had an obligation to understand and change the world by the power of his secular action.

Have I said anything more, however, than that the Christian Gospel is a renewed and intensified proscription of idolatry, a confirmation and (radical) reinterpretation of the first of the Ten Commandments? Surely, from a Christian perspective, nature *has* been freed from the elemental spirits whose worship is idolatry and thereby remains available for a more objective and detached study. But in accepting the Christian offer, the Christ event, that is, God giving himself for man, have we not simply recognized the redivinization of the world? Have we not recognized that the world is subject to the one God and dependent on Him for its immediate sustenance? Is not the God Who sustains it also present in its furthest and nearest constituent part? Is it not true then that a move toward radical "Christian" secularization is not a Christian move at all, but an attempt to ignore, and accordingly to establish man's independence of, the God Who is the ground of being of the cosmos itself?

Those advocating a Christian secularization would have a firm response to the above questions: To claim that true Christianity redivinizes the world is to make the mistake of confusing the power of the true God with the functions and activities of the elemental spirits. Such a claim essentially misunderstands the radical historical existence to which the Gospel calls us. It fails to grasp (or be grasped by) the grace of God, which frees man to respond to God and the world without coercion or manipulation *by* God. It is the failure to take seriously the Christian task of redemption of the world, a failure to follow our Elder Brother Who gave Himself to the world while in the world in order that He might be *for* the world. To presuppose that the world is divinized by the one God instead of the elemental spirits is to obviate the necessity for emulating the work of Christ, is to make unnecessary the "taking up our cross."

The above description of the position taken by those advocating a secularization of the Christian message, though, of course, not applying exactly to all such advocates but, I think, representing their religious intentions, is a "strong position" couched in terminology that would offend alike an orthodox or liberal believer in divine immanence. The question here theologically is not whether God dwells immanently in all parts of the cosmos in some general metaphysical sense, but whether dependence on such indwelling is appropriate to the soteriological aspects of the Christian gospel. It is on essentially religious grounds that the Christian secularists make their case, and on such grounds it must be criticized, at least from a theological perspective.

The claim that appropriate Christian secularization comes from forces *within* the religious Christian tradition may seem to the secular historian to be an incredibly obscurantist theological joust, for, if he is any historian at all, he knows from his studies that the great historical forces for secularization in Western culture have come *not* from the church, but from the Enlightenment, and particularly from the development of science itself. The church, through its representatives, has fought almost to an issue, not each development of science, but each development that seemed to it to enhance the powers of secularism. To claim now that it was the church's message, the Gospel of Christ, that precipitated the process of secularization, requires at a minimum some detailed justification. But this is precisely the claim of Gogarten, and a claim that is at least in part being recognized as legitimate. If man had not already become independent of the supernatural powers of the universe through the prophetic traditions of Judaism and the Gospel of Christ, he would not then have been able through processes *independent of the church* to free himself from organized religion and pietistic sensitivities engendered thereby. Contemporary secularization, according to Gogarten, is a result of a coming to fruition of man's new understanding of his *relationship to the world* brought about by the Judeo-Christian religion. The essentially secular movements in science and the humanities, divorced and separated from the church by its own choice, have aided in this essentially Christianizing development.

After all, Western science did arise in an essentially Christian environment. Prior to the theoretical breakthroughs that culminated in the Newtonian synthesis, Western European technical advances, especially in agriculture and weaponry, led the world, and accounted for the rising dominance and aggressive colonization by the European nations.[4] The essential insight that the world was to be *understood*, to be *used for* man, and not *placated* religiously; that the world had been neutralized from dominance by capricious evil spirits and could be investigated and manipulated for its own treasures, contributed significantly to the rise of organized European science.

But no matter how closely we may associate the religious assumptions of Christianity and the rise of scientific mentality, either through the historical study of the (Judaic and Christian) men of science or in the compatability of religious and scientific assumptions and ideas, we must recognise that there is a thrust toward secularization coming from a discipline that antedated Christianity and developed in its own right apart from influence by Judaism. We may find a legitimate historical connection between the rise of an empirical method in science and the (antirational) emphasis of Christianity that, because God created the world according to *His* desires and not necessarily according to our *a priori* rational categories, we must look *at* the world to see how, in fact, He did create it. But we cannot claim an essentially Judaic or Christian source for the secularizing force of *rationality* itself in Greek philosophy precipitated by the science of mathematics. I am claiming that one of the most potent forces for secularization of Western society has been the discipline of mathematics, and that historically it was separate from the sources of Judaism and Christianity. Mathematics was the first of the scientific disciplines to become both desacralized and "deorganicized," and it has contributed continually to the depersonalization

[4] Lynn White, Jr., "The Historical Roots of Our Ecologic Crisis," *Science* 155, no. 3767 (10 March, 1967): 1203–7.

and desacralization of nature as science itself has become more mathematical. The secular aspects of mathematics, though similar in some ways to early Christianity, have always differed from it in ways that constitute the very conflict between faith and reason discussed in chapter 1.

Any discussion of the problem of faith and reason in regard to the secularizing forces of mathematics, either in ancient or contemporary thought, comes up against another major Western tendency of thought that has both religious and antireligious impact, namely skepticism. In order to facilitate this discussion of the relationship of mathematics to secularization and skepticism, I need to make some essential distinctions between the two.

Secularization and Skepticism

Skepticism differs from secularization in emphasis and degree. In emphasis, skepticism has a decided and ever-present epistemological character that secularization need not have. A skeptic is one who questions the validity or authenticity of something purporting to be *knowledge*. Skepticism is a secularization of knowledge; a relativizing of the content of knowledge of some previously accepted authoritative position. But skepticism need not serve an overall secularizing function. One may doubt, for example, whether any propositional statements express what actually transpires in the sacrament of the Lord's Supper or Eucharist without relativizing its authority. Indeed, a position of skepticism may be necessary in order to uphold its authority.

In some degree, a radical secularization leads to an ultimate skepticism, for it then relativizes all knowledge. But the fact is that most secularization is not radical. The acts of secularization precipitated by science or the Judeo-Christian faith against old authorities presuppose an established value in some new (or rediscovered old) authority. There is even a *content of knowledge* usually associated with the new authority that clashes with the content of knowledge of the old. Secularization by its very nature, if it is to have any positive function, must be a halfway procedure.

There are built-in boundaries of "no further" in any religiously acceptable secularization, which often seem strange to the natural skeptic. Skepticism tends to go much further than secularization in relativizing knowledge, though it may not go so far in its religious usage as secularization in its total relativizing of old religious authorities.

In religion, philosophy, and science, skepticism has a long history. Its degree of popularity is often proportional to the degree of conflict of an established culture with conflicting knowledge, social systems, and religious values. The book of Ecclesiastes, as well as portions of the book of Job, maintain a skeptical position of high intensity, probably occasioned by the tensions and disillusionments accompanying the influence of Hellenism on Hebrew religion and thought. Skeptical positions were developed by both Catholics and Protestants after the Reformation.[5] The scientific community has often reacted skeptically to new and legitimate discoveries because the theory in which the discoveries were presented challenged old theories of highest authority.[6] Cultivation of skepticism became a religious or scientific necessity in order to hold onto one's own essential and convictional position. The greatest skeptic of all, perhaps, was Pascal—who was also a radical fideist. In his thought, Christian belief and radical skepticism were not contradictory. Kierkegaard was in this tradition.

There are, basically, three interpretations of skepticism: (1) that some knowledge is possible, that is, one's doubting is selective, (2) that no knowledge is possible, and (3) that there is insufficient evidence to determine whether any knowledge is possible. The first is the most frequently employed position. The second position, which can be called academic skepticism, if affirmed with any vigor at all, becomes implicitly contradictory, for if one knows that no knowledge is possible, he certainly knows something. The

[5] See Richard H. Popkin, *The History of Scepticism from Erasmus to Descartes* (New York: Harper & Row, 1968), chap. 1.
[6] The scientific community would not accept the existence of meteorites, nor the factual evidence of hypnosis. See Michael Polanyi, *Personal Knowledge* (New York: Harper & Row. 1964), pp. 51–52.

last position, which is classical Pyrrhonian skepticism, is, perhaps, the most devastating for religious assurance. It has, however, been used to bolster religious conviction.

Mathematics and the Forces of Secularization and Skepticism

The influence of mathematics on skeptical developments and secularizing tendencies within the Christian religion is manifold. Underlying most of the successful secularizing forces, however, is the authority of science through technology to explain, control, and use the world for man's benefit. The ordinary life of the average man in the developed countries has been so changed *within his lifetime by* the application of technology that he sees, not the hand of God affecting his life, but primarily the intelligence and application of man himself. I shall begin the discussion of how mathematics secularizes with another look at Newtonian mechanics.

In our ordinary experience we find that abstraction appears to entail limitation. For example, if we view any particular physical object and abstract from it the qualities of location and geometrical figure, mass and temporal movement, and describe each mathematically, by virtue of our attention on these factors we have ignored or eliminated from consideration the qualities of color, taste, aesthetic appeal, value, teleological considerations, and so on. Furthermore, if we extend these considerations of figure, mass, and movement to apply to a large number of things, or, perhaps, to all of them in their mutual relatedness, we shall have confirmed the irrelevance of other sense experience and goals, at least while engaged in this theoretical exercise. Try holding up a book, for example, and consider only its shape, position, weight, and movement. Try turning its pages and again consider only the shape of the written characters, the movement of its pages, and the like. Does it not seem clear that you have eliminated much that is of interest and value by the narrowness of focus. Colors, the *feel* of the texture of the binding, and the meaning of the words have all been relativized.

We might employ a skeptical attitude at this stage and claim that, in reality, as opposed to the appearances during a particular intellectual exercise, knowledge of the nonabstracted (but apparently more interesting) qualities, goals, and feelings was, in fact, misleading—was illusory and not primary. But such an attitude would seem to be patently a false position. On this minimal analysis, we would be probably sympathetic to Aristotle's claim that physical movement, and spatial and temporal location are *accidental* qualities and not so important as goals or purposes or the true essential nature of a substance. The true nature of a book, or its impact upon men or society, does not lie in the peripheral characteristics of its location or its shape, nor can it be interpreted significantly by these characteristics.

Or can it? Suppose that in the extension of the original Newtonian mathematical system that employed the parameters of geometrical extension and time we were able to characterize the "true" properties of colors (in terms of a wave or particle theory of light), tastes and feelings (in terms of the mathematically described chemical compositions of the elements in conjunction with a mathematically described physiological theory), meanings (in terms of the mathematically possible but highly intricate description of the human brain), and even intentions (in terms of the mathematization of psychological physiology). We would have "got back" those qualities that lay outside our original limitation in terms of the limited parameters. And our resulting theory would have the advantages of mathematical precision. Such precision gives power to control the cosmos.

We could then affirm a legitimate secularization where the authority of religious and philosophical explanation is undermined in terms of the mathematically expressible new physics and biology. Since we are dealing with knowledge in this case, we could also affirm the action of a legitimate skepticism of variety, which "doubts" the original modes of investigation, reception, and handling of data in favor of the new mathematical ones. Our original processes of limitation would appear fruitful, in that new knowledge above and beyond that of the original could be had and would constitute the authority for replacing the old.

Although general opinion will admit that this is what has happened historically—a secularization of both scientific and common attitudes as a result of the Newtonian mathematical presentation and its extension (and modification) into contemporary physics, chemistry, biology, and the other sciences as they employ mathematical techniques—the process of mathematization that necessarily employs the limiting procedures mentioned above, or ones like them, has been minimized as the source of secularization in favor of the general *empirical method*, which relies on neutral, that is, nonphilosophical or nontheological "facts." The very focus on "mere" sense experience or "bare" fact, in order to construct or justify a scientific system, seems by its very nature to restrict the modes of knowledge and authority to the "no more" of such analysis and give challenge to the authority of philosophical and religious metaphysical analysis alike. The claim that a chief source of secularization has been the general empirical method of science would of course be true if, in fact, science is based upon, or could be based upon, the collection of facts or the organization of sense experience. But it patently can not be so based, or at least not exclusively so based. One of the things we have learned in this century, and I think learned conclusively in spite of dominant prejudice to the contrary, is that both fact and sense experience are in large measure ambiguous. Neither can be clearly known, or unambiguously asserted, without some antecedent context, either in consciousness or language. In fact, scientific theory itself plays a crucial role in establishing what a relevant fact is and in some important experimental contexts whether a given aspect of the physical world is a fact at all. Fact and theory appear inextricably related in science, and the correct establishment of their appropriate and mutually dependent relationship constitutes one of the major problems of what "truth" is in science. It may be, however, that the general misconception that science is based primarily upon naked fact (that is declothed from philosophical and religious interpretation) has in fact unduly and illegitimately accelerated the secularizing tendency. An awareness of the crucial role of theory may serve to reduce the rate of such rapid secularization—provided the theory itself does not, on its own, serve a secularizing function. It appears to me that the theory itself, especially as it becomes mathematical, has been as potent a source of secularization as any of the host of historical positions of empiricism. In fact, a good case can be made that historically the various empirical positions themselves depended upon a successful mathematization of some aspects of the physical world.[7]

In claiming that mathematical theory has served as a potent condition for secularization, I do not want to obscure its frequent association with the religious and the occult. Its use in numerology and astrology is ancient. The recent revival of both cultic disciplines, even among those who are well trained mathematically, emphasizes the endemic use of mathematics for such purposes. Whenever mathematics has been identified with the realm of primary ontological structure, it has been seen to possess theological or ethical dimensions.[8] That is, it has been seen to possess these dimensions until its own sufficient development allows distinction from these dimensions. The general tendency has then been to secularize the religious and ethical dimensions in favor of the mathematical ones, although the progression in this direction is not linear, but subject to ups and downs and at times to intense revivals of the old. Claudius Ptolemy of Alexandria wrote not only the *Mathematical Syntaxis*, later called *Almagest*, that is, the greatest (of such mathematical collections), the brilliant mathematical work that dominated and, indeed, was astronomy for a millennium and a half, but also the *Mathematical Treatise in Four Books*, the well-known *Tetrabiblos*, which is an introduction to *astrology*. Ptolemy clearly distinguished between mathematical astronomy and astrology—although he sought the diminution of

---

[7] English empiricism developed in close association with Newtonian mechanics. Logical empiricism developed according to the mathematization of logic.

[8] Examples: Pythagorean justice, Platonic beauty, Kepler's regular solids, the earlier theology of Newton.

neither in importance or applicability. He recognized the unassailable position of his mathematical astronomy, since it had been demonstrated geometrically (!), but was well aware of the legitimate attacks on astrology because of its vagueness. He sought to justify "good" astrology by philosophical means for the purpose of making *astronomy* relevant. For of what good is it to know the accurate present and future positions of the stars if we have no means of correlating their positions with human concerns—like sexual happiness, the predicted nature of children, economic success, the state of happiness in old age, and death. Of course, astronomy could help one navigate, but such use was restricted to a minuscule part of the population and was considered of peripheral benefit. I cannot claim that the subsequent secularization of astrology due to the adequate distinction of Ptolemy occurred apace or progressed in some downward linear fashion. I can claim that the more adequate *mathematics* of Ptolemy allowed a clear distinction in kind between astronomy and astrology and caused subsequent thinkers who knew mathematics to claim the ontological supremacy of astronomy over astrology.[9] As the heavens became mathematized, the limiting aspects of mathematics itself secularized what had been an immensely important concern of mankind.

With the secularization of nature under the mathematical Newtonian paradigm and the secularization of astrology as a result of Ptolemy's distinctions as our models, we can see a number of contemporary secularizing tendencies associated with mathematics that have affected contemporary religion and theology. Language has suffered a secularization, due, of course, to the secularizing tendencies of Newtonian science, but also in recent years to the mathematization of logic. If one assumes that there is one true, universal, human logic, an assumption modeled after the Euclidean perspective that has been endemic in Western thought, he tends to see, at least at first, a successful mathematization of such logic as presenting the true structures of the logic. It

[9] Even Kepler, who was known to practice astrology for money, in no way confused the priority of the two.

is then but a short step to seeing only those propositions that conform to the mathematical structures of logic as meaningful. The conflict between theologians and the logical positivists was made inevitable by the secularization of language that occurred due to the positivists' insistence that the only propositions of language that *made sense* were interpretations of a precise logical or mathematical language. Although Wittgenstein reversed the order of priority and made precise mathematics dependent on and a part of certain kinds of ordinary language games, he held these language games to be secular in order to insure the essential secularity of the multiplicity of varied mathematical structures that were part of the language games. Mathematical logic, through its assumed universality in language, has cast a pall of secularity over language itself and has challenged the theological community to justify theological language about God and the language of ritual and worship, which it had previously held to be nonsecular. I am not affirming that logic itself is basically secular. Logic has in the past been used effectively to bolster the faith. It has spoken on matters mysterious and divine and often successfully. But, as logic has become mathematized—a process that can be dated and located within the history of mathematics—it then became secularized. And as mathematized, it has had a disastrous affect on Christian theology.

The most pernicious effect of secularization by mathematics has been the quantification of value through use of money. It is not only that the "everything has its price" attitude has increased, typified by the man who knows the price of everything and the value of nothing, but that the very facility with which money is transmitted has been enhanced by devices (data processing machines and computers primarily), business procedures, and consumer attitudes—as influenced by advertising—and has thereby intensified the more intricate and authoritative mathematization of money (=value) itself. It is quite a common practice in the industrialized countries for men to handle almost all financial transactions through the writing of checks or the use of credit cards. Except for small change and minor, almost peripheral purchases, the use of money in the form of the physical symbols of legal tender has been dispensed with. One receives each month a statement of the *number* (of dollars) sent to the bank. The economic task then becomes the mathematical partition of a subset of money available for various items. More often than not it also involves interest on savings or payments on loans, each of which is determined by the exponential and logarithmic mathematical properties of interest. But in each of these cases it is the numerical symbols that are of importance, especially as they become part of the more difficult and complicated mathematics of loans, interest, discounted dollar values for the future, mathematical prediction of market activities, and so forth. The man involved in business activities as his essential work is even more dominated by the quantificational aspects of money and the intricate mathematization involved therein than those who are not. His very livelihood depends upon it. And so he uses whatever influence is at his disposal to convince others through advertising (which is a manipulation of value) that they should invest in or purchase his goods or services.

Is there nothing, then, that is *priceless,* that is, without price? Notice that in the vernacular "priceless" means of astronomical quantitative value, and not that the item transcends quantificational pricing. To many of the young, and also, unfortunately, to many older people, the idea of a painting that is literally without price is an unintelligible notion. The feeling is that nothing transcends quantification by money. Else how could we then assign it a value? This attitude is far from exclusive to those who know *little* of art. It permeates the very art market itself.

Human worth is secularized by quantification in many ways: I. Q. tests, examinations for entrance to college or graduate school, the increasing use by computers and data processing units to handle, store, and manipulate both information and action of human clients. It is increasingly difficult to get a *human* response to any complaint these days. The computers are immensely clever in preventing one from dealing with anyone but the computer. They are *programmed* to act within certain rigid rules and assumptions, but their immense ability to create options within and according to these assumptions creates an unknown factor that is often not controllable by those who "care" for them. Thus one often settles a complaint "out of court" with a human representative, since to register and "measure" the complaint within the system that is normative, that is, the computer and its program, is too difficult. The point here is that the very success of the computers to handle all contingencies, which computer science and the business community are working toward, further quantifies human action and worth. The present foibles of the computers and their operators are the "cracks" within the machine through which human contact is possible.

The present ecological crisis resulting from a failure to recognize the rights of the subhuman world attributable to a combination of factors including the rise of technology, the assumptions of the Christian faith, the secularization of science, and the like, results also from the secularization of the world due to mathematics. We can recognize that Newtonian *science* made the world seem a machine and thereby secularized its value in many ways. And we have examined how mathematics contributed toward such secularization. But there are potent forces in Western thought where mathematics contributed to an understanding of the secularized world where there was little concern for empirical fact. This happened in Plato's philosophy and I think one could make a good case showing how mathematics began a secularizing function within his philosophy. The chief contributor to an understanding of a secularized nature, however, was Descartes. It was mathematics, remember, that prompted Descartes to formulate his "method." It was mathematics that gave him the criterion for a clear and distinct idea. It was a mathematical formulation of the traditional arguments for God's existence that allowed him to escape the solipsism of his discovery of "thinking substance" and "get back" to God. The crucial transition, however, is his move back to the existence of extended things in the world. Believing that God would not deceive him, Descartes claimed that his perception of physical things was valid. But he held God accountable only for guaranteeing that which appeared to Descartes clearly and distinctly, namely *mathematical extension*. The world that Descartes got back was a world of *geometrical figure*. That which was most real—indeed, perhaps the only real aspect of subhuman existence—was its geometrical relationship. Animals, therefore, were automata. The neutrality of mathematics was used to secularize the cosmos.

I can imagine the outcry of many of my readers to my making mathematics the villain in these cases, when to all intents and purposes the pure discipline of mathematics seems utterly transparent and could have been used for good or evil. My task here is to challenge this viewpoint of the neutrality of mathematics by pointing out that mathematics has contributed increasingly to continuing secularizing tendencies within Western culture (whether considered good or bad). In rationalistic times, when some philosophical and religious perspective has been integrated with some mathematical position, the mathematics has seemed to confirm only the "good" in the religious perspective, but essentially it has secularized other options by its own authority of reason. In more confused times (like the present), when there is no dominant or generally acceptable religious perspective, the successful quantification of the world by mathematics as it pervades the sciences allows people to believe at least something with assurance. In each case the tendency has been a decisive cutting away of nonmathematical options—at least within the established doctrines and disciplines. No wonder there continues to be a great interest in the nonmathematical occult.

The facts that the Newtonian parameters of time, space, and location are no longer considered exclusively paramount in contemporary physics, and that field theories, quantum theories—each with probabilistic interpretations mathematically—have achieved prominence, do not alter the fundamental problem or direction of secularization. Nor have new developments in astronomy, logic, economics, and computer science, significant though they be, changed the momentum toward further secularization. The very fact of the ever-more-complete mathematization in each of these fields, where essentially mathematical connections constitute the theory even though they ostensibly represent some undetermined and nonexperiential but real connections, further reduces the range of the applicability of sense experience, human emotion, and religious feeling. There is a basic limitation on the amount of nonmathematical content that the sterile literal variables of mathematical theory can bear. And the professionalization that these disciplines entail carries with it the price of further secularization.

Is there no lower bound to the process of secularization? The process of secularization *through mathematics* can be challenged by an appropriate skepticism directed *toward* mathematics. But why should we do this? If the Christian secularists are right, why should we move to a nonsecularist interpretation when the movement of the Christian faith insures, by its internal development and fruition, an ultimate and religiously appropriate secularization?

The answer, I think, may come from an examination of the direction and movement of science and mathematics itself. If the Christian faith follows too closely the movement of science toward further secularization, it moves beyond what it can possibly endure and becomes mere secularism. But it really cannot oppose this secularization based on quantification as it works in science. We have been struck over and over again by the ability of the mathematized sciences to interpret structures of the world more adequateley than we had dreamed possible, and with an insight and precision in no way approachable by the other disciplines. Also, the scientific disciplines seem to make the most progress, even in the fields of biology and genetics, by assuming that quantification mathematically is and will be the appropriate route of scientific progress. Reductionism mathematically is not just a philosophical perspective, it seems to be the most productive route for scientific research. On this route Christianity cannot follow too far. It quickly dissolves any true religious content.

The mathematical reductionism in the sciences, however, has produced certain limitation theorems from the disciplines themselves, which demand self-imposed limitations of interpretation on the scientific disciplines *in order to insure the accuracy, adequacy, and precision of the mathematical sciences.* Thus, as one pushes toward ultimate secularization, he is pushed back out of it by the success of its mathematical precision—entailing ultimately a philosophical analysis that does not exclude a purely religious one. The mathematical exactness and focused narrowness of the scientific disciplines insure *from their own theory* that these disciplines be taken not as ultimately comprehensive. This skepticism developed by the scientific disciplines must be grasped by the Christian faith and interpreted religiously. I think we need an appropriate Christian skepticism that does employ metaphysics more than a continued movement of Christian secularization.

Skepticism and the "New Paradigm"

We are in an age of relativism even for children. For those who have grown up under the presence of television there is an almost instant gratification available through the turning of a knob. Trained professionals insure appropriate gratification for the child provided that they can also influence him to buy or cause him to manipulate his parents to do so. But does the child *believe* what he sees on television; that is, does he both assent to the claims of factual truth and act upon such assent? Seeing may not really be believing. The child may want to believe all that he sees, and naturally does so at an early stage. But he quickly learns that he cannot believe *all* of the advertisements. He develops a necessary process of *epochē*, of abstention, not from all that television delivers, but from selective portions. By this means he may be able to obtain that which he truly desires.

Television does affect behavior. Billions are spent in advertising to confirm this fact. How then can we claim that children, and others, do not *believe* when in fact they do act by *buying* based on what they see? They may buy and act based upon a stimulation that is essentially noncognitive. An age of relativism is one in which action is initiated and prolonged without benefit of an agreed cognitive system that is thought true.

Images of the wars of Southeast Asia, mainland Asia, the Holy

Land, Ireland, and other places, and of political confrontations and campus unrest, that come to a viewer via the memorably stimulating vista of the visual structure of television presentation combine to insist that he develop both the ability to distance himself from a presentation and identify with some other. The inherent skepticism of our youth, as affected by the multiple claims laid on them by media aggressiveness, is not, however, dissociated from conviction or religion. We see this in the newer generation grown articulate, where a kind of skepticism has inhibited (and at times destroyed) the means and devices of reasonable argument or controlled and moderate change based on rational cognitive models and substituted in their place a kind of true belief that is most comfortable in a revolutionary or eschatological stance.

Such selective skeptical decision (literally *a cutting away*) has not been uncommon in religious and scientific societies in the past. Participation in any religious orthodoxy, as well as in any scientific orthodoxy, requires feeling at home with the *accepted* patterns of skeptical distancing. Such distancing has as much importance, especially for the religious, as affirming that which is positively believed. For inevitably, that which is truly believed and thought most important to believe has an elusive quality of cognitive precision, whereas that which is not believed, or distanced because of skeptical interposition, has a much more structured character. *Believing* in transubstantiation, for example, is quite different from both a rejection of the doctrine and a holding back of cognitive assent to the doctrine in some precisely stated form. The latter may be compatible with both a belief in and a rejection of transubstantiation.

Religion has traditionally employed skepticism against science when science seemed to conflict with important beliefs. White's *A History of the Warfare of Science with Theology in Christendom* is a documentary of such attempts. Interpreters of science have also freely employed skepticism to discredit or distance religion. Bertrand Russell's *Religion and Science*,[10] a most enjoyable attack

[10] Bertrand Russell, *Religion and Science* (New York: Oxford University Press, 1961).

on religion accomplished primarily by skeptical humor—"The moon was found [by telescope] to have mountains, which for some reason was thought shocking. More dreadful still, the sun had spots!"[11]—but for some reason the same canons of thought and standards of humor were not directed against science itself. Science, for Russell, was *a very serious matter*.

The relativism of our age, where there is no overarching cognitive system to give direction and values, is probably due as much to the skeptical attacks against science that had previously been directed toward religion, as to any other factor. Very few of us realized how vulnerable the enterprise of science is to such a perspective of skepticism and humor when science acquires a convictional status. We have in contemporary society a growing and deepening skepticism directed against both science and religion.

A significant part of the skeptical attitudes directed against science may be due, however, to what Kuhn calls a paradigm change. During such changes a general confusion and skepticism strike what had previously been a stable and secure science.[12] We may be in such a paradigm change right now, where the old is obviously unsatisfactory and the new has not yet appeared. The apparent chaos in understanding the elementary particles awaits with an attendant massive supply of factual data some new and probably mathematically simple paradigm to "put it all together." The anomalies at the "edge" of relativity theory, for example, an acknowledgement of both the possibility and the evidence (?) of factual data that some entities may exceed the speed of light, seek similar new theoretical grounding. The discovery of energy sources in deep space that presently defy adequate interpretation by contemporary physics, apparently point to modes of energy generation that are different from the sun's atomic fusion, and different to such an extent as to require new theoretical underpinnings.

[11] *Ibid.*, p. 36.
[12] Thomas S. Kuhn, *The Structure of Scientific Revolutions* (Chicago: The University of Chicago Press, 1962), chaps. 6 and 7.

If the history of science in the past is any guarantor of future trends in Western thought, the present age of relativism is but a prelude to the future success of some new scientific paradigm. And this paradigm will probably be far more comprehensive and simple than we had dreamed possible.

Not only are we in need of the new paradigm scientifically, but we are preparing and conditioning ourselves for its acceptance at a philosophical and religious level. In the community of religion, the general thrust of theological development toward first, the separation of religion from science in the nineteenth century in the work of Schleiermacher *et al.,* and second, the separation of religion from metaphysics in the twentieth century in the work of Barth, Brunner, Bultmann, and others of the so called Neo-orthodox movement, has about run its course. There is a renewed interest in metaphysics, and especially in the Whiteheadian variety that has generated contemporary process theology, but there is also a considerable revaluation and new use of Hegel in continental theology. In both cases, however, and particularly in the Whiteheadian version, metaphysical theology is tied to a contemporary scientific paradigm which, compared to past systems, is immensely useful, but which probably must be modified in order to handle, say, the new evidence that some things may travel faster than light (if indeed this evidence is confirmed). Those who eschew the new metaphysics, preferring to be caught in the present relativism, and those who espouse the new metaphysics will probably both capitulate to the beauty, usefulness, and explanatory value of the new paradigm—especially if they are caught unawares by it. It will probably be heralded by many theologians as new evidence of grace.

At another level, the present technical difficulties of both the average scientist and the modal theologian create a need for, and a propensity to accept the coming new synthesis. Neither the scientist nor theologian can keep up within his own field. Most have difficulty keeping up with but a narrow portion of it. Scientists, on the whole, read philosophy as laymen. They may have many ideas about relationships between science and religion that could be structured philosophically, but they normally consider such speculation to have less authority than their primary professional knowledge with its narrow confines. How can we expect the theologian to keep up with theology, much less with philosophy and science? Is not this an approaching hopeless situation, where both scientist and theologian are further isolated by the "information explosion." How can the situation be reversed? Only by the advent of new major comprehensive theories, that is, by a successful new major paradigm. Such a paradigm may be created either within or for philosophy or religion, but will probably, in continuity with past Western thought, come primarily from science. It has happened before. A general relativism, the intense preoccupation with specialities, and a mounting mass of incompatible factual knowledge, have been swept aside by the clear perception of a new theory.

The new paradigm will probably come replete with philosophical positions that can only later be successfully isolated. We appear now to be on the verge of a new, major, cosmological synthesis.

The Christian religion must learn to live not only in an age of relativism—to which most of the theological literature today is addressed—but also in the age of the new, successful, and apparently rigid paradigm. It is quite possible that the new paradigm may go hand in hand with a new puritanism, like the old moralistic Newtonianism. If the projections are true concerning population expansion, we can expect a worldwide crisis that will leave few of the old institutions and stratified modes of thought intact. But the political crisis may require, for the sustaining of a minimal quality of human existence and of some hope for the future, a moralism tied to the new synthesis of science. Thus, the Christian religion must cultivate, from its own well-endowed sources, an apropriate *skepticism* by which it can handle the age of the new paradigm. Though it will probably choose to be relevant by adapting itself to the dominant temporal, philosophical, and scientific viewpoints, it must continue to have some isolation to develop and transmit its own nature and maintain continuity with its past—especially in an age of profound crisis.

In this chapter I have attempted to show how the use of mathematics in science and theology has had a natural secularizing function. In the last chapter I attempted to show that Whitehead's metaphysical categories, as well as the intentional objects of phenomenology, could be classed as a subpart of Whitehead's realm of eternal objects. Thus, even within process theology, a full theological objectification of God is difficult because, as made precise by metaphysical structure, the entity God becomes relativized by being part of a mathematical structure. In short, an understanding of the reality and objectivity of God is secularized by the mathematical nature of process metaphysics—as well as by other highly structured metaphysical systems.

I think that a Christian attitude toward present metaphysics should be similar to that which I recommend toward the coming new paradigm. Both can be fully appreciated for their simplicity, their beauty, and their ability to bring order in understanding and experience. The activities and procedures that lead to both must be maintained, for science, on the one hand, cán give meaning to the cosmos, and metaphysics, on the other hand, can give meaning to religion—especially as religion is understood to be related to science. But both must be distanced by an appropriate religious skepticism that allows a full range of causal experiences, of cultic and mythological reality, to impinge on the believer.

Mathematics has been involved in past systems in both skeptical stances and rationalistic ones. In the next chapter let us look at *contemporary* developments in mathematics that may affect contemporary and future theology. The religious skepticism advocated here ought, I believe, to come primarily from religious sources. Some of the *new* mathematics, however, can aid in interpreting a Christian skeptical position.

7

Contemporary Mathematics and Future Theology

In an earlier chapter, I claimed that philosophers' and mathematicians' conceptions of and attitudes toward a general mathematical *all* precipitated and conditioned necessary responses from theologians and affected the general structures of the problem of faith and reason. Examples from traditional theology were given that showed how mathematical conceptions had affected a doctrine of God and doctrines of Christology, and from contemporary theology that showed how specific theologians had been affected by the tools of language analysis, phenomenology, and the metaphysical analysis of process philosophy. I attempted to outline, at least in a general way, how theological changes were conditioned by mathematical developments.

Are there mathematical developments of the last few decades that again have modified or changed our attitudes toward the content of mathematics and that thereby demand a response from theologians and philosophers concerning their categories of philosophical and theological *all*? I think that there are, and the

296

purpose of this chapter is to outline some of them, and then to show their possible relevance for *future* theology.

Chief among the developments that appear to me to be relevant is the creation (or discovery) of a multiplicity of different models for the real numbers. There are apparently a number of *different* real number systems, all of which characterize real numbers in that they satisfy all the accepted axioms of real numbers, but differ among themselves in specific and exact details. This is like telling the number theorist that there is no *one* arithmetic but a number of different arithmetics possessing different properties. And one can say that also! The *mathematical* authority that allows the claim of the existence of a multiplicity of different real number models also provides for a multiplicity of different arithmetics, and vice versa. In fact, if we accept any axiomatization for the real numbers or for arithmetic, there are an infinite number of different real-number systems and an infinite number of different arithmetics that satisfy the respective axiomatizations.

The discovery of nonstandard models for arithmetic and real numbers differs in degree and kind from the discovery of non-Euclidean geometries. Non-Euclidean geometries were formulated by *changing the axioms* of Euclidean geometry, and in particular the parallel-postulate axiom of Euclid. Each of the resulting different geometries had its own axiom system that was understood to characterize its own specific properties. Once one had the axioms, he had, presumably, the system "wrapped up," provided that he had the skill and the means to deduce the theorems from it. The different geometries were clearly distinguishable from each other in terms of clearly discernible sets of different axioms. This is not the case for nonstandard models, for within any one given family of models, they all have the *same* axioms.

The discovery of non-Euclidean geometries in the nineteenth century confirmed (what was already well known) that there are a multiplicity of different axiomatic systems. I have hesitated to emphasize the creation of non-Euclidean geometries as *the* central event precipitating major philosophical response and revision, for it was but one among many events that showed previous understandings of the *unity* of mathematics to be in error. It was, however, the most dramatic event, especially as it was communicated to nonmathematicians, by providing examples of new systems of space itself. Non-Euclidean geometries showed the possibility of the existence of new kinds of relationships and demanded responses from those who were interested in outlining the extent and nature of *all* formal possibilities—namely, those with philosophical and metaphysical interests.

Although nonstandard models differ in kind from non-Euclidean geometries, they did grow out of techniques that were originally established to test whether new mathematical systems, like non-Euclidean geometries, were consistent. If one possesses a "strange" mathematical system, he must wonder whether the unusual theorems of the system are due simply to an inconsistency in the axioms. The difficult results might be attributable solely to a contradiction in the theory, which allows the proof of nonintuitive and incompatible theorems. It became a paramount mathematical problem to show whether non-Euclidean geometries are consistent. One can show them consistent by constructing some model, or interpretation, that makes all the axioms of the non-Euclidean geometry true. These models for showing the consistency of non-Euclidean geometry, depend, however, on the consistency of Euclidean geometry. For if Euclidean geometry is consistent then we can show by constructing models in this geometry that the axioms of non-Euclidean geometry are consistent. We have thereby shifted the problem of the consistency of non-Euclidean geometries to the problem of the consistency of Euclidean geometry. Is Euclidean geometry consistent? It is, provided that we can assume the consistency of algebra. Algebra is consistent if we can show that arithmetic is consistent. Here, however, we must stop, for Gödel has *proved* that any techniques employed for the demonstration of the consistency of arithmetic are as problematical in their own consistency as is arithmetic itself. Mathematicians seem convinced, however, that arithmetic, in the standard model, *is* consistent. No contradiction has ever been found. The proofs for the consistency of arithmetic, though containing some suspect moves and assumptions, appear correct. It will be a very great surprise if arithemtic turns out to be inconsistent. The whole edifice of mathematics will tumble.

Gödel's results point out an aspect of the authority of experience in mathematics. Ultimately we think we know arithmetic to be consistent because we have experienced, in some way, its properties. The authority for its consistency is not ultimately based on proof but upon what we see, that is, what we know to be the case through our familiarity with the standard model of arithmetic. The only possible way we can settle the question absolutely about the consistency of arithmetic is to come up with some actual contradiction. Until that time (which most believe will never be) arithmetic is assumed consistent on a nonprovable but weighty basis of cumulative experience.

Mathematical intuition and experience, of course, are fallible. The whole thrust of rigor in mathematics is directed toward eliminating the errors in what *we think* we see mathematically. Although a good case could be made for the unanimity of vision of the great mathematicians, there are notable exceptions. One such exception has to do with the notion of *completeness*. An axiomatic system is complete if there is no statement in the *given* body of mathematical content that it describes which cannot be derived from the axioms.

Traditionally, mathematical content, that is, the structures of number and space, were seen as somehow given. The task of the mathematician was to characterize this content formally by relating the welter of disparate though interrelated theorems to some few statements by deduction. The theory of geometry, which was presumed to characterize spatial (and number) relationships, was axiomatized by Euclid and was generally thought complete in regard to the properties of space. Had some true statement about space been discovered that was not deducible from the axioms, Euclidean geometry as traditionally axiomatized would have then been understood to be incomplete. If this true statement were consistent with the other theorems of geometry, an attempt would have been made to make Euclidean geometry complete by the addition of this statement as an axiom or of some other statement from which the given statement would follow. The pressing question in any kind of axiomatization is whether the axioms that are used do in fact allow one to deduce all known (true) theorems. Such a question as raised in the past has had an experiential basis, for it has depended on mathematicians who know the theorems that ought to be able to be demonstrated. It would certainly be pleasant to conclude that the experiental conviction that elementary geometry is complete has now been vindicated by a proof. And one can make this claim. Tarski has a proof that *an* elementary geometry is complete. The problem, however, is that *another* so-called elementary geometry, differing slightly in axiomatic structure, is *not* complete. We do not know which corresponds most nearly to traditional elementary geometry. "The problem of deciding which of the various formal conceptions of elementary geometry is closer to the historical tradition and the colloquial usage of this notion seems to be rather hopeless and deprived of broader interest."[1] The very precision of expression that the new formal mathematical logic gives us, in a way prohibits an answer to the original question of completeness. This precision also changes the meaning of *completeness,* for the terms I have used "true for the properties of space" become unacceptably vague when asked in relationship to the new formalized elementary geometries. Still, a definition of completeness can be gained that captures the idea of an axiomatic system being adequate to give by deduction all true theorems in models that apply to it. We can say, following Tarski, that a theory is called complete if every sentence (formulated in the symbolism of the theory) holds either in every model of this theory or in no such model.[2] In terms of this more precise understanding of completeness, we now know that the traditional conviction and

---

[1] Alfred Tarski, "What is Elementary Geometry?" *The Axiomatic Method, with Special Reference to Geometry and Physics,* ed. L. Henkin, P. Suppes, and A. Tarski (Amsterdam; North-Holland Publishing Co., 1959), p. 29. Reproduced in Jaakko Hintikka, ed. *The Philosophy of Mathematics* (London: Oxford University Press, 1969), pp. 164–75.

[2] *Ibid.,* p. 22.

understanding that arithmetic is complete is wrong! There are true theorems in the standard model of arithmetic that cannot be derived from the axioms of arithmetic, and there are models of the arithmetical axioms in which these same theorems are false.

The possibility of the existence of nonstandard models has been evident since the announcement by Gödel to the Vienna Academy of Sciences in 1930 of his now famous Incompleteness Theorem. This theorem is an effective proof by metamathematical considerations that arithmetic is essentially incomplete: that not only are there true theorems in arithmetic that can not be proved from the axioms of arithmetic but also that, no matter how many axioms are added, there always remain "true" theorems that cannot be proved. If one finds some true theorem that cannot be proved from the axioms, then neither can its negation be proved. What if one adds to the set of axioms not the unproved "true" theorem but its negation. We know that in any consistent first-order theory, if some theorem A is not provable from the axioms, then the theory with the negation of A affixed to the axioms is itself consistent. Obviously this new system, or more accurately an *interpretation* or *model* of this system, is different from the previously accepted one. It differs exactly in that the accepted unprovable but true theorem in the original system is false in the newly constructed one. Yet both theories conform to the previously accepted axiom system.

In the decade of the thirties, Gödel's theorem stimulated interest in the basic limitations of the axiomatic method, further impelled mathematicians and logicians to investigate the status of metamathematics, but did not produce a driving thrust toward creation of nonstandard models. These were regarded more as curiosities than new tools for basic mathematical research.[3] In our day, not only have numerous nonstandard models been produced, but they are being used effectively to solve major problems in pure mathematics itself. Cohen has shown the independence of the continuum hypothesis by producing a nonstandard model of

[3] The first explicit construction of a nonstandard model of arithmetic was produced by Skolem in 1934.

the real numbers in which the continuum hypothesis is not true.[4] Gödel had previously produced a model in which it was true —thereby showing its consistency with the axioms of the real numbers. Robinson has introduced a nonstandard model of the real numbers that contains infinitesimals, those "vanishing ghosts of departed quantities" introduced by Newton and Leibniz and finally banned from the calculus by the rigor of the nineteenth century. These developments are both dramatic and surprising.

What might a nonstandard model of arithmetic look like? If we could find some true but unprovable theorem that we could easily understand, then a nonstandard model could be demonstrated that would contain the negation of the theorem. But such theorems are notoriously difficult to find. They are available, but involve the complexities of the Gödel sentences themselves. It is as easy (or as difficult) to understand Gödel's proof as it is to find and understand sentences that are true but unprovable. We can approach the problem, however, by examining a weaker axiomatization of arithmetic and showing what a nonstandard model would be like in that axiom system.

The natural numbers (plus zero) and their properties are normally developed axiomatically from a revision of Peano's postulates. These postulates state essentially that:

1. Zero is a natural number.
2. If x is a natural number, there is another natural number denoted by x′, the successor of x.
3. O is not the successor of any natural number.
4. If the successor of x is equal to the successor of y then x is equal to y.
5. For any property P, if (I) O has the property P, and (II) whenever a natural number x has the property P, then x′ has the property P, then all natural numbers have the property P (Principal of Induction).

---

[4] See Paul J. Cohen, *Set Theory and the Continuum Hypothesis* (New York: Benjamin, 1966). For a highly readable exposition of Cohen's results see Paul J. Cohen and Reuben Hersh, "Non-Cantorian Set Theory," *Scientific American* 217, no. 6 (December 1967): 104–16.

A more rigorous revision of Peano's postulates is required because, as they stand above, they contain certain intuitive notions like set and property which, unless themselves formalized axiomatically, contain contradictions. The Principle of Induction must be formalized by an infinite set of axioms determined by an axiom scheme. In each case, however, one can tell whether a given sentence is an axiom or not—thereby making the system *axiomatic*.

Let us consider a finite axiomatization of arithmetic that leaves out the Principle of Induction. Obviously this system, first presented by Rafael M. Robinson,[5] will be much weaker than any strict formalization of all *five* of Peano's postulates. The axioms of Robinson arithmetic, appropriately formalized are:

1. $(x) \ (y) \ (x'=y' \rightarrow x=y)$
2. $(x) \ (x \neq O \rightarrow (\exists y) \ x=y')$
3. $(x) \ O \neq x'$
4. $(x) \ x+O=x$
5. $(x) \ (y) \ x+y' = (x+y)'$
6. $(x) \ x \cdot O = O$
7. $(x) \ (y) \ x \cdot y' = (x \cdot y) + x$

Notice that axiom 2 corresponds to Peano's 2, axiom 3 to Peano's 3, and axiom 1 to Peano's 4. The axioms 4–7 are recursive equations for addition and multiplication that Peano did not have to have since his use of (intuitive) set theory allowed their use without formalization. Peano's axiom 1 is taken care of by the presence of O as an individual constant.

In this axiomatization we can give certain objects *names* from the axiom system itself. O as a constant has a name; its successor, what we would call the number 1, has a name, O'; its successor has a name, O'', and so on. These named objects stand for the set of natural numbers, 0, 1, 2, 3, 4, and so forth, and form the constants for what we call the *standard model* for an interpretation of these axioms.

This model is a model also for stronger systems of axioms that

[5] Rafael M. Robinson, "An Essentially Undecidable Axiom System," *Proceedings of the International Congress of Mathematicians* (Cambridge, 1950), 1: 729–30.

formalize and include the fifth Peano axiom. Some things can be proved in the stronger systems that cannot be proved in the weaker Robinson arithmetic. But nothing provable in the weaker system or the stronger system is false in the model of the natural numbers I have chosen, that is, the standard model. For example, we can prove in the stronger system the general commutative law for addition, for any numbers x and y, $x + y = y + x$. This theorem is true in the standard model. But it cannot be proved from Robinson's arithmetic. The best that we can do from Robinson's system is to prove that given any specific (named) numbers, that is numbers in the standard model, say O'''''''' and O''''', then their sum is commutative.

If Gödel's theorem is true for a stronger axiomatization of arithmetic, then it is true of a weaker form of the axioms. For, if there is some true theorem (in the standard model) that cannot be proved in the stronger axiomatization, it therefore also cannot be proved in the weaker form. The converse, of course, is not true. We have an example in the form of the general commutative law, which is not provable in the weaker but provable in the stronger. But does not the Robinson system behave in regard to the stronger axiomatization as the stronger axiomatization behaves in regard to even stronger axiomatizations? Remember that Gödel's theorem states the essential incompleteness of arithmetic axioms. No matter how many additional axioms we add, that is, no matter how strong we make the system, there are still true statements in the standard model that cannot be proved from the axioms. So, for some theorem not provable in the standard axiomatization, there is an axiomatization in which it is provable, namely, an axiomatization that contains the theorem as an axiom.

The reason that the formal revisions of Peano's postulates occupy the place of standard axioms for arithmetic is that they *appear* to be adequate for a deduction of all true theorems about arithmetic. True but nonderivable theorems were discovered only after Gödel's theorem was made public, only after their possibility was made apparent. They would probably never have been discovered without Gödel's theorem or some theorem comparable to it, whereas it is *obvious* that Robinson's system is not complete, for the commutative law is a known property of the natural numbers. The increased strength of an axiom system only makes it more difficult for us to find true but unprovable statements, but as there is an arithmetic statement, for example, the commutative law, that is true in the standard model but unprovable in Robinson arithmetic, so, given any stronger axiomatization, there is a statement, indeed an infinite number of statements, that are true in the standard model of arithmetic but unprovable in this axiomatization.

For us, a focus on Robinson arithmetic as if it were the axiomatization for arithmetic, helps us see what a nonprovable but true theorem might look like. Such a focus on Robinson arithmetic is legitimate, however, only if it has the expressive powers to allow Gödel's Incompleteness theorem to be proved in terms of its symbolism. Fortunately this can be done, and it is one of the easiest ways to get at Gödel's theorem. We can prove that no (decidable) set of axioms in the notation of quantificational logic can entail all of the true statements of the standard model of arithmetic expressible in the language used for Robinson arithmetic. And this is sufficient to declare the essential incompleteness of arithmetic.

If we take the negation of the sentence that for all x and for all y, x + y = y + x, and affix it to the axioms of Robinson arithmetic, we would have a consistent system that would have models different from the standard model. In addition to the elements of the standard model (0, 1, 2, 3, etc.), which the original axioms of Robinson's arithmetic *guarantee*, there would be some elements that would not be commutative, that is, some elements satisfying our additional axiom. We would then have a nonstandard model of Robinson arithmetic. Both models make true the original Robinson axioms. When we look at standard axiomatizations of arithmetic that include axiom schemes for the Principle of Induction, we know that a similar situation exists. There are an infinite number of nonstandard models that can be generated by affixing the negation of a true but unprovable theorem to the original axioms.

We have created a nonstandard model of Robinson arithmetic

by adding elements to the standard model that do not satisfy the commutative law. The general situation for nonstandard models of arithmetic based upon standard axioms is similar to the situation observed for a nonstandard model of Robinson arithmetic. With the addition of elements to the standard model, we can violate some "for all" statement that is true in the standard model. We can add additional elements to the standard model with their appropriate structure and relationships and have a nonstandard model of arithmetic that still conforms to the original axioms, whether Robinson axioms or some stronger set of axioms. The axioms of Robinson arithmetic, or the standard axioms following all five postulates of Peano, allow us to generate the standard model. The perplexing problem is that from the axioms themselves we cannot be altogether sure what else we have got. An axiom system for arithmetic simply cannot capture only the properties of the standard model. This is insured by the Incompleteness Theorem.

If the situation of the natural numbers, in regard to their nonstandard models that we have observed, held throughout the theory of non-standard models, namely, that the nonstandard models of an axiomatic theory rest on a standard model of equal or smaller cardinal number, that is, on a more intuitive and more readily available familiar standard model, then we might feel that we had not lost much in our discovery of the limitations of the axiomatic method. For although the axiomatization might not give us all the properties of the more complex and difficult nonstandard models, it could give us most of the properties of the standard one. But what if there were a nonstandard model of arithmetic that had noticeably fewer elements than the standard one—say, a finite number of elements. (There exists no such model. We can prove that any model of arithmetic must contain an infinite number of elements.) We should then have to consider that all of the properties and relationships expressed *by the axiomatic system* for the standard model were included also within the finite model.

There is an almost comparable situation in regard to set theory.

There are nonstandard models that have a smaller cardinal number of elements than the standard model. Within set theory we can form subsets of any given set. Given the set of natural numbers, that is, the constants in the standard model of arithmetic, we can form subsets of this set, for example, the finite set {3, 5. 7} or the infinite set of all even numbers. The set of all subsets of the natural numbers has a cardinal number larger than the number of objects in the set itself. This is a result of a famous proof by Cantor. There is no one-to-one correspondence between the set of all subsets of the natural numbers and the natural numbers themselves. The set of subsets of the natural numbers is uncountably infinite, whereas the set of natural numbers is countably infinite. Axiomatizations of set theory are designed to capture the properties of sets of sets like our set of all subsets of the natural numbers, but without contradiction. The standard model of set theory, the one that axiomatization was designed to describe, has an uncountable number of elements (sets). For if set theory is adequate, as most mathematicians believe, to present all known mathematics, then it must be capable of characterizing mathematical systems, the real numbers, for example, that contain an uncountably infinite number of elements.

A theorem by Skolem-Löwenheim (1915, 1919) proves that any (first order) axiomatic theory that has a model has a countable one. Set theory has a model, namely, an uncountable one, hence it must also have a countable one. Axiomatizations of the real numbers have a standard model, an uncountable one, hence they also have a countable one. What this means is that all the properties, that is, all the mathematical structures that can be shown (deduced) as theorems from the axiomatic system of set theory or the axiomatic system of the real numbers, hold in some countable model. This is again to confirm, by a different method, that no axiomatic system can give us *all* the properties of an uncountable number of sets in their relationships. For whatever these properties be, at least as captured by an axiomatic system, they can be obtained in a countable set of objects.

The Skolem-Löwenheim theorem is not a contradiction, nor

even a true paradox, as some have claimed. It does not say that an uncountable number of elements can be made countable, nor even that the true relationships among an uncountable number of elements can be structured exactly in terms of a countable number. It does point out that the axiomatic method, any axiomatic system, can represent only some of the statements true of uncountable sets, and that these statements can be expressed in terms of a restructured model of a countable number of elements. Both the Skolem-Löwenheim theorem and Gödel's Incompleteness theorem demonstrate the possibility of a multiplicity of nonstandard models.

Mathematical Platonism and Christian Theology

Does the existence of nonstandard models shed light on the ancient question whether mathematical entities exist in their own right independently of the creative activities of man. Do the results of Gödel, Skolem-Löwenheim and others tip the balance toward an understanding of the discovered nature of mathematics or do they confirm its created nature? The discovery that the axiomatic method has implicit limitations, as well as the recognition that certain models stand out with a clarity that can not be represented by the axiomatic method, might well tend to confirm a platonic view of mathematics. This is certainly the case for the position of Gödel himself, who accepts a kind of platonic realism as the best philosophical orientation toward mathematics.

> Classes and concepts may . . . be conceived as real objects . . . existing independently of our definitions and constructions. . . . It seems to me that the assumption of such objects is quite as legitimate as the assumption of physical bodies and there is quite as much reason to believe in their existence. They are in the same sense necessary to obtain a satisfactory theory of mathematics as physical bodies are necessary to obtain a satisfactory theory of our sense perception.[6]

[6] Kurt Gödel, "Russell's Mathematical Logic," *The Philosophy of Bertrand Russell*, ed. Paul Schillp (New York: Tudor, 1944), p. 137.

Gödel is asserting that there are kinds of real objects that form the subject matter of mathematics and that this assumption that they are real and independent of mathematicians' creation most nearly allows us to understand the significance of mathematics.

Although Gödel may represent the majority opinion of working mathematicians, he probably does not represent the majority opinion of those who have considered the philosophical implications of the existence of nonstandard models. Abraham Robinson, for example, the rediscoverer of infinitesimals by means of nonstandard models, does not believe that infinitesimals exist. In fact, he does not believe that any *infinite* models, standard or nonstandard, exist. His basic position is that "infinite totalities do not exist in any sense of the word."[7] Yet he affirms, "Nevertheless, we should continue the business of Mathematics 'as usual,' i.e., we should act *as if* infinite totalities really existed."[8] The discovery of nonstandard models stands as evidence to Robinson that platonic entities do *not* exist. The complementary results by Gödel and Cohen that the continuum hypothesis and its negation are compatible with all known "natural assumptions regarding the universe of sets" suggests to Robinson that the notion of the entire universe of sets is meaningless. Lynn Arthur Steen, in an excellent expository article on "New Models of the Real Number Line," has observed the irony that the "re-creator of infinitesimals does not believe they really exist, whereas Gödel, the prophet of undecidability, believes in a Platonic universe in which the properties of mathematical objects are visible for those who have eyes to see."[9]

One can understand the respective positions of Gödel and Robinson and see how aspects of contemporary mathematics

[7] Abraham Robinson, "Formalism 64," *Logic, Methodology and Philosophy of Science ; Proceedings of the 1964 International Congress,* ed. Yehoshua Bar-Hillel (Amsterdam: North-Holland Publishing Company, 1965), p. 230.

[8] *Ibid.*

[9] Lynn Arthur Steen, "New Models of the Real Number Line," *Scientific American* 225, no. 2 (August 1971): 99.

provide evidence both for and against a platonic viewpoint concerning mathematics. It seems quite safe to say that although these new results are quite unsettling for any philosophy of mathematics, and hence for philosophy proper, the evidence as presently seen does not allow mathematicians or philosophers to come to any agreement concerning the nature of mathematical existence. It may be quite some time before the situation begins to clear up, and what clarity is obtained will be due both to new mathematical results and further interpretations of present results.

For Christian theology, however, these new mathematical developments may have something quite immediate to say. This is not because they confirm or deny a platonic or nonplatonic position in mathematics, but because they may have an effect on an already assumed platonic position concerning mathematics. Christian theology has tended to view mathematical relationships in a platonic fashion, if for no other reason than the assumption that God knows and understands mathematical relationships, thereby giving them some kind of existence independent of man's creation.

I have examined how the moves toward a more "objective" understanding of mathematics conditioned the philosophies of Husserl, Whitehead, and Wittgenstein and thereby affected theology. My analysis assumed a previous use of an objective and platonically understood mathematics within Christian theology, and it was this previous use that was modified by the new developments. I can now claim that contemporary mathematics ought to affect assumptions in contemporary Christian theology concerning the platonic nature of mathematics. Process theology is particularly vulnerable here, for in following Whitehead, it assumes the existence of ideal entities (eternal objects) of which mathematics is a part.

Revisions of Process Theology [10]

If we assume, or believe, that God exists, and further assume that He has attributes appropriate to Him under a Christian

[10] See Granville C. Henry, Jr., "Nonstandard Mathematics and a Doctrine of God," *Process Studies* 3, no. 1 (Spring 1973).

perspective, namely, for example, that he knows the *possibilities* for existence, we can view mathematical potentials in some platonic form as part of His knowledge. We cannot, however, move in an opposite direction from contemporary developments in mathematics to the platonic reality of mathematical relationships, or further, to the fact that they insure a Christian God. The Christian God is not known in this manner.

In assuming that mathematical relationships have a kind of platonic reality at least in terms of being potentials for matters of fact as known by God, we recognize that these relationships may be structures of that which is known—or part of the structures of knowing itself. The structures of knowing, at least the means by which one can know mathematics, have traditionally been known as logic. It is a well-known fact that these structures have been objectified and made epistemological objects whose nature can be examined mathematically as structures of the known. Gödel's theorem points out that the structures of knowing can not all be formalized mathematically.

The new developments in mathematics of the last few decades seem to me to allow a better understanding of what it might mean for God to have the freedom *to change* the totality of potentials—both in terms of the structures of knowing within human consciousness and in terms of the objects known. This would mean that man's consciousness, as well as other structures of the world, could evolve not only in ways hitherto unknown, but in ways that might be even a surprise to God—a surprise in the sense that the potential mathematical structural relationships that could characterize (in part) such consciousness might not even *be* at present. My viewpoint here is a departure from a strictly Whiteheadian process theology that could understand God's surprise at the way Beethoven's Fifth Symphony turned out, but in this thought it would be a surprise that it turned out *this* way and not *that* way, or some other way, all ways being known as strict potentials. There may be no surprise to God at new potentials added, however, for God may create and add them Himself. But we should not limit new potentials solely to God; they may come also from God's interaction with the world or from the world itself, that is, by creative power given to the world by God.

Almost all traditional and contemporary theologies that maintain a platonic reality for mathematical potentials insist both that the mathematical structures do not change and that they are complete in their totality as understood or envisioned by God. This doctrine is found in Augustine as well as in contemporary Process Theology. God, though changing in His actual consequent nature in process theology, does not change in His essential nature, that aspect of Him called the primordial nature. The eternal objects that constitute the primordial nature are fixed; they are pure potentials and as such have a rigid logical structure. God may establish possibilities for actual entities by selective envisionment of, or ordering of, the realm of eternal objects, and in this role He acts as *destiny* or *providence* for actual entities. From the perspective of the actual entity, there are multiple routes to the future in terms of different potentials for actualization, but each of these routes, as in the completion of Beethoven's symphony, is a choice of *this* route or *that* route, each of which is known to God. God is the ground of an individual's possibility in traditional process theology. He provides the options. But He may not create new pure possibilities (i.e., eternal objects) or destroy old ones. This is a fixed aspect of His own nature.

I would like to maintain the emphasis that "platonic" mathematical structures do not change, as affirmed by Whitehead and Augustine, but relax the requirement that no new potentials or structures be added to the realm of eternal objects. This relaxation is based on the simple observation that it has been primarily the axiomatic method that has given mathematicians and philosophers the authority for stabilizing the mathematical realm, for claiming it to be complete as related logically to a few unquestionable assumptions. What we have learned about mathematics since the advent of Whitehead's philosophy is that the axiomatic method can not adequately characterize the nature of mathematical structures that are presently known. It is true that we may know *some aspects* of these structures apart from the axiomatic method. This is essential. But we still know the unity of mathematics, or the unity of mathematical systems, primarily through axiomatic investigation. It may be that what unity we know, we know through axiomatic systems, but that this unity is not complete.

The claim that individual mathematical structures are unchanging but that new ones may be formed, new potentials added to the realm of eternal objects, entails some kind of evolution in the realm of eternal objects itself—at least it does so within the remainder of Whiteheadian assumptions. Under the principle that actuality determines (at least) potentiality, I would maintain that all actual relationships in the past of the cosmos are now potential. The realm of eternal objects is comprised at least of those relationships that were (or are) actual (of course, understood now as potential). In addition, the realm of eternal objects is comprised of all known potential relationships and especially that vast welter of mathematical relationships created by the imagination and consciousness of man. For as known by man, these relationships do have a tie to the actual world, even though in their objective status they do not now characterize, or may have never characterized, any particular complex of events. I am sure that the realm of potentials, that is, eternal objects, is greatly enlarged by God's knowledge of potentials. He knows (I believe) the mathematical structures that we could know but now in fact do not know. In addition, I think His presence and activity is the primary source of structured relationships in the realm of eternal objects and that those relationships coming from the world, if any, probably constitute only a small portion of the total. What am I claiming? That in terms of our knowledge of structured potentials, there is no reason to assume that new relationships may not be added. Those that are present, however, are fixed and eternal.

We may get some insight into the *possibility* of a changing realm of eternal objects by referring to recent statements made by mathematicians as they consider the new foundational developments. At the International Congress for Logic, Methodology and Philosophy of Science held in Jerusalem in 1964, Abraham Robinson made the statement:

> As far as I know, only a small minority of mathematicians, even of those with platonist views, accept the idea that there may be mathematical facts which are *true* but unknowable.[11]

In a 1971 expository article on "New Models of the Real-Number Line," Lynn Arthur Steen comments:

> It seems unlikely, however, that within the next few generations mathematicians will be able to agree on whether every mathematical statement that is true is also knowable.[12]

Are there mathematical structures that are true but unknowable? This is, indeed, a new question for the foundations of mathematics. How could any *mathematical* structure be true but unknowable? We can understand Robinson's incredulity and Steen's more cautious skepticism about the existence of such structures, for traditional Western mathematics has operated in almost the opposite direction. The truth of a mathematical relationship, theorem, or claim has been primarily a function of its *knowability*. We know it as true because it is known in a certain way—through deduction or insight. Indeed, in my analysis of the relationship of mathematics to theology and philosophy, it is the changing qualities and ways of knowing mathematical structures that have influenced the ways of knowing theological objectivities. I have found this to be true from the Pythagoreans to the latest phenomenological analysis. And the truth claims for theological objectivities are often modeled after similar truth claims for mathematical ones, each of which is based on ways of knowing.

The reason why Robinson and Steen raise the question can be seen in the developments, or ones like them, that I have outlined in the first part of this chapter. If we *know* by mathematical proof

[11] Robinson, p. 232.
[12] Steen, p. 99.

that there are true statements in the standard model of arithmetic that cannot be deduced from any given axiom set, how can we be assured that our ways of knowing apart from axiomatic deduction are comprehensive? If we, by an axiomatic system, cannot uniquely determine a model, how do we know that there are not models that do in fact satisfy the axioms but that cannot be known at all (ever) by mathematicians? At the present state of knowledge in the foundations of mathematics, we cannot answer these questions definitively.

I share Steen's and Robinson's skepticism about the existence of platonic mathematical structures that are true but unknowable. There is something presumptuous, I think, about affirming the existence of a platonic mathematical form that cannot be known —either within a Platonic perspective or outside of it. In principle, one could never have any evidence of the form's positive existence. I also find somewhat presumptuous the affirmation that there is a platonic realm of mathematical structures, eternally fixed in their relationship to each other, changing perhaps in their *relationship* to the world but never growing or diminishing in totality. The evidence historically, certainly in terms of what we *know,* is almost exclusively of a changing domain of mathematical structures, a domain that changes primarily by addition to itself. Of course, it may be claimed that this is simply a growth of our knowledge, and I would certainly acknowledge the fact of our increased ability to perceive mathematical relationships. But this does not mean that the mathematical potential relationships for matters of fact are not themselves being added to in order to allow more complexity.

If one conceives and affirms any platonically understood mathematical structures, it seems to me far less presumptuous to understand them as a loosely knit multiplicity that is incapable of unification axiomatically and to which new relationships may be added. The addition of any new relationship would, of course, be compatible with some structures and incompatible with others. But this is the case with the presently understood Whiteheadian eternal objects. Any new structure would immediately have an cxact relationship with all other given structures and would, when added (from whatever source), be indistinguishable in kind from all other mathematical eternal objects.

What motivation could we, as philosophers or theologians, have to claim that God might add potentials, might create them or choose them to be a part of the available future of the world? Why not assume that God knows them all, whatever they be, and understand our restrictions found in terms of the restrictions of the axiomatic method to be the restrictions of our being somehow finite? This may be ultimately, as it has been in the past, the best way for Christian theology to go. But in contemporary process theology there is a tension that seeks reconciliation, a tension that has produced a division between those who follow Whitehead strictly on his doctrine of eternal objects and those who follow a modification of his position as espoused by Hartshorne. I think that a new position on eternal objects, patterned after what we know about the new mathematics, may not only effect a reconciliation of their positions, but capture an emphasis that they both insist is necessary.

Whitehead, as I have indicated in an earlier chapter, did model his understanding of eternal objects after his understanding of mathematical existence. Eternal objects, therefore, according to Whitehead, are exact, discrete, individual, objective, and existing in themselves, apart from any relationship to particular actual entities. Whitehead's God, though not fully developed in *Process and Reality,* is described characteristically as a nontemporal actual entity whose primordial nature—the realm of eternal objects—is given primacy over His consequent nature. For Hartshorne, however, who emphasizes that the concrete contains the abstract, the temporal includes the atemporal; eternal objects are given less emphasis than actual entities. It is the becoming of actual entities that determines their being, and especially that being which is characterized by (mathematical) eternal objects. Consequently Hartshorne's God is much more temporal than Whitehead's God; God's consequent nature is understood to embody concretely His primordial nature as abstract essence.

The issue here between the two philosophers is one, I think, primarily of emphasis. In writing *Process and Reality*, Whitehead was so preoccupied with establishing the nature of actual entities that he gave eternal objects, their structure and nature, only cursory attention. But the structure that he gave them has allowed, with subsequent philosophical development, a challenge to the very historical character of reality that he so painstakingly sought to present in his concept of actual entities.

Consider a realm of eternal objects that contains every possible potential and aspect of potential that any actual entity can have. How is it possible to differentiate between an actual entity and that set of eternal objects which characterizes it? Do we require an additional property or quality of "existence" to make the distinction? In recent literature it has been noticed, and with considerable justification, that there is a symmetry in Whitehead's thought between eternal objects and actual entities.[13] One may shift the primacy to eternal objects away from actual entities, and still have much of process thought intact, although this is clearly not what Whitehead intended. In order to maintain clearly the historical and causal, Hartshorne has taken the direction in Whitehead's thought that emphasizes actual entities *over* eternal objects and forged a cogent, logical, and apparently adequate philosophical system out of this emphasis.

For the person, however, who comes to Whitehead's thought from mathematics, Whitehead's description of the nature of mathematical eternal objects can appear quite precise. These objects do, in fact, seem to have the independence from actual existence that Whitehead specified.

How can one differentiate between an actual entity and the eternal objects that characterize it? In process thought, as I have emphasized perhaps all too often, there is a claim that one knows the difference in terms of an experiential causal prehension. In no way seeking to deny this, nor reduce the emphasis on experiential feelings, I can, I think, make some claims in this regard on

---

[13] See Justus Buchler, "On a Strain of Arbitrariness in Whitehead's System," *The Journal of Philosophy* 66, no. 19 (Oct. 2, 1969): 589–601.

the basis of the mathematical analysis in this chapter. One can say, for example, that the mathematical characteristics of an actual entity cannot be described completely by known mathematical means. I am maintaining that even for the mathematical characteristics of an actual entity, a prehension of this actual entity by another concrescent one may contain more of actual mathematical knowledge—though in its own assimilation unconscious for its own being—than it is possible to know *ever* by formal mathematical means. We know the exact logical properties of infinite totalities by axiomatic means. We know, as we could never know otherwise, the properties of all right triangles, for example, by deductive axiomatic means. Although we can know properties of infinite sets by deduction, we have seen that we can not know all the properties and relations of infinite sets of things by axiomatic means. Do we run into this kind of problem when we examine an individual actual entity? Do we run into an analysis of an infinitude that cannot be actually described by axiomatic mathematical means—even in regard to mathematical properties?

If we can answer Yes to these questions, then we may see our way clear to understand prehension to include more than can be known axiomatically, that is, to include an infinitude of aspects that are impossible to characterize logically. For if we limit prehension to include only that (mathematical) information that can be characterized axiomatically, we then force the actual entity prehending to generate its own noncharacterizable infinitude without reference to its past—that is, provided that we do answer Yes to the question.

In order to see whether an individual actual entity may itself involve the kinds of infinitude that cannot be characterized axiomatically, let me point out first that science itself has not succeeded in such an axiomatic analysis. If we look at any object, say, a glass in the hand, and ask what science has to say about it, we cannot respond with an axiomatic system that will describe all of its properties and relations. We can describe its spatial characteristics in terms of an axiomatized space, or its kinematic properties in terms of an axiomatized mechanics, or its statistical characteristics in terms of an axiomatized probability. And we could go on and on in terms of this description, showing that whatever scientific characteristics were applicable could themselves, in most cases, be found part of some axiomatic theory. What we get is a multiplicity of theories used to correlate information that we have, and never any one theory that claims to be completely adequate.

Let us shift the examination and consider making *all* possible mathematical statements about some object. And this time let us consider as the subject of examination a true actual entity (the glass above was not a true Whiteheadian actual entity), say, the event that constitutes some person's immediate past experience, that is, who he was (in totality) in his immediate past. If we try to make all possible scientific mathematical statements about him, we would have to include, for example, his position in time-space, the activities of the molecules of his brain, the theoretical (mathematical and scientific) considerations of evolution that have affected him, the relationship of him as event to all interstellar activity, even the potentialities that he had as an event, i.e., that vast multiplicity of if-then statements which characterized his actual possibilities. We can see immediately how limited we are in ability actually to form these statements, even if we were to assume that the whole force of present scientific endeavor is focused on this one event. But let us try to consider in abstract that *all* such true statements have been made about this event, and that these statements have been reduced to some recognizable logical-mathematical form. For further simplicity let us say that they have been reduced to some equivalent (as far as possible) expression in the first-order predicate calculus. And now to the question that we want to ask. Can this multiplicity of statements be put in axiomatic form? That is, is there a set of them so that for any given sentence we can tell whether it is an axiom or not and tell that the other sentences all follow logically from this set of axioms?

We should not have any problem with inconsistency among our statements, for we have, after all, made them true about some actual event. We do have a model. To have a logical model we would have to decide on some universe of discourse, that is, some logical domain in which all the statements would have interpretation in the normal manner. In our case, the establishment of such a domain would be a solid metaphysical task. But let us assume that we have a logical model, and ask the question again about our now (assumed) consistent set of sentences. Are they axiomatic?

Notice the kinds of conditions that would prohibit us from having an axiomatic system. If our sentences involved the full properties of any incomplete theory, say arithmetic, we could not order them (in totality) axiomatically. If our sentences involved (in completeness) any uncountable domain, for example, that of the continuum itself, it would force us, in order to get *all* true sentences about the event, to have an uncountable domain for the sentences—which in turn would mean that no axiomatic system would be adequate to derive all sentences. The kinds of sentences that could easily constitute a sufficient number to prevent complete axiomatization would be, for example, conditionals, those which state that if certain conditions hold then certain events will follow. These can easily be seen to be infinite, provided again that we agree to get *all* such sentences, for we could specify what physical forces would change the entities' position. And the possibilities for physical spatial change are infinite, even over a finite space and, depending upon our perspective, are uncountably infinite.

I am pointing out here, what Leibniz knew so well, that to characterize any individual substance or entity *in totality*, we must mirror, as it were, the whole universe in the entity. And certainly this is true in Whiteheadian process philosophy and theology, for any actual entity is conceived as related intimately to its whole past, which includes the whole past of the universe, and related to the complete future of the universe through its intention and that of God. To completely describe any specific entity, therefore, would seem to require so much information as to prohibit axiomatization.

It is obvious, I think, that I have not made here a detailed metaphysical and logical analysis that would show conclusively that the complete description of any entity in terms of its mathematical aspects could not be axiomatized. Such an analysis would necessarily be metaphysical and therefore would not be logically conclusive—that is, one could challenge the analysis from another metaphysical perspective. I am not sure whether it would be proper, or indeed helpful, to make a *responsible* metaphysical analysis of this problem, for such an analysis might ultimately be so obscure and so technically detailed as to cloud the theological advantages of relaxing the restrictions on the rigidity of the eternal objects.

If, as in my argument, there is no axiomatic possibility of characterizing even the mathematical characteristics of a complex actual entity and, of course, no possibility of axiomatically characterizing all mathematical eternal objects—I have proved the latter—then I have relaxed the restriction that only those "presently existing" eternal objects may characterize the future of the entity. There may be genuinely unknown potentials that may draw the entity to some future event. In what sense are these unknown? Do they exist as eternal objects and are they simply unknown or unknowable to us? This could be the case, and in most analysis would be the case. I am also allowing, and proposing for general consideration, that these unknown structures or relationships may not exist as Whiteheadian eternal objects but may *come to be* as potentials, that is, eternal objects through the activity of God or through His gift of creativity to the world itself. Whitehead maintains that eternal objects are structured for actual entities by God's envisionment. I am extending this and saying that eternal objects may themselves actually come to be by God's action.

In the sense that logical structure itself seems to prohibit the claim that any event can be characterized (totally) by existent and known logical structures, we can then see one way in which any event of a complex sort must be *more than* any set of (presently available) eternal objects. Any complex event may not only be structured in terms of available eternal objects, it may draw, from the future as given by God, some new eternal object for the concrescence of its own being, or it may by virtue of what it is and becomes, and by its own activity, add to the domain of eternal objects some new group of them. Here I am trying to maintain the emphasis of Hartshorne, and indeed of Whitehead as I interpret him, that actuality ontologically precedes potentiality; that of the two—actual entities and eternal objects—precedence must go to actual entities.

As I have mentioned, this theory entails ascribing an evolutionary aspect to the realm of eternal objects. God's freedom extends to His influence not only on actualities but also on the limitation of that which is possible, not just in the sense of choosing those possibilities which may be most relevant in a particular set, but in creating the possibilities themselves. The realm of eternal objects grows as history progresses. Things in their true possibility literally become more complex. Actual mathematical structure evolves ontologically. Not only can God point out possibilities that we do not know of, but He can create them. Thus, in a genuinely new sense, at least in process theology, the future is His.

This revision of process theology that I am proposing presents, at least to me, two attractive answers to two fundamental problems that have recurred throughout this study, namely, the place of metaphysics and the question of the unity of Logos.

The Place of Metaphysics and the Question of the Unity of Logos

In chapter 5, I tried to point out the similarity of nature and function between overarching metaphysical principles and mathematical structures, and stated that most metaphysical principles can be reduced to or translated into essentially mathematical ones. This seems to me to entail that there are no necessary metaphysical principles, that is, because of the multiplicity of mathematical and metaphysical structures, we must ultimately affirm the *relativity* of metaphysics. Such a position is commensurate with the historical emphasis of the Christian faith. One chooses metaphysical positions in terms of adequacy. A Christian metaphysics is one that is more adequate to Christian experience and

Christian historical communal belief than another. There may be, however, an altogether true metaphysics as mathematical structure that is at present unknown, or at least unknown as true. It may be existent as potential structure and we have not yet discovered it. We may have discovered it and not found its applicability. Non-Euclidean geometries, for example, thought of as curiosities for many decades, now describe some of the most universal aspects of relativity theory. We have not found physical interpretations yet of nonstandard models, but they could be, perhaps, as powerfully used in some scientific or philosophical field as have the non-Euclidean geometric models. The irony may be, and indeed it would be an irony appropriate to God, that the true metaphysics is a (mathematical) structure *yet to be evolved*. Metaphysical truth may come from the hands of God *in the future*.

This new, true, and future metaphysics, even though perhaps recognized as *the answer*, need not be adequate to describe all aspects of all things. Indeed, if our presently understood epistemological restrictions on precise mathematical structure continue to hold, it cannot be a complete description. I have discussed in this chapter our inability to characterize completely any one actual entity by axiomatic method. And we know of no other procedure or method that is adequate. Surely, then, epistemological restrictions that apply to the knowledge of an actual entity also apply to the cosmos as a whole. What I am saying is that the cosmos has no *essence*, where by *essence* I mean a precise, rational—and mathematical—description that is adequate to characterize *all* aspects of it. Or, if it does have an essence in this sense, not only are we presently ignorant of it, but, in fact, we can never know it according to present restrictions.

How firmly, however, should we hold to present epistemological restrictions in the foundations of mathematics? The answer is, I think, a rule of safety. Anyone who attempts to relax the restrictions must state precisely and exactly what he means. And this, of course, would be *very* difficult. For it is the precision of concept that has inexorably led to the restrictions. The two go clearly hand in hand. As one says exactly and with mathematical precision what he means, the restrictions are necessarily there. One may perceive an essence of the cosmos in a holistic "right-lobe" vision. Many have claimed to do so. But such a vision is not amenable to precise, mathematical, "left-lobe" expression. Indeed, when so expressed, the cosmic essence does not seem to exist. But might there not emerge in the future some new mathematical structure, according to the new doctrine about eternal objects, a structure that relates to procedures of knowing, a structure that would relax restrictions, a structure that could allow us to know what we meant by a complete essence or a true and complete metaphysics? This could, of course, happen. We have no assurance of it. And we have *absolutely no way* of saying what such a mathematical structure would be. In looking over mathematical concepts whose change would affect the epistemological restrictions, one is struck by the sensitive position of recursive functions or the idea of mechanical procedures. These ideas have their initial basis in intuition but have been characterized, apparently completely, by the brilliant work of Gödel, Church, and Turing, and are used effectively to present the limitation theorems. Any mathematician reading these lines will be especially appreciative of the difficulty of saying what some *new* and now *unknown* type of mechanical procedure would be—without in fact declaring what it is and thereby specifying it. And yet, according to the position of the evolution of eternal objects as outlined above, it is possible to conceive that God could, by adding appropriate mathematical structures, unify the cosmos as essence, an essence that would be not only exact but complete. At that time, one could approach the Christian religion, and the Christian God, primarily through *reason*. Perhaps this would be part of the "great consummation," a time, or out of time, when faith and reason are unified. But that time, if ever, is not yet our time. Our time, and the historicity of the Christian religion, require us to accept the epistemological restrictions imposed by contemporary mathematics, to recognize that there is no precise and complete essence to the cosmos—or at least none that can be presently known.

In chapter 1, I attempted to develop a concept of Logos, compatible with contemporary mathematics, that represented possibilities of obedience. I began the investigation with the unity of the person Jesus, as characterized by the substantial unity of the events in his life, described what a mathematical characterization of these events would be like, and then described how, understood as possibilities (that were in fact actualized), these characterizations could be associated mathematically with all other possibilities having to do with obedience past and future, and thus would form, at least as modeled on mathematical structure, the Logos of God. Jesus as the Logos become flesh did not possess as knowledge the abstract relationships of Logos but *was* (and *is*) the Word as action, that is as fulfillment of God's standard of obedience (love, self-giving, etc.). In terms of the subsequent development of the book, my inability to characterize the *unity* of Logos was not an accident, but now seems a necessity in the light of the epistemological restrictions that are imposed on an individual actual entity as well as the cosmos. If we accept that there is no essence to the cosmos and no knowable essence of God, and here I remind the reader of the characteristics of the word *essence* used here—that of strict mathematical clarity and of complete mathematical description—then neither can Logos have an essence. Logos is of such complexity that it is impossible to describe it fully or adequately. And, of course, one cannot approach it significantly through reason alone.

Understanding the unity of God as well as understanding the unity of Logos is dependent upon a religious tradition. It should be clear by now that my position is one of radical skepticism concerning the abilities of natural (mathematical) reason to establish God's existence, His unity, or His action in Christ. But one can know, I fully believe, God's unity and objectivity in terms of His causal efficacy in a manner that I have attempted to outline in chapter 5.[14] Causal experiences, as interpreted within the Christian tradition, indicate the One Who has acted.

What both causal experiences and the tradition tell us is that

[14] See section "Metaphysics and a Theological Objectification of God," chap. 5.

the One Who acts also knows; the One Who creates also under-stands His creation. This is a religious presupposition attendant on the Jewish and Christian tradition, which claims that God knows all knowable things. In particular, we assumed earlier, God knows all mathematics.

The unity of mathematical structures, and hence the unity of possibilities, can be understood within the religious tradition to be effected because of the *substantial* unity of God. Mathematical structures are unified because God views them or envisions them. The unity of Logos is established by God, Who chooses the possibilities of obedience according to His standards. I have main-tained in chapter 1 that Logos also has a *substantial* unity in Jesus Christ. Any adequate doctrine of Logos similar to the one I have proposed must consider the metaphysical structures of such unity. I have not done so in this book.

But the point here is to indicate an advantage that the revision of process theology, which allows an addition to the realm of eternal objects, might have for an understanding of the unity of Logos. If we understand that new, mathematical, eternal objects may be added by God to the existing realm, we must allow the possibility of the addition of *new* relationships to Logos, relation-ships that may be added by God and possibly by the church fellowship in its relationship to Christ. This would not affect the validity of the existent, eternal structures of Logos "begotten of the Father before all ages," but would add dimensions to the eschatological consummation undreamed of now and perhaps not even now existing as possibilities. In the same manner that I indicated for the possible, coming, true metaphysics, the new mathematical structures could be of a sort that would allow for the *essential* unification of Logos.

In summary, contemporary discoveries in mathematics place necessary restrictions on our abilities to characterize completely the essence of an actual entity, of the cosmos, of God, or of Logos by rational mathematical means. These limitations on mathematical knowledge, imposed by the preciseness of mathematics itself, con-firm a traditional posture in the Christian religion concerning the priority of "faith" as the vehicle of appropriate religious knowledge, which may then, and perhaps only then, be buttressed by the full powers of reason. They further confirm an ontological emphasis within process theology on actual entities as contrasted with eternal objects, on "existence" as contrasted with "essence." I find this to be a normative and very healthy perspective for the Church.

But reason seems to have the seeds of its own completion. Man's thrust toward understanding is God-given and God-commanded. The enterprise of science and the discipline of metaphysics are both future-oriented toward a comprehensive grasp of the structures of the cosmos. Christ Jesus as Logos has promised through church and Scripture to find completion in all things—even the rational. The relaxation of the rigid restrictions within process theology on the domain of eternal objects, and an allowing of an addition of new ones, provide a means for an understanding of the possibility of the consummation of *reason* in the Christian faith, a consummation brought about by the activity of God in His relationship to the world.

In the first part of this chapter, I indicated the nature of contemporary developments in mathematics that I thought would have an effect on contemporary and future theology. In the second part I attempted to show how these developments could affect only one of a number of theological options, namely, process theology. Process theology is, of course, not the only contemporary theology that is susceptible to influence by these developments. Any theology that has developed under an assumption of the platonic nature of mathematical relationships, and assumed them to be unified under some mathematical, logical, or intuitional ground, is sensitive to modification. I challenge those readers who may have an allegiance to philosophical and theological beliefs other than those espoused in process theology to work out what might be the consequences to their theology if the traditional understanding that mathematical structures are complete, unified, and eternal in nature were relaxed.

In closing, I want to point out again the aesthetic and utilitarian function of mathematics for Christian existence. Mathematics is not necessary for salvation—of course. Neither is painting, sculpture, music, or literature. But each of these may indicate truly meaningful aspects of God's world and the Christian Gospel, and can give pleasure and enjoyment. On a recent Sunday during the season of Pentecost, one of the members of our parish uttered the following prayer during the time for thanksgiving: "Thank you for the simple joys of mathematics." He is a physicist for whom mathematics is a professional tool. But it is also an aesthetic medium, and a reason for giving thanks.

The ultilitarian function of mathematics can be seen primarily in the applications of science. I began this book with a mathematical example from population studies. It is in these and similar studies, where mathematics is now applicable to the social sciences, that I see a use of mathematics most relevant for contemporary Christian *action*. Christians must know the variety of mathematical characterizations of urban growth and decline. They must understand the general patterns and limits to population, industrial, and pollution growth, and the consequences of natural resource depletion. These are forces that appear to be having a most powerful effect on the future of man. They are not mechanistically determined, however, and can be modified by individual and collective Christian action.

In addition to the aesthetic and utilitarian uses of mathematics, there are theological and metaphysical ones. I have maintained that mathematics has been a traditional adjunct to Christian theology. It can be an important aid to future theology, especially as it contributes to a legitimate synthesis of science and religion, aids in a reconciliation of the faith-reason problem, and enhances the aesthetic and utilitarian function, through this theological use, that mathematics itself serves.

Bibliography

Albright, W. F. "Some Canaanite Phoenician Sources of Hebrew Wisdom," in *Wisdom in Israel and in the Ancient Near East.* Edited by M. Noth and D. W. Thomas. Leiden: E. J. Brill, 1960.

Allman, G. J. *Greek Geometry from Thales to Euclid.* Dublin: Dublin University Press, 1889.

Altizer, T. J. J. *The Gospel of Christian Atheism.* Philadelphia: Westminster, 1966.

———— and Hamilton, William. *Radical Theology and the Death of God.* Indianapolis, Ind.: Bobbs-Merrill, 1966.

Anton, J. P. *Aristotle's Theory of Contrariety.* New York: Humanities Press, 1957.

Apostle, H. G., trans. *Aristotle's Metaphysics.* Bloomington, Ind.: Indiana University Press, 1966.

————. *Aristotle's Philosophy of Mathematics.* Chicago: The University of Chicago Press, 1952.

Aquinas, Thomas. *On the Truth of the Catholic Faith: Summa Contra Gentiles.* Translated by A. C. Pegis. 3 vols. Garden City, N.Y.: Image Books, 1957.

Ashley Montagu, M. F., ed. *Studies and Essays in the History of Science and Learning in Honor of George Sarton.* New York: Shuman, 1946.

Augustine, Saint. *The City of God.* Translated by George Wilson. New York: Modern Library, 1950.

Ayer, A. J. *Language, Truth and Logic.* New York: Dover, n.d.

Baillie, John. *The Idea of Revelation in Recent Thought.* New York: Columbia University Press, 1956.

————. *Natural Science and the Spiritual Life.* London: Oxford University Press, 1951.

Barbour, Ian G. *Issues in Science and Religion.* Englewood Cliffs, N.J.: Prentice-Hall, 1966.

————, ed. *Science and Religion: New Perspectives on the Dialogue.* New York: Harper & Row, 1968.

Bar-Hillel, Y., ed. *Logic, Methodology and Philosophy of Science: Proceedings of the 1964 International Congress.* Amsterdam: North-Holland, 1965.

————, Posnanski, E. I. J., Rabin, M. O., and Robinson, A., eds. *Essays on the Foundations of Mathematics, Dedicated to A. A. Fraenkel.* Jerusalem: The Magnes Press, 1961.

Bartsch, H. W., ed. *Kerygma and Myth: A Theolog'cal Debate.* Translated by R. H. Fuller. London: S. P. C. K., 1953.

Bell, E. T. *Men of Mathematics.* New York: Simon & Schuster, Inc., 1937.

Benacerraf, Paul and Putnam, Hilary, eds. *Philosophy of Mathematics: Selected Readings.* Englewood Cliffs, N.J.: Prentice-Hall, 1964.

Bernays, Paul and Fraenkel, A. A. *Axiomatic Set Theory.* Amsterdam: North-Holland, 1968.

Beth, E. W. *The Foundations of Mathematics.* New York: Harper & Row, 1964.

Birkhoff, Garrett and MacLane, Saunders. *A Survey of Modern Algebra.* 2nd ed. rev. New York: Macmillan, 1959.

Bohm, D. *Causality and Chance in Modern Physics.* London: Routledge and Kegan Paul, 1957.

Bonhoeffer, Dietrich. *Act and Being.* Translated by Bernard Noble. New York: Harper & Row, 1956.

Boole, George. *An Investigation of the Laws of Thought on Which Are Founded the Mathematical Theories of Logic and Probabilities.* New York: Dover, n.d.

————. *The Mathematical Analysis of Logic.* Cambridge: n.p., 1847.

Boyer, C. B. *A History of Mathematics.* New York: John Wiley & Sons, 1968.

————. *The History of the Calculus and Its Conceptual Development.* New York: Dover, 1949.

Bronowski, J. *Science and Human Values.* New York: Julian Messner, 1956.

Brown, D., James, R. E. and Reeves, G., eds. *Process Philosophy and Christian Thought.* Indianapolis, Ind.: Bobbs-Merrill, 1971.

Brumbaugh, R. S. *Plato's Mathematical Imagination.* Bloomington, Ind.: Indiana University Press, 1954.

————. *The Role of Mathematics in Plato's Dialectic.* Chicago: The University of Chicago Libraries, 1942.

Buchler, Justus. "On a Strain of Arbitrariness in Whitehead's System." *The Journal of Philosophy.* 66, no. 19: 589–601.

Bultmann, Rudolf. *Essays: Philosophical and Theological.* Translated by James Grieg. London: Student Christian Movement Press, 1955.

————. *Glauben und Verstehen: Gesammelte Aufsatze.* vol. 1. Tubingen: Mohr, 1954.

————. *Jesus Christ and Mythology.* New York: Charles Scribner's Sons, 1958.

————. *Theology of the New Testament.* 2 vols. Translated by K. Grovel. New York: Charles Scribner's Sons, 1951–1955.

Bunge, Mario. *Causality—The Place of the Causal Principle in Modern Science.* Cambridge, Mass.: Harvard University Press, 1959.

————. *Philosophy of Physics.* Dordrecht-Holland: D. Reidel, 1973.

Burnet, John. *Early Greek Philosophy.* 4th ed. London: A. and C. Black, 1930.

Burtt, E. A., ed. *The English Philosophers from Bacon to Mill.* New York: The Modern Library, 1939.

————. *The Metaphysical Foundations of Modern Physical Science*. London: Routledge & Kegan Paul, 1959.

Caldin, E. F. *The Power and Limits of Science*. London: Chapman & Hall. 1956.

Cantor, Georg. *Contributions to the Found:ng of the Theory of Transfinite Numbers*. Translated by P. E. B. Jourdain. New York: Dover, 1915.

Cantor, Moritz. *Vorlesungen Uber Geschicte der Mathematik*. 4 vols. Leipzig: 1873.

Capak, Milič. *The Philosophical Impact of Modern Physics*. Princeton, N. J.: D. Van Nostrand, 1961.

Cassirer, Ernst. *Determinism and Indeterminism in Modern Physics*. New Haven, Conn.: Yale University Press, 1956.

————. *An Essay on Man: An Introduction to a Philosophy of Human Culture*. New Haven, Conn.: Yale University Press, 1944.

————. *The Philosophy of the Enlightenment*. Translated by F. C. A. Koelln and J. P. Pettegrove. Boston: Beacon Press, 1951.

————. *The Problem of Knowledge: Philosophy, Science, and History since Hegel*. Translated by W. H. Woglom and C. W. Hendel. New Haven, Conn.: Yale University Press, 1950.

Church, A. *Introduction to Mathematical Logic*. Princeton, N. J.: Princeton University Press, 1944.

Chardin, Pierre Teilhard de. *The Phenomenon of Man*. Translated by B. Wall. New York: Harper & Brothers, 1959.

Cleve, Felix. *The Giants of Prehistoric Greek Philosophy: An Attempt To Reconstruct Their Thoughts*. 2 vols. 2nd ed. The Hague: Martinus Nijhoff, 1969.

Cobb, John, B., Jr. "Freedom in Whitehead's Philosophy: A Response to Edward Pols." *The Southern Journal of Philosophy* 7, no. 4 (Winter 1969–70).

————. *Living Options in Protestant Theology*. Philadelphia: The Westminster Press, 1962.

————. *The Structure of Christian Existence*. Philadelphia: The Westminster Press, 1967.

———. "A Whiteheadian Christology," in *Process Philosophy and Christian Thought.* Edited by Brown, James and Reeves, Indianapolis, Ind.: Bobbs-Merrill Co., 1971.

Cohen, I. B. *The Birth of the New Physics.* New York: Doubleday Anchor, 1960.

Cohen, M. R. and Nagel, E. *An Introduction to Logic and Scientific Method.* New York: Harcourt Brace, 1934.

Cohen, P. J. *Set Theory and the Continuum Hypothesis.* New York: Benjamin, 1966.

——— and Hersh, Reuben. "Non-Cantorian Set Theory." *Scientific American* 217, no. 6 (Dec. 1967): 104–16

Collingwood, R. G. *The Idea of Nature.* Oxford: Clarendon Press, 1945.

Cooper, Lane, trans. *Plato: On the Trial and Death of Socrates.* Ithaca, N.Y.: Cornell University Press, 1941.

Copi, I. M. *Symbolic Logic.* New York: The Macmillan Co., 1954.

Cornford, F. M. *From Religion to Philosophy in Ancient Greece.* New York: Harper Torchbooks, 1957.

———. *Plato's Theory of Knowledge.* London: Routledge & Kegan Paul.

———, ed. and trans. *Plato and Parmenides.* London: K. Paul, Trench, Trubner & Co., 1939.

Coulson, C. A. *Science and Christian Belief.* Chapel Hill, N.C.: University of North Carolina Press, 1955.

———. *Science and the Idea of God.* Cambridge: Cambridge University Press, 1958.

Cowan, J. L. "Wittgenstein's Philosophy of Logic." *The Philosophical Review* 70 (July 1961): 362–75.

Cox, Harvey. *The Secular City: Secularization and Urbanization in Theological Perspective.* Rev. ed. New York: Macmillan, 1969.

Cullman, Oscar. *Christ and Time: The Primitive Christian Conception of Time and History.* Rev. ed. Translated by F. V. Filson. Philadelphia: Westminster, 1964.

Curry, H. B. *Foundations of Mathematical Logic*. New York: McGraw-Hill, 1963.

D'Arcy, M. P. "The Philosophy of St. Augustine," *Saint Augustine*. New York: Meridian Books, 1957.

Dampier, W. C. *A History of Science and its Relations With Philosophy and Religion*. 4th ed. Cambridge: Cambridge University Press, 1948.

Dantzig, Tobias. *Number, the Language of Science*. 4th ed. rev. Garden City, N.Y.: Doubleday & Co., 1954.

De Boer, P. A. H. "The Counsellor," in *Wisdom in Israel and in the Ancient Near East*. Edited by Martin Noth and D. W. Thomas. Leiden: E. J. Brill, 1960.

Dedekind, Richard. *Essays on the Theory of Numbers*. Translated by W. W. Beman. New York: Dover, 1963.

Descartes, Rene. *Geometry*. Translated by D. E. Smith and M. L. Latham. La Salle: Open Court, 1924.

Dillenberger, John. *Protestant Thought and Natural Science, A Historical Interpretation*. Garden City, N.Y.: Doubleday & Co., 1960.

Dodds, E. R. *The Greeks and the Irrational*. Berkeley, Calif.: University of California Press, 1951.

Driver, S. R. *An Introduction to the Literature of the Old Testament*. New York: Meridian Library, 1956.

Ehrlich, P. R. *The Population Bomb*. New York: Ballantine Books, 1968.

Eichrodt, Walter. *Theology of the Old Testament*. 2 vols. Translated by J. A. Baker. Philadelphia: Westminster Press, 1967.

Elder, Leo. *Aristotle's Theory of the One: A Commentary on Book X of the Metaphysics*. Netherlands: Van Gorcum, 1961.

Elwes, R. H. M., ed. *The Chief Works of Benedict de Spinoza*. 2 vols. New York: Dover, 1951.

Eves, Howard. *An Introduction to the History of Mathematics*. New York: Rinehart & Co., 1959.

Farber, Marvin. *The Foundation of Phenomenology: Edmund*

Husserl and the Quest for a Rigorous Science of Philosophy. Cambridge, Mass.: Harvard University Press, 1943.

Farrer, Austin. *Finite and Infinite: A Philosophical Essay.* London: Dacre Press, 1959.

Ferre, Frederick. *Language, Logic and God.* New York: Harper & Brothers, 1961.

Flew, Antony, editor. *Logic and Language.* Oxford: Basil Blackwell, First Series, 1951. Second Series, 1955.

Ford, Lewis. "Can Whitehead Provide for Real Subjective Agency? A Reply to Edward Pols' Critique." *The Modern Schoolman* (Jan. 1970).

Fraenkel, A. A. *Abstract Set Theory.* 3rd ed. Amsterdam: North-Holland, 1966.

———. Bar-Hillel, Y., and Levy, A. *Foundations of Set Theory.* 2nd rev. ed. Amsterdam: North Holland, 1973.

Frank, Philip. *Philosophy of Science: The Link between Science and Philosophy.* Englewood Cliffs, N.Y.: Prentice-Hall, 1957.

Frege, G. *The Foundations of Arithmetic.* Translated by J. L. Austin. New York: Philosophical Library, 1950.

Freud, Sigmund. *The Future of an Illusion.* New York: Doubleday, 1957.

Flew, Antony and MacIntyre, Alasdair, eds. *New Essays in Philosophical Theology.* London: S. C. M. Press, 1955.

Forrester, J. W. *Industrial Dynamics.* Cambridge, Mass.: M.I.T. Press, 1961.

———. *World Dynamics.* Cambridge, Mass.: Wright-Allen Press, 1971.

———. *Urban Dynamics.* Cambridge, Mass.: M.I.T. Press, 1969.

Galilei, Galileo. *Dialogues Concerning Two New Sciences.* Translated by Henry Crew and A. De Salvio. New York: Dover, 1914.

Gilkey, Langdon. *Maker of Heaven and Earth.* New York: Doubleday, 1959.

Gillispie, Charles. *The Edge of Objectivity.* Princeton, N.J.: Princeton University Press, 1960.

Gilson, Etienne. *The Christian Philosophy of Saint Thomas Aquinas*. Translated by L. K. Shook. New York; Random House, 1956.

———. *God and Philosophy*. New Haven: Yale University Press, 1941.

———. *Reason and Revelation in the Middle Ages*. New York: Charles Scribner's Sons, 1938.

Gödel, Kurt. *On Formally Undecidable Propositions of Principia Mathematica and Related Systems*. Translated by B. Meltzer. Edinburgh: Oliver & Boyd, 1962.

———. "Russell's Mathematical Logic," *The Philosophy of Bertrand Russell*. Edited by Paul Schillp. New York: Tudor, 1944.

Gogarten, Friedrich. *Demythologizing and History*. Translated by N. H. Smith. London: S. C. M. Press, 1955.

Gow, James. *A Short History of Greek Mathematics*. New York: Hafner, 1923.

Grant, Edward. *Physical Science in the Middle Ages*. New York: Wiley, 1971.

Grunbaum, A. *Philosophical Problems of Space and Time*. New York: Knopf, 1963.

Guthrie, W. K. C. *A History of Greek Philosophy*. 3 vols. Cambridge: Cambridge University Press, 1962.

Haldane, E. S. and Ross, G. R. T., trans. *The Philosophical Works of Descartes*. 2 vols. New York: Dover, 1931.

Halmos, P. R. *Algebraic Logic*. New York: Chelsea, 1962.

Hardin, Garrett, ed. *Population, Evolution, and Birth Control*. 2nd ed. San Francisco, Calif.: W. H. Freeman, 1969.

———. "The Tragedy of the Commons," *Science* 162 (Dec. 1968): 1243–48.

Hartshorne, Charles. *The Logic of Perfection, and Other Essays in Neoclassical Metaphysics*. La Salle, Ill.: Open Court, 1962.

———. *Man's Vision of God, and the Logic of Theism*. Willett, Clark & Co., 1941.

————. "Ontological Primacy; A Reply to Buchler." *The Journal of Philosophy* 65 (Dec. 10, 1970): 981.

———— and Reese, W. L. *Philosophers Speak of God.* Chicago: University of Chicago Press, 1953.

Hazelton, Roger. *On Proving God: A Handbook in Christian Conversation.* New York: Harper & Brothers, 1952.

Heath, T. L. *Diophantus of Alexandria.* New York: Cambridge University Press, 1910.

————. *History of Greek Mathematics.* vol. 1. New York: Oxford University Press, 1921.

————. *Mathematics in Aristotle.* New York: Oxford University Press, 1949.

————. *The Thirteen Books of Euclid's Elements.* 3 vols. 2nd ed., rev. New York: Dover, 1956.

————. *The Works of Archimedes.* New York: Dover, 1912.

Heidegger, Martin. *Being and Time.* Translated by J. Macquarrie and E. Robinson. New York: Harper and Brothers, 1961.

————. *An Introduction to Metaphysics.* Translated by R. Manheim. Garden City: Doubleday, 1961.

Heim, Karl. *Christian Faith and Natural Science.* New York: Harper & Brothers, 1953.

Heisenberg, Werner. *Physics and Philosophy: The Revolution in Modern Science.* New York: Harper & Row, 1962.

Henkin, Leon. "Mathematical Foundations for Mathematics." *The American Mathematical Monthly* 78, no. 5 (May 1971).

————, Suppes, P., and Tarski, A., eds. *The Axiomatic Method with Special Reference to Geometry and Physics.* Amsterdam: North-Holland, 1959.

Heyting, A., ed. *Constructivity in Mathematics.* Amsterdam: North-Holland, 1959.

Hick, John. *Faith and Knowledge.* Ithaca, N.Y.: Cornell University Press, 1957.

Hilbert, David. *Foundations of Geometry.* Translated by L. Unger. Revised by P. Bernays. La Salle, Ill.: Open Court, 1971.

———— and Ackermann, W. *Principles of Mathematical Logic.*

Translated by L. M. Hammond, G. G. Leckie, and F. Steinhardt. Edited by Robert Luce. New York: Chelsea Publishing Co., 1950.

Hintikka, Jaakko. *The Philosophy of Mathematics.* London: Oxford University Press, 1969.

Hodgson, Leonard. *Theology in an Age of Science.* Oxford: Clarenden Press, 1944.

Hume, David. *An Enquiry Concerning Human Understanding.* Indianapolis, Ind.: Bobbs-Merrill, 1955.

Husserl, Edmund. *Cartesian Meditations.* Translated by Dorion Cairns. The Hague: Martinus Nijhoff, 1960.

―――. *Formal and Transcendental Logic.* Translated by Dorion Cairns. The Hague: Martinus Nijhoff, 1969.

―――. *Ideas.* Translated by W. R. B. Gibson. New York: Collier Books, 1962.

―――. *Logische Untersuchungen.* Halle: Niemeyer, vol. 1, 1900. vol. 2, 1901.

―――. *Phenomenology and the Crisis of Philosophy.* Translated by Quentin Lauer. New York: Harper Torchbooks, 1965.

―――. *Philosophie der Arithmetik: Psychologische und Logische Untersuchungen.* Halle: C. E. M. Pfeffer, 1891.

Jaeger, W. W. *The Theology of the Early Greek Philosophers.* Oxford: Clarendon Press, 1947.

Jaki, S. L. *The Relevance of Physics.* Chicago: University of Chicago Press, 1966.

Jeffrey, Richard. *Formal Logic: Its Scope and Limits.* New York: McGraw-Hill, 1967.

Johnson, R. C. *Authority in Protestant Theology.* Philadelphia: Westminster, 1959.

Jonas, Hans. "Is God a Mathematician? The Meaning of Metabolism," in *The Phenomenon of Life: Toward a Philosophical Biology.* New York: Harper & Row, 1966.

Kant, Immanuel. *Critique of Pure Reason.* Translated by F. M. Müller. Garden City: Doubleday, 1966.

————. *Prolegomena to Any Future Metaphysics.* Edited by Oskar Piest. Indianapolis: Bobbs-Merrill, 1950.

Kegley, C. W. and Bretall, R. W., eds. *The Theology of Paul Tillich.* New York: Macmillan, 1952.

Kirk, G. S. *Heraclitus: The Cosmic Fragments.* Cambridge. Cambridge University Press, 1954.

———— and Raven, J. E. *The Presocratic Philosophers: A Critical History with a Selection of Texts.* Cambridge: Cambridge University Press, 1962.

Kittel, G., ed. and Bromiley, G. W., trans. *Theological Dictionary of the New Testament.* vol. 4. Grand Rapids: Eerdmans, 1967.

Kleene, S. C. *Introduction to Metamathematics.* Princeton: D. Van Nostrand, 1950.

Klein, Jacob. *Greek Mathematical Thought and the Origin of Algebra.* Translated by Eva Braun. Cambridge, Mass.: M.I.T. Press, 1968.

Kline, Morris. *Mathematical Thought from Ancient to Modern Times.* New York: Oxford University Press, 1972.

————. *Mathematics in Western Culture.* New York: Oxford University Press, 1964.

Koestler, Arthur. *The Sleep Walkers.* New York: Macmillan, 1959.

Korner, Stephen. *The Philosophy of Mathematics: An Introduction.* New York: Harper Torchbooks, 1960.

Kraft, Victor. *The Vienna Circle: The Origin of Neo-Positivism.* New York: Philosophical Library, 1958.

Kuhn, T. S. *The Copernican Revolution.* Cambridge, Mass.: Harvard University Press, 1957.

————. *The Structure of Scientific Revolutions.* Chicago: The University of Chicago Press, 1962.

Lakatos, Imre, ed. *Problems in the Philosophy of Mathematics.* Amsterdam: North-Holland, 1967.

Langer, Susanne. *Philosophy in a New Key.* New York: The New American Library of World Literature, 1961.

Lauer, Quentin. *The Triumph of Subjectivity: An Introduction* to *Transcendental Phenomenology*. New York: Fordham University Press, 1958.

Leclerc, Ivor. *Whitehead's Metaphysics: An Introductory Exposition*. New York: Macmillan, 1958.

Leeuw, G. Van Der. *Religion in Essence and Manifestation*. Translated by J. E. Turner. London: George Allen & Unwin, 1938.

Leibniz, G. W. *Philosophical Papers and Letters*. 2 vols. Translated and edited by L. E. Loemker. Chicago: University of Chicago Press, 1956.

Locke, John. *An Essay Concerning Human Understanding*. 2 vols. New York: Dover, 1959.

Lovejoy, A. O. *The Great Chain of Being*. Cambridge, Mass.: Harvard University Press, 1936.

Lowe, Victor. "Whitehead's Metaphysical System," in *Process Philosophy and Christian Thought*. Edited by Brown, James and Reeves. Indianapolis: Bobbs-Merrill, 1971.

Lukasiewicz, Jan. *Aristotle's Syllogistic, from the Standpoint of Modern Formal Logic*. London: Oxford University Press, 1951.

Lutoslawski, Wincenty. *The Origin and Growth of Plato's Logic*. New York: Longman's, Green, 1905.

Lyon, Ardon. "Causality," *The British Journal for the Philosophy of Science* 18 (1967).

Macquarrie, John. *Twentieth-Century Religious Thought: The Frontiers of Philosophy and Theology, 1900-1960*.

Malcolm, Norman and Von Wright, G. H. *Ludwig Wittgenstein: A Memoir*. London: Oxford University Press, 1958.

Malthus, T. R. *An Essay on the Principle of Population as it Affects the Future Improvement of Society*. London: J. Johnson in St. Paul's Church Yard, 1798. Reprinted as *First Essay on Population*. New York: Augustus M. Kelley, 1965.

Mascall, E. L. *Christian Theology and Natural Science*. London: Longman's, Green, 1956.

———. *Existence and Analogy*. London: Longman's Green, 1949.

———. *He Who Is: A Study in Traditional Theism.* London: Longman's, Green, 1943.

———. *The Secularization of Christianity: An Analysis and a Critique.* London: Darton, Longman & Todd, 1965.

Mates, Benson. *Stoic Logic.* Berkeley, Calif.: University of California Press, 1961.

Mays, W. *The Philosophy of Whitehead.* New York: Collier Books, 1962.

Meadows, Meadows, Randers and Behrens. *The Limits to Growth.* New York: Universe, 1972.

Meadows, D. L. and Meadows, D. H., eds. *Toward Global Equilibrium: Collected Papers.* Cambridge, Mass.: Wright-Allen Press, 1973.

Merleau-Ponty, M. *Phenomenology of Perception.* London: Routledge and Kegan Paul, 1967.

Merlin, Philip. *From Platonism to Neoplatonism.* 3rd edition. The Hague: Martinus Nijhoff, 1968.

Metzger, Bruce. *An Introduction to the Apocrypha.* New York: Oxford University Press, 1957.

Michalson, Carl. *The Rationality of Faith.* New York: Charles Scribner's Sons, 1963.

Miller, I. E. *The Significance of the Mathematical Element in the Philosophy of Plato.* Chicago: University of Chicago Press, 1904.

Molina, Fernando. *Existentialism as Philosophy.* Englewood Cliffs, N.J.: Prentice-Hall, 1962.

Moltmann, Juergen. *Theology of Hope.* Translated by J. W. Leitch. New York: Harper & Row, 1967.

Moore, G. E. *Philosophical Studies.* New York: Harcourt, Brace, 1922.

Morgenbesser, Sidney, ed. *Philosophy of Science Today.* New York: Basic Books, 1967.

Most, W. G. "The Scriptural Basis of Saint Augustine's Arithmology." *The Catholic Biblical Quarterly* 13 (1951): 284–95.

Nagel, Ernest. *Logic without Metaphysics.* New York: Free Press, 1956.

—— and Newman, J. R. *Gödel's Proof.* New York: New York University Press, 1958.

——, Suppes, P., Tarski, A., eds. *Logic, Methodology and Philosophy of Science, Proceedings of the 1960 International Congress.* Stanford, Calif.: Stanford University Press, 1962.

Neugebauer, O. *The Exact Sciences in Antiquity.* Princeton, N.J.: Princeton University Press, 1952.

Neve, J. L. *A History of Christian Thought.* 2 vols. Philadelphia: The Muhlenberg Press, 1946.

Newman, J. R. *The World of Mathematics.* 4 vols. New York: Simon & Schuster, 1956.

Newton, Isaac. *Principia.* 2 vols. Translated by Andrew Motte. Revised by Florian Cajori. Berkeley, Calif.: University of California Press, 1962.

——. *Universal Arithmetick.* Translated by Raphson. London: J. Senex, 1720.

Northrop, F. S. C. *The Logic of the Sciences and the Humanities.* New York: Macmillan, 1947.

—— and Cross, Mason W., eds. *Alfred North Whitehead: An Anthology.* New York: Macmillan, 1961.

Noth, Martin and Thomas, D. W., eds. *Wisdom in Israel and in the Ancient Near East.* Leiden: E. J. Brill, 1960.

Oates, W. J., ed. and Leckie, G. G., trans. *Basic Writings of Saint Augustine.* New York: Random House, 1948.

Ogden, S. M. *Christ without Myth.* New York: Harper & Brothers, 1961.

——. *The Reality of God, and Other Essays.* New York: Harper & Row, 1963.

Osborn, A. D. *The Philosophy of Edmund Husserl in its Development from His Mathematical Interests to His First Conception of Phenomenology in Logical Investigations.* New York: International Press, 1934.

Otto, Rudolf. *The Idea of the Holy.* Translated by John Harvey. New York: Oxford University Press, 1958.

Pascal, Blaise. *Oeuvres Complètes de Blaise Pascal*. 2 vols. Paris: n.p., 1860.

———. *Pensées, The Provincial Letters*. Translated by W. F. Trotter. New York: The Modern Library, 1941.

Philip, J. A. *Pythagoras and Early Pythagoreanism*. Toronto: University Press, 1966.

Plotinus. *The Enneads*. Translated by S. MacKenna. London: Faber & Faber, 1956.

Polanyi, Michael. *Personal Knowledge*. Chicago: University of Chicago Press, 1958.

———. *The Study of Man*. Chicago: University of Chicago Press, 1960.

Pole, David. *The Later Philosophy of Wittgenstein*. London: Athlone Press, 1958.

Pollard, William. *The Cosmic Drama*. New York: National Council of the Episcopal Church, 1955.

———. *Chance and Providence*. New York: Charles Scribner's Sons, 1958.

———. *Physicist and Christian*. Greenwich, Conn.: Seabury Press, 1961.

Pols, Edward. *Whitehead's Metaphysics: A Critical Examination of* Process and Reality. Carbondale: Southern Illinois University Press, 1967.

Popkin, R. H. *The History of Skepticism from Erasmus to Descartes*. New York: Harper & Row, 1968.

Ptolemy, C. *Tetrabiblos*. English translation by J. M. Ashmand. London: Davis & Dickson, 1822.

Quine, W. V. *Methods of Logic*. New York: Henry Holt, 1950.

———. *Set Theory and Its Logic*. rev. ed. Cambridge, Mass.: Belknap Press, 1971.

Rad, Gerhad von. *Old Testament Theology*. 2 vols. Translated by D. M. G. Stalker. New York: Harper & Row, 1962.

Radhakrisnan, S., ed. and trans. *The Principal Upanisads*. New York: Harper & Brothers, 1953.

Ramsey, F. P. *Foundations of Mathematics*. New York: Humanities Press, 1950.

Ramsey, I. T. *Models and Mystery*. London: Oxford University Press, 1964.

Raven, C. E. *Natural Religion and Christian Theology*. 2 vols. Cambridge: Cambridge University Press, 1953.

Ringgren, Helmer. *Word and Wisdom, Studies in the Hypostatization of Divine Qualities and Functions in the Ancient Near East*. Lund: n.p., 1947.

Robinson, Abraham. "Formalism 64," in *Log.c, Methodology and Philosophy of Science: Proceedings of the 1964 International Congress*. Edited by Yehoshua Bar-Hillel. Amsterdam: North-Holland, 1965.

———. *Introduction to Model Theory and to the Metamathematics of Algebra*. Amsterdam: North-Holland, 1965.

———. *Non-Standard Analysis*. Amsterdam: North-Holland, 1966.

Robinson, J. A. T. *Honest to God*. London: S. C.M. Press, 1963.

Robinson, J. M. *A New Quest of the Historical Jesus*. Naperville, Ill.: Alec R. Allenson, Inc., 1959.

——— and Cobb, J. B., Jr., eds. *The Later Heidegger and Theology*. New York: Harper & Row, 1963.

Robinson, Rafael. "An Essentially Undecidable Axiom System," *Proceedings of the International Congress of Mathematicians*. Cambridge, 1950. 1: 729–30.

Rosenbloom, Paul. *The Elements of Mathematical Logic*. New York: Dover, 1950.

Ross, W. D. *Aristotle*. New York: Oxford University Press, 1924.

———. *Plato's Theory of Ideas*. Oxford: Clarendon Press, 1951.

Runyon, Theodore. "Secularization and Sacrament: Reflections on the Theology of Friedrich Gogarten," in *Spirit and Power of Christian Secularity*, edited by Albert Schlitzer. Notre Dame, Ind.: University of Notre Dame Press, 1969.

Russell, Bertrand. *Mysticism and Logic*. New York: Doubleday, 1957.

———. *Principles of Mathematics I*. Cambridge: Norton, 1903.

————. *Religion and Science*. New York: Oxford University Press, 1961.

————. "On the Notion of Cause." *Proceedings of the Aristotelian Society* 13 (1913): 1–26.

———— and Whitehead, A. N. *Principia Mathematica*. Cambridge: University Press, vol. 1, 1910; vol. 2, 1911; vol. 3, 1912.

Russell, E. J. *World Population and World Food Supplies*. London: George Allen and Unwin, 1954.

Saaty, T. L. and Weyl, F. J., eds. *The Spirit and the Uses of the Mathematical Sciences*. New York: McGraw-Hill, 1969.

Sarton, George. *Ancient Science and Modern Civilization*. New York: Harper Torchbooks, 1954.

Sartre, Jean-Paul. *The Transcendence of the Ego: An Existentialist Theory of Consciousness*. Translated by Forrest Williams and Robert Kirkpatrick. New York: Noonday Press, 1957.

Schleiermacher, Friedrich. *The Christian Faith*. Translated by H. R. Mackintosh and J. S. Stewart. Edinburgh: T. & T. Clark, 1928.

Schillp, Paul, editor. *The Philosophy of Bertrand Russell*. New York: Tudor, 1944.

Schrecker, Paul. "On the Infinite Number of Infinite Orders; a Chapter of the Pre-history of Transfinite Numbers," in *Studies and Essays in the History of Science and Learning in Honor of George Sarton*. Edited by M. F. Ashley Montagu. New York: Shuman, 1946.

Sellars, Wilfrid. *Science, Perception and Reality*. London: Routledge and Kegan Paul, 1963.

Shapere, Dudley. *Philosophical Problems of Natural Science*. New York: Macmillan, 1965.

Sheffer, H. M. "A Set of Five Independent Postulates for Boolean Algebras." *Transactions of the American Mathematical Society* 14 (1913): 481–88.

Shiner, Larry. *The Secularization of History: An Introduction to the Theology of Friedrich Gogarten*. Nashville, Tenn.: Abingdon, 1966.

Smith, D. E. *History of Mathematics*. 2 vols. New York: Dover, 1958.

Snow, C. P. *The Two Cultures and the Scientific Revolution*. Cambridge: Cambridge University Press, 1961.

Spiegelberg, Herbert. *The Phenomenological Movement: A Historical Introduction*. 2 vols. The Hague: Martinus Nijhoff, 1960.

Steen, L. A. "New Models of the Real Number Line." *Scientific American* 225, no. 2 (Aug. 1971).

Strawson, P. F. *Introduction to Logical Theory*. London: Methuen, 1952.

Suppes, Patrick. *A Probabilistic Theory of Causality*. Amsterdam: North-Holland, 1970.

———. *Introduction to Logic*. Princeton, N.J.: Van Nostrand, 1957.

Tarski, Alfred. "What is Elementary Geometry?" in *The Axiomatic Method, with Special Reference to Geometry and Physics*. Edited by Henkin, Suppes and Tarski. Amsterdam: North-Holland, 1959.

Taylor, A. E. *Varia Socratica*. Oxford: James Parker, 1911.

Temple, William. *Nature, Man and God*. London: Macmillan, 1934.

Tillich, Paul. *Systematic Theology*. Chicago: University of Chicago Press, vol. 1, 1951; vol. 2, 1957; vol. 3, 1963.

Toulmin, Stephen. *Foresight and Understanding*. Bloomington, Ind.: Indiana University Press, 1961.

Van Buren, P. M. *The Secular Meaning of the Gospel Based on an Analysis of its Language*. New York: Macmillan, 1963.

Wach, Joachim. *The Comparative Study of Religions*. New York: Columbia University Press, 1958.

Vahanian, Gabriel. *The Death of God: The Culture of Our Post-Christian Era*. New York: George Braziller, 1961.

Wartofsky, M. W. *Conceptual Foundations of Scientific Thought: An Introduction to the Philosophy of Science*. London: Macmillan, 1969.

Wedberg, Anders. *Plato's Philosophy of Mathematics.* Stockholm: Almquizt and Wixkel, 1955.

Weizsacker, C. F. von. *The Relevance of Science: Creation and Cosmogony.* New York: Harper, 1964.

Weyl, Hermann. *Philosophy of Mathematics and Natural Science.* Translated by Olaf Helmer. Princeton, N.J.: Princeton University Press, 1949.

White, A. D. *A History of the Warfare of Science with Theology in Christendom.* New York: Free Press, 1965.

Whitehead, A. N. *The Aims of Education.* New York: Macmillan, 1929.

――――. *Adventures of Ideas.* New York: Macmillan, 1933.

――――. "Axioms of Geometry," *Encyclopaedia Britannica.* 11th ed.

――――. *The Concept of Nature.* Cambridge: Cambridge University Press, 1920.

――――. *An Introduction to Mathematics.* New York: Henry Holt, 1911.

――――. *Essays in Science and Philosophy.* New York: The Philosophical Library, 1948.

――――. "Mathematics," *Encyclopaedia Britannica.* 11th ed.

――――. "Mathematics and the Good," in *Essays in Science and Philosophy.* New York: The Philosophical Library, 1948.

――――. *Modes of Thought.* New York: Macmillan, 1938.

――――. "On Mathematical Concepts of the Material World," in *Alfred North Whitehead: An Anthology.* Edited by Northrop and Gross. New York: Macmillan, 1961.

――――. *An Enquiry Concerning the Principles of Natural Knowledge.* Cambridge: Cambridge University Press, 1919.

――――. *Process and Reality.* New York: Macmillan, 1929.

――――. *The Principle of Relativity.* Cambridge: Cambridge University Press, 1922.

――――. *Religion in The Making.* New York: Macmillan, 1926.

――――. *Science and the Modern World.* New York: Macmillan, 1926.

————. *Symbolism, Its Meaning and Effect.* New York: Macmillan, 1927.

————. *A Treatise on Universal Algebra with Applications.* New York: Hafner, 1960.

Whitehouse, W. A. *Christian Faith and the Scientific Attitude.* New York: Philosophical Library, 1952.

Whybury, R. N. *Wisdom in Proverbs, the Concept of Wisdom in Proverbs 1 through 9.* London: S. C. M. Press, 1965.

Wieman, H. N. *The Source of Human Good.* Chicago: University of Chicago Press, 1946.

Wigner, Eugene. "The Unreasonable Effectiveness of Mathematics in the Natural Sciences." *Communications on Pure and Applied Mathematics* 13 (Jan. 1960).

Wilder, R. L. *Introduction to the Foundations of Mathematics.* New York: John Wiley & Sons, 1952.

Willard, Dallas. "Husserl's Essay 'On the Concept of Numbers.' " *Philosophia Mathematica* 9, no. 1 (Summer 1972): 40–52.

Winance, E. "Intention and Nature of Husserl's Logic." *Philosophia Mathematica* 2 (Dec. 1965): 69–85.

Wisdom, John. "Gods," in *Logic and Language.* Edited by A. G. N. Flew. Oxford: Basil Blackwell, 1951.

————. *Philosophy and Psycho-Analysis.* Oxford: Basil Blackwell, 1957.

Wittgenstein, Ludwig. *The Blue and Brown Books.* Oxford: Basil Blackwell, 1960.

————. *Philosophical Investigations.* Translated by G. E. M. Anscombe. New York: Macmillan, 1953.

————. *Remarks on the Foundations of Mathematics.* Edited by G. H. von Wright, R. Rhees and G. E. M. Anscombe. Oxford: Basil Blackwell, 1956.

————. *Tractatus Logico-Philosophicus.* Translated by D. F. Pears and B. F. McGuinness. London: Routledge & Kegan Paul, 1961.

Wolfson, L. A. *Philo.* 2 vols. Cambridge, Mass.: Harvard University Press, 1948.

Zeller, Edward. *Outlines of the History of Greek Philosophy.* Translated by L. R. Palmer. Revised by Wilhelm Nestle. London: Kegan Paul, 1931.

Index